MOLLY!
YOU'RE A PEACH,
AND NO PITS!
HAPPY COOKING -

SLIM MAN COOKS

The Adventures and Recipes of Mr. Man

52 Dishes, 52 Stories, One Manly Man

SLIMMANCOOKS.COM

ISBN: 978-1-4951-8129-0
LCCN: PENDING

Printed by Sheridan Books, Inc.
Designed by Soundview Design Studio

Printed in the United States of America

Contents

Acknowledgements

Special Thanks to:

Aaron and Katie

Abe Goldman

Barbara O. Caton

Benicio del Toro

Big Nick and Han

Bob and Judi Griffiths

Bob and Wendy Perrigo

Brad Woods and Lisa Masters

C.C.

Carly and Greg Patronik

Charlene Palmer and Gary Barth

Coral Haug Blanchard

Dave Love of Listen 2 Entertainment Group

David and Maria Grden

Deb and Gregg Little

Deby Thayer

Dick Huddleston

Ellen and Scott Ward

Faith and Dan McCarthy

Frenchy le French

Georgi Matsunaga

Hal Ryman at Na-Pali Productions

Harry and Liza

Jazzy Valerie

Jennifer Cunha

Kathy and Denny Bierl

Kay Burns

Liz Porter

Lovely Leslie

Madonna Hitchcock

Michael J

Mike "Chef" Hignite

Mindy Camponeschi

Mitch Mitch

Myrna Ross

Pamela and Paul Johnson

Paul and Leslie Doty

Perrie Patterson

Phil and Shari Zongker

Rei Peri

Richie Sweet and Lexus Lexi

Rudolf Peschek

Scrap Dog and Jules Camponeschi

Soundview Design Studio (Dave & Amy)

Stephen and Jack

Sue Forrest

Tom "TR" Roberts

Extra-special thanks to Carl Griffin!

I've got a big, crazy, wonderful family, and the best friends a man could ask for. A big hug and a huge thanks to all. Who loves ya?

Introduction

One Christmas a while ago, I got a dog named Batu. I also got a video camera.

I started filming cooking videos, silly little five-minute videos that I posted on YouTube. They featured my recipes, my songs, as well as stories about my crazy Italian family, my loony life in the music biz, and growing up in Baltimore, Maryland.

The videos also featured Batu. They caught the attention of the Italian American Network, and they asked me to make more, so I started making a couple videos a month, and that's how this cookbook got started.

Cooking. Music. Stories.

I come from a family of cooks. I've been cooking most of my life. When I was starting out in the music biz, and needed to feed the band, we'd scrape up a couple of bucks, buy some garlic, vegetables, and pasta, and I'd whip up a little something for dinner.

I've been creating dishes ever since.

A few things you should know . . .

I wrote this cookbook with my nieces and nephews in mind. If those numbskulls ever get into cooking, I want to make it easy for them to get started, so I explain everything in clear and simple terms, with lots of practical advice and sensible substitutions.

Most of these recipes are quick, easy, and use ingredients that you can find in almost any grocery store. A few of the dishes are involved, but you're gonna have to show off every once in a while! All of these recipes are delicious; I love each and every one of them, and know you will, too.

You can do this. I can show you how.

These dishes are my own creations—recipes I've come up with over the past few years. I've also included my versions of some classic Italian dishes, as well as some family favorites that I managed to Slimmify. They have yet to forgive me.

Lots of the recipes have videos; you scan the QR code with your phone, and it takes you to a quick YouTube video that shows you how to cook that dish.

The stories that accompany each recipe are part of a new literary genre that I created—I call it "faction." It's a combination of fact and fiction. The stories are all based on real occurrences, but have been embellished over time with a dash of Italian exaggeration, and a splash of jazz improvisation.

I love cooking. I love music. I love telling stories.

These three go together in my book, which you are now holding in your hands.

Let me know what you think.

Who loves ya?

Slim Man

PAP'S PESTO
and SONNUVABITCH

REFRIGERATE

The basil in this pesto is home grown and handpicked at Rat Tail Ridge, a farm in the northwest Catskills. The cheeses, parmesan and pecorino, come from Italy as does the olive oil. The pine nuts are from China and the garlic from Hoboken, N.J.

8 OZ. NET WT.

My dad walked into the TV room on the second floor, and his head was bleeding; we three kids were trying not to laugh.

My dad had a workbench in the basement, the ceiling was low, and there were two large iron water pipes right behind the work area. When you turned around to go upstairs, you had to duck under the pipes to avoid cracking your skull. My dad hit his head all the time; you could hear the "BOING!" all the way up on the second floor. It was always followed by a yell.

"SONNUVABITCH!"

We three kids thought it was the funniest thing in the world. Maybe it was because we loved the Three Stooges so much. Maybe it was something else. Whatever it was, when our dad hurt himself, we found it hilarious.

We called my dad "Paps." He was a professor of literature at the State University of New York, and one of his favorite books was *The Adventures of Huckleberry Finn*. Huck had an alcoholic father who used to get drunk, beat him, and chain him to chairs. Huck called his Dad "Pap." I read the book and thought it would be funny if we called our dad "Pap," too. We changed "Pap" to "Paps," hoping maybe nobody would find us out. For the record, our Paps did not get drunk, beat us, and chain us to chairs. But I'm sure he might have felt like it when we laughed at his bleeding head.

Paps used to take us fishing—it was a lot of fun for us kids. It couldn't have been fun for him. One summer, my dad and mom rented a small house near the beach on Fenwick Island, Delaware. It wasn't fancy; just a simple, small, white cottage on stilts by the Atlantic Ocean. The bay was on the other side of the island; there was a boat rental place on the bayside not far from the house. We had the place for a week.

One sunny summer day, Paps piled us three monsters into the back of the pale-green Plymouth station wagon and drove over to the boat rental place. He rented a small wooden boat with an eggbeater engine on the back. He grabbed his rods and reels, the bait, and us three knuckleheads, and we walked out on the pier. There was a boat ramp on one side of the pier; the tide was high, and the ramp was covered in water. People were slowly backing their boats down the ramp and into the bay.

On the other side of the pier were the rental boats. We all piled into one, Paps pulled the starter cord, and the motor revved up. We went motoring away, out into the wild blue yonder.

Little Assawoman Bay. That really was the name of the bay. Big Assawoman Bay was the larger one, right next to it. It sounds like I'm kidding, but I'm not. We motored out for quite a ways and dropped anchor in Little Assawoman. My dad got all of our rods baited up, and we dropped our lines into the water. Then he got his rod, attached his brand new lure, and casted. He slowly drew the line in. We kids sat and waited for the fish to bite; we were not patient children.

Paps usually stood at the front of the boat, his back would be to us. I would sneak up behind my dad and jiggle the butt-end of his fishing rod, so it felt like he had a fish. Paps would jerk his rod suddenly and pull his line toward him like he was landing a blue marlin.

"SONNUVABITCH!"

Then he would realize I'd played a joke. I'm surprised he didn't throw me overboard. We didn't take fishing very seriously, but my dad did. Anything my dad caught, he'd keep. He once caught an eel, kept it, and made a tomato sauce with it. It was awful. Paps would catch blowfish and keep them. Blowfish puff up like balloons when you catch them; most people don't eat them—my dad did. We didn't. Paps could have pulled an old tire into the boat, and I'm pretty sure he would have tried to make a sauce out of it. Just about anything he caught, he'd keep.

Except once.

That day on Little Assawoman Bay, when we were fishing off the side of the boat, my dad's rod bent over. He must have hooked something big. Or heavy. Or both. He reeled it in; it took him a while. Keep in mind; we're in Little Assawoman Bay. Not a lot of real big fish in there. When Paps got the fish to the side of the boat, he screamed for us to get the net. We scrambled, and the boat started rocking, almost knocking him into the water.

I got the net and pulled this big, ugly fish on board. It was the ugliest fish I'd ever seen—it had a big, wide, mouth with nasty-looking sharp teeth. My dad's brand new and very expensive lure was stuck in the back of the fish's mouth, right behind all those sharp teeth.

Paps decided to cut off the fish's head right then and there and retrieve the lure later. He cut off the head, and tossed the body of the fish back in the water and threw the bloody, severed fish head on the bottom of the boat. It was definitely a joy-killer. We kids wanted to go back in.

Paps didn't look too happy as we pulled in our lines; he pulled up the small anchor, and we headed back to the pier. My dad wasn't the greatest captain in the world; it took us a while to get back to the rental place, but we eventually found our way after hitting a couple of sand bars and missing a couple buoys.

Paps was looking might surly as he pulled the boat up to the pier and tied it up. We three kids got out and stood on the pier and watched as Paps grabbed the dead, bloody fish head from the bottom of the boat, and stuck his hand inside its mouth to pull out his pricey lure. The severed fish head clamped down on my dad's hand.

"SONNUVABITCH!"

Paps let out a yell, and tried to shake off the fish head. It wouldn't release its grip. Here was Paps, waving his hand in the air and thrashing his arm around, but the severed fish head wouldn't let go. We would have tried to help him, but we were laughing too hard.

The dead fish head finally released its grip, and got flung way up in the air. It landed in the water with a splash. My dad's very expensive lure was gone; his hand was bleeding. He got out of the boat and walked past us hyenas to the boat ramp. Paps walked down the boat ramp toward the water to rinse off his bloody hand. Only problem was . . . the tide had gone out; the ramp was covered in slick wet moss. When my dad hit the slippery part, his feet flew up in the air, and he let out a yell.

"SONNUVABITCH!"

He landed on his ass with a thud you could hear across the ocean. People in Paris felt a rumble. We saw the whole thing. We could not stop laughing; I'm surprised we didn't roll off the pier and fall into Little Assawoman Bay.

Paps was lying there on his ass, hand bleeding, and having trouble getting back up—he kept slipping. All we could do was laugh. Seriously.

This was probably one of those times when Paps might have felt like getting drunk, beating us, and chaining us to a chair. But he didn't. Whenever I told that story, he'd be the one laughing the hardest.

PAP'S PESTO

Paps made pesto before pesto was cool. He had a bunch of basil beds in front of his cabin on top of the Catskill Mountains. Rat Tail Ridge; that's what his place was called.

When the basil was ready, we'd pick it and go back to the house; we'd wash the leaves, and Paps would make pesto. He put it in small jars and sold it to local food stores. It was really delicious.

Pesto in Italian means "paste," and this blend of basil, cheese, garlic, pine nuts, and olive oil is *delizioso*. The recipe originates in Genoa, Italy. I had to Slimmify it a bit.

I like to use toasted pine nuts, rather than plain. Toasted pine nuts taste better, that's all. I place a dry skillet over medium-high heat, toss in the nuts, and flip them around 'til they're light brown. Keep an eye on your nuts—don't burn 'em!

This recipe calls for both Parmigiano-Reggiano and Pecorino Romano cheese. Parmigiano is a sweeter cheese. Pecorino is saltier. The blend of the two is wonderful. However, in a pinch I have used just Parmigiano, and it tastes great like that, too.

Paps used pesto in all kinds of dishes. He put it over pasta. He used a dollop in soups. He made omelettes with it. Use your imagination—I've put it on chicken and fish. I once made shrimp with pesto for the Food Network.

Makes 1 generous cup of pesto.

INGREDIENTS

2 cups fresh basil leaves, cleaned

½ cup extra-virgin olive oil

8 tablespoons of pine nuts (pignoli), toasted (½ cup)

2 cloves garlic, peeled

½ teaspoon of salt

½ cup freshly grated Parmigiano-Reggiano cheese

½ cup freshly grated Pecorino Romano cheese

HERE WE GO!

Put the basil, ½ cup of olive oil, 4 tablespoons of the toasted pine nuts, the garlic and the salt in a blender and blend, baby, blend. You can also use a food processor.

When everything is smooth, transfer to a bowl and slowly blend in the grated cheeses by hand. Or better yet, use a spatula.

That's it.

If you want to serve it over pasta, *farfalle* works well.

Get a large pot, fill it with cold water, and put it on the highest heat. When it boils rapidly, toss in 2 tablespoons of Kosher salt and a pound of pasta.

Follow the cooking instructions on the side of the pasta box. When the pasta is supposed to be done, start tasting. Take a piece of pasta and bite into it. If it's chalky in the center, it is not done. Check the pasta every 2 minutes or so.

When the pasta is firm to the bite (*al dente*), drain and transfer it to a warm bowl. Drizzle with 1 tablespoon of olive oil and mix.

Scoop some of the pesto sauce from its bowl, about ¼ cup, and add it to the pasta. Toss well, but be gentle. You can add some more pesto if it doesn't look like there's enough.

Dish it up! Put a small amount of pasta on a plate. Add a little sprinkle of grated cheese, Parmigiano or Romano or both.

Take some of the remaining toasted pine nuts, and sprinkle on top.

VARIATION:

Sometimes I'll broil or sauté a couple chicken breasts, chop 'em up, and add them to the pasta and pesto. *Delizioso*!

MANGIAMO!

MEATBALLS
and Motown

Griff

When I was a kid, fresh out of school, a friend of a friend got me an appointment in New York City with a pretty big publisher. I had written some songs, which I recorded and produced at a studio in my hometown of Baltimore, Maryland. I had my little demo tape all ready for the Big Time. In the Big Apple. With a Big Publisher.

I got all dressed up in my white, three-piece, *Saturday Night Fever* suit, complete with the John Travolta hair-do. I used so much hairspray, you could have hit me in the head with a baseball bat, and I wouldn't have felt it. I took the train from Baltimore to Manhattan. I walked uptown from Penn Station, figured I'd save money on a cab.

The building was on 54th Street. I walked in, gave the doorman my name, and took the elevator to one of the top floors. I got off the elevator and gave the receptionist my name. I waited for a while, taking in the views of Manhattan, dreaming about what kind of deal I was gonna be offered. The receptionist led me into the guy's office.

He was probably in his 50s. I shook his hand. He looked me up and down then told me that his friend—the guy who set-up the meeting—mentioned that I was "quite attractive."

Welcome to the music binniz. Maybe I was reading the guy the wrong way. So I let it go. But over the next few minutes, it became painfully obvious that the guy was interested in one thing, and it wasn't my music. He kept moving in closer to me, and I kept stepping back. He'd move in, I'd move back. We were doing this strange little tango around the room; I finally walked over to the couch and sat down. The guy sat on the edge of his desk, staring at me. I was getting a very strange vibe.

When he walked over and started to sit down on my lap, I decided it might be best to just skedaddle out of there. I walked outside onto the streets of Manhattan. It started to rain. Then it started pouring down.

He hadn't listened to one song. I'd put every last penny I had into making those demos. I played a lot of dives to come up with that cash.

I was supposed to meet my dad at a French restaurant for a victory lunch. It's hard to catch a cab in NYC in the rain, so I walked the few blocks to the restaurant—Café Brittany—in the upper 50s, on the west side of town.

My dad was a World War II veteran. He followed Patton's army across France, liberating town after town. He spoke French, was a charming raconteur, and would tell the French women who worked at Café Brittany his war stories. They loved him; no wonder he went there so often.

I walked in, all wet. My white suit was splattered with muddy water that a taxi had splashed on me. I was a mess. It hadn't been a great day. When my dad asked how it went, I told him it went okay. I didn't tell him the whole story. I was kinda embarrassed. I just kept my mouth shut. Like my dad used to say, "Nobody gets in trouble by keeping their mouth shut." Lunch was quick and quiet. I left my dad with his admirers and went back out into the rain.

I started cold-calling publishers. One of the first calls I made was the Motown office in New York. Motown had some of my favorite songwriters—Stevie Wonder, Marvin Gaye, Smokey Robinson, Holland-Dozier-Holland—and they had some of my favorite songs. To my surprise, a gal named Roxanna Gordy answered the phone. I asked for an appointment. She asked when. Hesitating as I mustered up my courage, I said, "How about right now?"

About thirty minutes later, I was in her office. It was on 57th Street, across from Carnegie Hall. I looked like shit, my suit was soaked and soiled, and my hair at this point looked more like Moe from the Three Stooges than John Travolta in *Saturday Night Fever*.

Roxanna Gordy took my tape and started playing it. I sat there in silence as we listened. Her office door was open a crack. A few minutes into the first song, the door cracked open a little more, and a man's head popped in. The guy asked Roxanna about the music, and she pointed at me. No surprise, he didn't appear too impressed with the way I looked. Can't blame him.

However, he liked what he heard and invited me into his office. His name was Carl Griffin, VP of Motown Publishing in New York. We hit it off. Carl signed me to a songwriting deal a few weeks later. I got paid a thousand bucks every month to write a song every two weeks. I was in heaven.

Right after I signed, Carl called and asked me to write a song for a new artist who had a debut CD coming out. I asked Carl when, and he told me, "Yesterday."

That didn't leave much time. I immediately wrote a song, and it sounded pretty good to me—it gave me the tingles, which is always a good omen—but how was I going to record it? I didn't have time to book a studio. All I had was an old cassette player with two inputs, and two microphones. So I hung one mic inside my upright piano, and sang into the other mic.

It was the worst recording I've ever done. On the playback, the piano came out of one speaker, and my voice came out of the other. I loved the song, but the recording made me want to hide in a cave in Afghanistan. I sent the tape to Carl.

A few weeks later, Carl came down to Baltimore to do a demo session with me. I'd written some new songs, and we needed to get them recorded. We went into the studio, which was pretty fancy. Carl sat me down in front of the speakers and told me he wanted me to listen to something.

He put on a tape, and what came out of those speakers was amazing.

It was my song, the one I had recorded into the cassette player. The new version sounded as good as anything I'd ever heard. Dave Grusin, one of my favorite producers, produced it. Dave wrote and produced the soundtracks for *Tootsie*, *The Graduate*, *On Golden Pond*, and lots of other movies.

The players were incredible—all the top session guys. Francisco Centena on bass, Eric Gale on guitar, Ralph MacDonald on percussion, and Dave Grusin himself played electric piano. I was absolutely floored. I could not believe my ears. They took that shitty little recording of my song and made it into this stupendous record, with a stunning new singer that had an amazing voice.

The singer was Angela Bofill. Her debut CD was *Angie*. My song was "Summer Days."

The album went on to get great reviews in the *New York Times*, and the *Los Angeles Times*. It was quite an auspicious debut. It sold quite a few copies and created a big buzz in the Biz.

I played the song for my dad. He was a rough, tough, and gruff guy that didn't radiate a lot of warmth, and didn't give out compliments. But I could tell he really liked it. Especially when he said, "I want you to play that at my funeral."

Keep in mind, my dad wasn't old, or sick, or close to death, or anything. But whenever I'd visit him, he'd remind me to play "Summer Days" at his funeral.

That was my dad's way of saying he liked it.

MEATBALLS

To this Italian kid, meatballs are a source of comfort. They remind me of Sunday at my grandmother Angela's house—the smell of the sauce, the warmth of the kitchen, the family drinking, and screaming, and throwing knives at each other.

Home sweet home.

When I need a little comfort, I make meatballs. A lot of Italians used to put bread soaked in milk in their meatballs. The reason was simple—you could make a lot more meatballs that way. And when you're poor and starving, you do what you can to extend a meal. I've cooked them both ways—with bread and without. And they're just plain better without the bread soaked in milk.

If you're worried about keeping your balls moist, just don't overcook them. About 3 or 4 minutes per side is plenty of time. I don't use lean meats. A lot of that juice makes things . . . juicy.

Traditional meatballs are made with equal amounts of ground beef, ground pork, and ground veal. If you have any objections to any of these meats, you can substitute.

I've made meatballs from ground turkey, and they were good; I used half dark and half white meat. I've made meatballs with just ground beef and pork, and they were good, too. Just make sure you end up with 3 pounds of meat, which should make about 60 small meatballs. Feeds 2, if you're in my family.

Freshly grated Parmigiano-Reggiano cheese is the way to go. The pre-grated stuff in a box is dry and tasteless and should be avoided if possible.

You can eat meatballs plain, but I put my meatballs in a tomato sauce. You will need about 6 cups of tomato sauce—I make my own, it's quick, simple, and easy.

I usually put my meatballs and tomato sauce over spaghetti. But what the hell do I know?

INGREDIENTS

6 cups tomato sauce (bottled is OK, homemade is best)

1 pound ground beef

1 pound ground pork

1 pound ground veal

3 eggs

3 tablespoons onion minced fine

3 tablespoons chopped fresh Italian flat-leaf parsley (you can use curly parsley in a pinch)

1½ cups breadcrumbs—don't use any that are heavily flavored—I use plain panko

¾ cup freshly grated Parmigiano-Reggiano cheese

Salt (I use 1 teaspoon of Kosher salt) and pepper

Extra-virgin olive oil (a tablespoon or so)

HERE WE GO!

Heat your tomato sauce in a large pot over high heat. When it starts to bubble, lower to a simmer.

SCAN THE QR CODE TO SEE THE YOUTUBE VIDEO

Get a big bowl. Put the meat in. Crack the eggs on top. Add the onion and parsley. Add the breadcrumbs, and the Parmigiano-Reggiano. Add some salt and fresh-cracked pepper.

Mix 'em up! I use my hands. Dig in, mix all the ingredients together. When it's all well-mixed, it's time to roll our balls! Grab a small amount of the mix, about the size of a golf ball. Roll it into a ball. Put it on a plate, and flatten it a bit. Do this with all the meat mixture.

Get a large sauté pan. Add a tablespoon of olive oil. Swirl it around the pan, and then wipe out the excess with a paper towel. Put the heat on medium, heat for 2 minutes.

Add as many meatballs as you can without crowding. No bunching! Cook for 4 minutes. Don't move them around! We want the bottoms of our balls to be brown. Pick up a meatball with some tongs. If the bottom is brown, turn all the meatballs over and cook for another 4 minutes until brown on the other side. Slice one open, take a look. If it's done, put the meatballs in the tomato sauce. If not, cook for another minute or so, and then place in the sauce when done.

Do this with all your meatballs. Drain the sauté pan of excess juices after each batch. When they've all cooked, let them simmer in the sauce for 10 minutes.

Dish it up! Put it over pasta, or serve as an appetizer with some crusty bread for your crusty friends, and . . .

MANGIAMO!

SLIM'S TOMATO SAUCE

with Bonnie Raitt
and Little Feat

In the mid-1970s, I was doing sound-alike records in a recording studio in Timonium, Maryland. The studio was Blue Seas, owned by Steve Boone, who was the bass player in the Lovin' Spoonful. Steve was from New York. How he ended up in Baltimore, I don't know.

I heard there was a woman involved.

I was in Studio B doing "sound-alike" songs for K-Tel Records. This is how it worked—K-Tel would keep their eyes on the pop charts. As soon as a song looked like it was gonna be a hit, they rushed you into the studio to do a cover version, which they would release as soon as possible. The song title would be the same, but where the band name was supposed to appear, they would put "Not the Original Artist."

At the time, I was doing a version of "Rock the Boat" by the Hues Corporation. I was trying to make my voice sound like that guy's voice. When he hits that really high note at the very end of the song? I tried to mimic it and almost gave myself a hernia.

So if you ever hear a version of "Rock the Boat" and the band is listed as "Not the Original Artist," that's me singing.

Who was in Studio A—the big studio with the grand piano and all the fancy gear?

Little Feat. One of my favorite bands. They were working on their album, *Feats Don't Fail Me Now*. Every now and then I would peek in the door; there was a lot of partying going on, right there in the control room. Don't get me wrong—some great music was being made, but the atmosphere in Studio A was completely different than Studio B. Studio A was definitely more festive.

I was in Studio B during the day; most nights I was playing a place called Mother Lode's Wild Cherry. It was a crazy rock and roll joint with a curving sliding board that started on the third-floor balcony, crossed the stage—which was on the second floor—and emptied out on to the dance floor.

The drummer in Little Feat, Richie Hayward, used to come and sit in with us at Mother Lode's. He was amazing. The club was open until 2:00 a.m., and the next day I'd go do sound-alikes in Studio B, and Richie would play drums with Little Feat in Studio A.

One day I got to the studio about an hour early. My mom had just brought home the *Rags to Rufus* record the day before. *Rags to Rufus* was the first record by a band called Rufus, Chaka Khan was the singer. My mom brought home lots of great music; there was a record store up the street from our house. My mom didn't drive, so she'd walk up to the store. The guy would tell her what was good; she'd buy the record and bring it home.

My mom brought home a wide variety of incredible music, way before anybody else discovered it. Aretha. Isaac Hayes. Judy Collins. The Beatles. The Band. Donovan. B.B. King. My mom had Bonnie Raitt records before anybody knew who Bonnie Raitt was.

So, I was sitting in Studio B, and I put the *Rags to Rufus* record on the turntable and turned it up. The first song came on. That's when Bonnie Raitt walked in. I knew who she was, and asked her what she was doing in Baltimore. She told me she was in Studio A, singing back-ups for Little Feat. She listened for a minute, and then asked me who the singer was. I told her, "Chaka Khan." That first song kicked us both in the head—"You Got the Love." It was rock, it was funk, it was soul. But the song that really knocked us out was a song called "Tell Me Something Good." When that tune came on, we both were floored.

Bonnie Raitt and I sat and listened to the whole *Rags to Rufus* album together. We didn't talk much; we just listened—Bonnie Raitt and Yours Truly. When the Rufus album ended, we said goodbye, and she walked out of the studio. I never saw her again.

About five years later, I met the guy who placed "Tell Me Something Good" with Rufus. Carl Griffin discovered that song. He was VP at Motown. He was going through old Stevie Wonder songs, and he heard this really rough demo that Stevie did of "Tell Me Something Good." Carl loved the song, saw its potential, and sent it over to Rufus.

The song won a Grammy.

I met Carl for the first time five years later. How I met him was a strange coincidence, but Carl ended up signing me as a songwriter to Motown—five years after I sat with Bonnie Raitt, listening to "Tell Me Something Good," a song Carl discovered.

One last crazy thing—

Blue Seas eventually moved their studio from Timonium to a barge in the Inner Harbor of Baltimore. Bonnie Raitt recorded an album there; so did Verdine White from Earth, Wind and Fire. On Christmas Day, 1977, the barge sank. It was not insured; there were rumors of drug debts, mob vengeance, and loan sharks. But not insurance fraud.

SLIM'S TOMATO SAUCE

If I ever have to face a firing squad, and they ask me what I want for my last meal, I'd ask for pasta with tomato sauce. Can I get a glass of wine with that? A couple meatballs? Take your time!

This is a simple sauce: tomatoes, basil, and garlic. It's quick, easy, healthy, and *delizioso*. It's also versatile—put it over pasta, and it takes on a starring role, like Marlon Brando in *The Godfather*. Use it in lasagna or eggplant Parmigiano, and it takes on a supporting role, like Robert Duvall in *The Godfather*. Use it on a pizza, and it takes on a smaller, but important role, like Diane Keaton in . . . *The Godfather*.

This recipe uses 2 (28-ounce) cans of whole, peeled, Italian tomatoes. San Marzano are best, but a little pricey. The yield is about 6 or 7 cups. In the video, I use a 6-pound can of tomatoes. I have since come to my senses.

INGREDIENTS

2 (28-ounce) cans of whole, peeled Italian tomatoes

3 tablespoons olive oil (extra-virgin, or at least one that hasn't been sleeping around)

6 cloves of garlic, sliced thin, about 3 tablespoons

Crushed red pepper to taste (I start off with ¼ teaspoon)

1 large handful fresh basil, about 1 cup, loosely packed

Kosher salt

HERE WE GO!

SCAN THE QR CODE TO SEE THE YOUTUBE VIDEO

Put the tomatoes in a large bowl.

Smoosh, yes, smoosh the tomatoes with your hands. Don't be afraid, dig in and squeeze your tomatoes; it's fun. There's a small, bitter V-shaped yellow core that needs to be removed. Also, get rid of any tomato skins, stems or other funky stuff that doesn't look like it belongs.

Put your olive oil in a large sauté pan over medium-low heat.

Put in the garlic and the crushed red pepper. Sauté a couple minutes until the garlic is pale gold. Stir occasionally. Don't burn your garlic! It tastes really bitter when burned.

Add your tomatoes. Turn the heat on high.

Grab half the basil leaves, and snip with scissors (or tear into small pieces by hand) right into the sauce.

Add salt to taste.

When the sauce comes to a boil, reduce to medium-low heat, and simmer for about 25 minutes. Stir every few minutes.

After 25 minutes, take the remaining basil leaves, and snip into the sauce. Stir it up.

Remove from heat. Taste for salt and pepper and adjust, if needed.

MANGIAMO!

PIZZA EGGS

at

My Brother's Wedding

The first time I ever drank tequila was with my uncle Oscar.

The second and last time was also with Oscar. It was the night before my brother's wedding. The family had flown in from the east coast—Baltimore and New York—to Cottonwood, Arizona, my brother's home at the time.

We all checked into a small motel, and then headed to a Mexican restaurant for a big dinner. Oscar didn't like Mexican food, but he liked tequila. He ordered margaritas for everybody, they came in glasses the size of goldfish bowls. If they were any bigger, they would have had to put filters on them. I drank mine, and it went right to my head. I hadn't had anything to eat, I had just flown across the country, and I was dead-tired. I had played until 2:00 a.m. the night before with my band, BootCamp.

Oscar ordered another round of margaritas. Wow! The last time I drank tequila with Unc, I swore I'd never do it again. I should have kept my promise.

The rest of the night is still really fuzzy; I remember some parts, and forget others. But I do remember this—at one point, my brother and I were in a pool hall in a funky part of town. We were playing pool with some banditos, and there was *dinero* involved.

My brother and I are not good pool-players, but that night, we made some incredible shots, which was amazing because we were both pretty whacked. Miraculously, we won the game, the bet, and the money. But the guys we beat wanted to play another game, to try and win back their money. We didn't; it came down to a Mexican stand-off.

I remember them slowly approaching us, pool cues in hand, and they didn't look overjoyed. I turned around to look for my brother, and he was gone. Disappeared. It was just me and the advancing desperados. I was facing them and walking slowly backwards until I felt my back touch the wall. I got lucky—I felt a door handle. I opened the door, and did what any brave soul would have done in those circumstances.

I ran like hell.

Only one small problem, I had no idea where I was. I had no idea how to get to the motel or to my brother's house. My memory gets a bit sketchy at this point. . . . I remember running like an escaped convict; and the next thing I remember, I was in my brother's house in the living room, and we were clowning around, ripping the shirts off each other's backs.

Literally. We looked like a couple of drunken, shipwrecked sailors. I have no idea why we were ripping the clothes off each other's backs. I don't know why we thought it was so funny. This I do know, I woke up the next morning feeling like someone was driving nails into my cranium, and it would have taken a crowbar to get my tongue unstuck from the roof of my mouth. If anyone had lit a match anywhere near me, I would have spontaneously combusted.

A woman priest was shaking me, trying to wake me up. I tried to focus my eyes, but my vision was a little blurry. I thought I was seeing things, or maybe I was dreaming. I was in bed; I looked next to me, and there was my brother, in his ripped-up clothes. Next to him was his wife-to-be, not looking real thrilled. The lady priest was standing next to me, looking down at us. Lord knows what she was thinking, seeing the three of us in bed together. For the record, we all had our clothes on.

I got out of bed and stood up. My shirt was hanging from my shoulders, ripped to shreds, both pant legs were torn and dangling, flapping in the breeze. I thought the priest was gonna read me my last rites. Or do an exorcism.

The wedding was in an hour; I had no clothes, except my ripped up shirt and shredded pants. I called my mom back at the hotel. Help, Ma! She couldn't find my suit. I then realized that I had forgotten to pack it. I may look like an idiot, and I may act like an idiot, but don't let that fool you.

I really am an idiot.

I had forgotten almost everything except my shaving kit and a Swiss Army knife. My mom was an angel; she really was. She pieced together an outfit from the various men in the wedding party. The only problem? I'm six feet two inches tall, I have really long arms, and really long legs, and really big feet. The pants she got for me were about six inches above my ankles, the arms of the sport coat came halfway up my forearms—I looked like Chico Marx. None of the colors matched.

The wedding took place on top of a mesa, which is a mountain that looks like the top has been chopped off. The long drive to the top of the mesa was swervy and curvy, and I wasn't feeling so great.

My brother had an old pickup truck, a beater with an old chair in the back. The woman priest sat in the chair in the back of the pickup truck, and my brother drove her like that up to the top of the mesa. The rest of the wedding party was already there. When I looked out over the panoramic view of the valley, with the incredibly beautiful town of Sedona in the distance, I didn't feel inspired, I didn't feel stirred.

I felt dizzy. For the whole wedding ceremony, I had my hands folded at my waist, looking down at the ground—not because I was being reverent or emotional. I was just thinking that if I had to throw up, maybe nobody would notice if my mouth was already pointing at my feet. I looked down at my shoes, which weren't actually mine, and were ridiculously silly-looking and way too small.

After the wedding, we all went to my brother's house. That's when he asked me if I'd tend bar. The thought of alcohol was enough to send me to the Betty Ford Center, but I said yes. I can't refuse my brother on his wedding day. Do you know what everybody wanted to drink?

Tequila. For what seemed like a couple of weeks, I made margaritas, and I poured shots. I didn't drink a drop. I don't think I've been near a shot of tequila since that crazy night in Cottonwood.

My brother and his wife have been married for years—the first marriage for both of them. They have one of the best relationships I've ever witnessed. I am extremely proud of them; it worked out so very well.

PIZZA EGGS

My brother created this recipe. It's the family go-to recipe for breakfast on holidays and birthdays, and of course, weddings. It's quick, it's easy, and it's *delizioso*. And great for hangovers.

I make my own tomato sauce from scratch. It takes about 30 minutes, start-to-finish, and it is so good and so healthy.

But if you're in a pinch, you can use store-bought tomato sauce.

Bufala mozzarella is made from the milk of water buffalos. Where the hell are they keeping these water buffalos? And who's milking them? Bufala mozzarella is quite expensive and not absolutely necessary for this dish—you can just use regular mozzarella if you want and save the Bufala for a Caprese salad.

INGREDIENTS

3 cups tomato sauce

6 eggs

1¼ cup shredded mozzarella

¼ cup grated Parmigiano-Reggiano cheese

Salt and fresh-cracked black pepper

HERE WE GO!

SCAN THE QR CODE TO SEE THE YOUTUBE VIDEO

Put a large sauté pan on high heat—I used a 12-inch pan.

Put in the 3 cups of tomato sauce.

When it starts bubbling, lower the heat to medium-low.

Break the eggs right into the sauce, but keep 'em separated from each other.

Add salt and pepper on top of each egg.

Add shredded mozzarella on top of each egg.

Cover and cook for about 5 minutes, until the eggs are done, and the cheese has melted.

Remove from heat.

Add a little grated Parmigiano on top of each egg.

Serve it up with crusty bread, to your crusty, dusty amigos, and . . .

MANGIAMO!

ROASTED VEGETABLE LASAGNA

at the Vatican
with Pope John Paul II

On Christmas Day, 1999, I sang for Pope John Paul II at the Vatican.

When you read that first line, you might get the impression that I was strumming my guitar at the Pope's bedside, singing Christmas songs as he dozed off to sleep.

That ain't what happened.

A friend of mine called from L.A. She was putting a choir together to sing two pieces of music written for Pope John Paul II. She was familiar with my music and thought I might like to be included as a vocalist. Yes, indeed! Both pieces were going to be performed at the Vatican on Christmas Day, 1999, the last Christmas of the 20th century. She asked me to be in the choir, to sing for the Pope.

You can't say "nope" to the Pope.

I drove over to my uncle Oscar's house, not far from my hometown of Baltimore, Maryland. I told him what was going on—I was flying to Rome for Christmas to sing for the Pope. He was so happy; you would have thought I'd just cured erectile dysfunction. Oscar insisted on paying for my hotel as a Christmas gift. He wanted me to stay at the Excelsior, a luxurious hotel in the heart of Rome. Fellini shot part of a movie there, *La Dolce Vita*.

A few days before Christmas, I flew to Rome. I had never been before. When I checked into the hotel, I was dazzled. It was beautiful. Elegant. I didn't get to see much of the hotel, though. Most of my days were spent at rehearsals. The two pieces of music we were doing for the Pope were called "Magnificat" and "Cantata Giubileo."

"Magnificat," was written by Beppe Cantarelli, an Italian guy who had written songs for Aretha and Mariah Carey. "Magnificat" is truly magnificent, one of my favorite pieces of choral music.

"Cantata Giubileo" was written by Maurice Jarre, a pretty famous and serious film composer. He won three Academy Awards for the music he wrote for *Lawrence of Arabia*, *Doctor Zhivago*, and *A Passage to India*.

Giubileo is the Italian word for "Jubilee." Every twenty-five years, the Roman Catholic Church celebrates Giubileo. *Cantare* is the Italian word for "sing." In other words, "Cantata Giubileo" was supposed to be a joyous piece of vocal music. It was a difficult piece of music—difficult to sing and difficult to like. There were so many key changes, time signature changes, and tempo changes. To top it off, the choir had to sing the word "peace" in thirty-three different languages. I like to joke a lot. But I ain't kidding, Maurice wanted us to learn how to sing "peace" in thirty-three languages. There were about fifty people in the choir, men and women, mostly from L.A.; a mixed bag of gospel singers, pop singers, R&B singers, and one lonely jazz guy—me. We were called the Millennium Choir.

We rehearsed in the Sala Nervi, the concert hall that had just been built next to St. Peter's Basilica. Sala Nervi was amazing. The acoustics, the mile-high ceilings, the marble floors, the masses of stained glass—they didn't get this stuff at Home Depot. It was really and truly stunning.

The orchestra was down in front in the pit. The choir was on stage in a semi-circle, on raised stands. I stood next to a well-dressed black guy, who introduced himself as Darryl Phinnesse. He had written the lyrics to the theme song for the TV show *Fraser*. I always wondered about the lyric in that song "tossed salads and scrambled eggs." I asked Darryl about it. He explained that "tossed salads and scrambled eggs" meant crazy people, people who were mixed up.

I didn't get it. I still don't get it. He had a real good voice, though.

Rehearsals for "Magnificat" were magnificent. The choir, the orchestra—everybody connected with that piece of music in a big way. It sounded glorious. To sing that incredible song, with a full choir and orchestra, in that amazing hall—I could have sung it a hundred times in a row. But "Cantata Giubileo"? Both the choir and orchestra were having a tough time. Even when we got it right, it didn't sound right—it sounded like an orchestra tuning up. Cacophonous.

Maurice Jarre was not happy. He didn't look like a real happy guy to begin with.

One night, after rehearsal, I was at the hotel bar in the Excelsior, singing "Blue Christmas" to a woman I was having a drink with, when a very stylish Italian guy came over and told me he liked my voice, told me I sounded like Elvis. I had been studying Italian for months. I knew enough to get around, especially when someone was talking about The King. He asked me my name. I was gonna say Slim Man, but I told him my real name. His eyes lit up. He told me about Ristorante Camponeschi in Rome. He told me I had to go there. He introduced himself—Federico.

Federico called me in my room the next morning to tell me he had made a reservation. I thanked him, hung up, and promptly forgot about it. I was focused on the Pope. I showered, dressed, and got in a taxi. I told the cab driver to take me to the Vatican. When he asked me why I was going there, I told him I was going to sing for the Pope. He laughed. I guess it did sound like a joke.

Rehearsal that day was no joke. "Cantata Giubeleo" was still not sounding right. Maurice worked us hard. Towards the end of the long day, Maurice stopped the choir to yell at us. He was a fiery Frenchman, and he wasn't happy with the way his masterpiece was sounding. In the middle of his hollering, I noticed a guy walking across the marble floor. He was about 100 yards away, but you could hear his footsteps echo in the hall, getting louder as he got closer. The guy stopped next to Maurice Jarre. He was dressed in a suit and tie with overcoat. He looked like a hit man. Maurice stopped yelling.

The guy said, to no one in particular, that he was looking for Signore Camponeschi. I looked around. There were no other Camponeschis. I raised my hand. He motioned for me to go with him. I had no idea what was going on. Maybe the Pope wanted me to make him some meatballs.

The orchestra, the choir, Maurice—everyone stood and stared in silence as I stepped down from the choir stand, walked off the stage, and followed the guy out of the Sala Nervi, our footsteps fading in the grand hall. We walked outside, and the guy opened the back door of a Mercedes limo. I got in. I knew he wasn't gonna kill me—he wouldn't have abducted me in front of a hundred witnesses if he were. But I was a bit curious as to where I was going. When I'd ask, he'd say "Camponeschi."

Ten minutes later, we pulled up in front of the French Embassy. I was really confused, until I saw a sign across the street from the Embassy. Ristorante Camponeschi. We walked in. I couldn't have had a better reception if I were the Pope. They had everything but a brass band playing the national anthem. Alessandro Camponeschi and his dad, Marino, owned the place, and they greeted me with hugs, and treated me like a long-lost son.

My grandfather, Romollo Camponeschi, was born in Rome. It's quite possible that Alessandro and I might be related. But what a welcome, regardless. Ristorante Camponeschi is very elegant. Alessandro and Marino wouldn't let me order from the menu. I must have had a hundred courses. They brought soups, salads and appetizers, lobsters, champagne, and desserts as well as flaming liqueurs.

When your name is Slim Man, it's not a good thing to stuff yourself like I did. Especially in public.

After dinner, I gave a warm goodbye to Alessandro and Marino. The Mercedes limo was waiting for me outside. He gave me a quick ride back to the Excelsior. I thanked him, walked inside, and went to sleep. I found out the next day that Federico had made all the arrangements—the limo pick-up from the Vatican, the dinner, the limo ride home. All because he liked the way I sang "Blue Christmas." Long Live The King!

On Christmas morning, I got all dressed up in my tuxedo. It took me a while to get my bow tie tied—I didn't want to use a clip-on for the Pope. I caught a cab to the Vatican and got ready for the Big Show. We took the stage, the lights went dim and . . .

The concert was amazing. The choir sounded great, so did the orchestra, and it all went really well—both pieces of music sounded exquisite. I was concentrating so hard on the sheet music, on getting everything right that I really didn't have time to look around and soak it all in. It all flew by right quickly. Before I knew it, it was over.

After the concert, I walked out of the Sala Nervi into the chilly Christmas night, and it was breathtaking. The streets of Rome were jam-packed with people, the church bells were ringing, voices were singing, the Christmas lights were twinkling, all the streetlamps were decorated, and it was glorious.

Absolutely glorious.

ROASTED VEGETABLE LASAGNA

I wanted to make a lasagna that was . . . Slim, so to speak. So I skipped the ricotta cheese, and just roasted some vegetables.

The first time I cooked this I used no-cook lasagna noodles in a 9 by 13-inch dish. The lasagna fit in the dish perfectly, but I didn't like the way they tasted. I know a lot of people use them. To me, no-cook lasagna don't taste right.

I prefer to boil the lasagna the old school way—in boiling water. What a concept. I boiled my lasagna noodles according to the instructions on the package, and they turned out so nice! It didn't add any additional time, I cooked the lasagna noodles as the vegetables roasted.

I used an 8 by 11-inch glass baking dish for the lasagna, because the traditional lasagna noodles fit perfectly in there. I used 9 sheets of lasagna—3 layers of 3.

I was gonna cook a tomato sauce for this, but then, in a stroke of genius, I decided to do a no-cook tomato sauce. When I usually cook a tomato sauce, I cook it for 20 minutes.

I figured, the tomato sauce was gonna bake in the oven with the lasagna for 20 minutes anyway, why cook the sauce beforehand. *Capisce*?

It saved a lot of time and effort, but the best thing about this no-cook tomato sauce? It tasted so fresh. Funky fresh!

You'll need 3 generous cups of tomato sauce. You can use bottled sauce, but my no-cook tomato sauce takes no time.

I found some organic mini-bell peppers on sale. They were beautiful—red, yellow, and orange—and added a nice color and flavor to this dish. If you can't find mini-bell peppers, you can use a regular orange, yellow or red bell pepper, or a combination of all three. Whatever combination you use, you'll need to end up with a cup and a half, chopped.

I found some multi-colored heirloom grape tomatoes on sale. They, too, were colorful and *delizioso*. And not expensive. I cut them in half, squeezed the seeds out, and they worked perfectly.

Cippolini onions are sweeter and milder than normal onions. They're good for roasting, and you can find them in normal grocery stores. If you can't find cippolini onions, use regular onions or shallots.

I always clean my vegetables. I clean everything. You gotta keep it clean, Slim People.

INGREDIENTS

For the lasagna:

3 cups (2 medium) zucchini cut in ¼ inch circular slices

1½ cups small cippolini onions (6), peeled and quartered

1½ cups bell peppers (red, orange, yellow) cored, seeded, cut into 1-inch pieces

5 tablespoons extra-virgin olive oil

4 cups (8 ounces) sliced portobello mushroom caps, cut into 1-inch pieces (a ¼ inch thick)

3 cups (2 small) yellow squash cut in ¼ inch circular slices

3 cups grape tomatoes, cut in half, insides/seeds squeezed out

1 package lasagna noodles (at least 9 sheets)

¼ cup basil, loosely packed, snipped with scissors or chopped gently—it bruises!

1 pound (or more!) mozzarella cheese, you'll need 1½ cups shredded, plus 12 circular ¼ inch slices

½ cup freshly grated Parmigiano-Reggiano cheese

Kosher salt and fresh-cracked black pepper

For the no-cook tomato sauce:

1 (28-ounce) can crushed Italian tomatoes (San Marzano are best)

1 tablespoon minced garlic

¼ cup basil leaves, loosely packed, snipped with scissors or chopped gently

½ teaspoon Kosher salt

¼ teaspoon crushed red pepper

Combine all the ingredients, stir, set aside. Taste for salt and pepper and adjust. This should make about 3 or 4 cups. How easy was that?

HERE WE GO!

SCAN THE QR CODE TO SEE THE YOUTUBE VIDEO

Pre-heat your oven to 400 degrees.

Put your zucchini, onion, and peppers in a bowl, drizzle with 1 to 2 tablespoons of olive oil, add some Kosher salt and fresh-cracked black pepper, and toss.

Get a large metal baking pan, line it with aluminum foil. Add the zucchini and onions and peppers to the pan.

Put your portobello mushrooms and yellow squash in the bowl. Add 1 to 2 tablespoons of olive oil, some Kosher salt and fresh-cracked black pepper, and toss.

Get another large metal baking pan, line it with aluminum foil. Add the portobello mushrooms and yellow squash to the pan.

Put both pans in the oven, as close to the middle as possible, and roast for 20 minutes. As the vegetables roast . . .

Take your 3 cups of halved grape tomatoes, put them in a bowl. Add a tablespoon of olive oil, some Kosher salt and fresh-cracked black pepper and toss. Set aside.

Now, for the lasagna noodles. Get a large pot, fill it full of cold water, put it on the highest heat ya got. When it comes to a full boil, add 2 tablespoons Kosher salt and the lasagna noodles.

Cook the lasagna noodles according to the directions on the package. I followed the instructions on a package of Barilla lasagna; I cooked them for 7 minutes, they turned out great.

But keep an eye on these guys, make sure they don't stick together. People should stick together, lasagna shouldn't. Use tongs. Be gentle. Be kind. But you gotta keep 'em separated.

When the lasagna noodles have cooked according to the instructions, drain gently.

When the vegetables have roasted, take them out of the oven.

Get a glass or ceramic baking dish; I used an 8 by 11-inch glass baking dish.

Put a generous cup of uncooked tomato sauce in the bottom, spread around evenly.

Add 3 pieces of lasagna, lay like shingles, overlapping.

Add the roasted zucchini, peppers, and onions.

Add a cup of tomato sauce.

Add ¾ cup shredded mozzarella, spread evenly and judiciously.

Add 3 more pieces of lasagna, layering like shingles.

Add the roasted yellow squash and portobellos. Spread 'em out even.

Add a cup of tomato sauce, spread evenly.

Add ¾ cup of shredded mozzarella, evenly—*capisce*?

Add another layer of lasagna noodles, 3, lay 'em down like shingles.

Add the tomato halves, distribute evenly. Any part of the lasagna noodles that are exposed, rub or brush with a little olive oil from the bowl that held the tomatoes. This will help keep the noodles from drying out.

Stick the baking dish in the oven on the middle rack for 20 minutes.

After 20 minutes, remove from the oven.

Sprinkle the ¼ cup of basil leaves on top of the tomatoes. Add the slices of mozzarella, make sure you cover all the tomatoes.

Top off with the grated Parmigiano-Reggiano cheese.

Turn the oven to broil. Put the lasagna in the oven and KEEP AN EYE ON THESE GUYS. Don't burn the cheese. You want it to get golden brown. It should only take a MINUTE OR TWO.

Maybe three . . .

When the mozzarella is golden and bubbly, remove. Let it sit for 10 minutes.

Dish it up! Make it look nice. Sprinkle with some snipped basil leaves, maybe some freshly grated Parmigiano-Reggiano cheese. She's a-so-nice!

MANGIAMO!

CHICKEN PICCATA

and Hobnobbin' with Slim Slimski

Follow a transvestite while he/she shops for clothes. Go to an underground tattoo parlor, get a tattoo, then go to a dermatologist and get it removed with a laser.

Those are just a few of the episodes we did for a TV show called *Hobnobbin' with Slim Slimski*.

Rei Peri was the director. He was the cameraman. He was also the editor, the light guy, the sound guy—he was the guy. The guy behind the camera. I was the guy in front of the camera. It was just the two of us, thinking up wacky segments to shoot.

We would then go around our hometown of Baltimore, Maryland, and film these episodes. Most of the stuff was completely spontaneous. Well, we'd make appointments; but what we did when we got there was just run and gun—improvise, see what happens. No script. It was a lot of fun. Nerve-wracking fun.

Rei had the idea to follow a transvestite while he/she shopped for clothes. "He" was a man dressed as a woman. He called himself Marilyn. Most of the clothes shops we visited were in Fells Point, which is a funkified neighborhood, deep in the heart of Baltimore. Marilyn seemed to like biker clothes—black leather motorcycle jackets, black leather chaps, things like that. A man, dressed as a woman, shopping for biker clothes.

In another episode, we went to an underground tattoo parlor. It was in this guy's kitchen, in his small apartment, in a nasty section of town. Strange-looking folks were waiting around to get tattoos. It wasn't the cleanest place in the world, and he was making some of the most bizarre tattoos I'd ever seen.

I got one, of course. The tattoo guy asked me what I wanted. I asked for a simple heart with "Mom" in the middle, on the inside of my forearm. I got tattooed. The guy didn't use any ink—he probably didn't want to waste it on a tattoo that was gonna get removed right away. So I felt the pain but got no stain. It didn't hurt as much as I thought it would. Even without the ink, you could clearly see the tattoo. The skin was raised and red and it looked like I had been branded with a branding iron.

I showed my mom and she thought it was real. Then she hit me in the head with a frying pan.

Just kidding. How could she be mad? I got "Mom" tattooed on my forearm.

I went to the dermatologist soon after to see what it was like to get a tattoo removed. I wasn't the first in line. There was a woman before me who wanted to get a big eagle tattoo removed from her chest. She was complaining that the wings of the eagle looked like chest hair when she wore low-cut shirts.

The dermatologist let Rei and I sit in on her tattoo removal. We all had to wear special goggles, so the laser wouldn't fry our eyeballs. We looked like mad scientists. The doctor placed the laser pen on her tattoo and zapped. She flinched, like she'd just been tasered. He put the pen back on the tattoo and zapped. She flinched again. He'd zap, she'd flinch; it went on way too long, like a torture session. She looked like she was having some kind of strange conniptions every couple seconds. Rei and I were filming and watching all this play out with our mad scientist goggles on. I wanted to jump in, wave the white flag, blow the whistle, toss in the towel, call off the dogs!

The doctor finally relented. The woman got out of her chair. The tattoo was still visible. Doctor Dude told us that a tattoo that big and dark would need a couple of sessions to remove. The gal didn't look too happy. Plus, she had to pay for all this. She zombie-walked out of there.

I sat down in the chair. The doctor revved up the laser and zapped me. It didn't hurt as much as the time I got my genitalia caught in my zipper, but it was close. The laser hurt more than getting the tattoo. After a bunch of zaps, my skin was on fire.

No wonder that poor woman was flailing around like that.

For another episode of *Hobnobbin' with Slim Slimski*, we went to the Timonium Fairgrounds for the 4-H festival. 4-H stands for Head, Heart, Health, and Hands. It's a collection of young folks trying to improve urban, suburban, and rural communities. I walked into a large barn, with Rei following and filming. Some of these young folks were demonstrating how to milk a cow.

I like farm animals. They look okay from a distance. But I've never felt the strong urge to get real close to any of them, let alone start mangling their mammaries. They wanted me to milk a cow named Leslie. Really. I walked up to Leslie and sat down on a stool by her rear legs. She turned her huge head around and stared me up and down with these big dark eyeballs. I looked her in the eye, and then looked down at her udders and . . .

It was a little too soon for me. Call me old-fashioned, but I think it's more appropriate to go out on a few dates, get to know a female before you start yanking on her breastages.

Then Leslie winked. I think she liked me. I liked her, too. But sadly, that was the end of our relationship. I walked away, knowing I did the honorable thing.

The highlight of the 4-H festival was Rei following me around, cameras rolling, as I walked around the fairgrounds, checking out the games—you know the kind—games where you throw a hardball and try to knock down some pins, or you try to shoot a basketball into a hoop a million times in a row, or you throw darts at balloons, or toss Ping-Pong balls into small gold fish bowls. If you win, they give you prizes, like huge stuffed animals. Those kinds of games.

As we were checking out the games, I walked by a dunking booth. Let me explain the dunking booth. A guy sits in a chair over a pool of water. There is a target over his head. You buy three hardballs, and if you hit the target, the guy gets dunked in the water. This guy was hurling insults at people as they passed by. Calling people all kinds of nasty names. "Hey Fatso, get your big butt over here!" As I walked by, the guy got quiet. Then, all of a sudden I heard . . .

"Hey, you! Donkey Face!"

That's what he said. Donkey Face. I kept walking. I had long hair in a ponytail. The guy kept shouting,

"Hey you! Donkey Face! With the ponytail! You can't cut off that pony tail 'cause it goes with your donkey head!"

That's what he said. I stopped walking.

"That's right, Donkey Face! I'm talkin' to YOU! Uno, dos, tres, come on, hit me Donkey Face!"

He kept chanting.

"Uno, dos, tres, come on, hit me Donkey Face!"

A crowd started to gather. That made him scream louder.

"Uno, dos, tres, come on, hit me Donkey Face!"

I calmly walked over to the booth and bought three balls. He kept chanting. I reared my arm back and threw as hard as I could. I nailed the target with the first throw. Bulls-eye. He fell in the water with a huge splash. But the damage was done. When my friends and family saw that video footage, they didn't say, "That's not funny. That guy was way out of line. Glad you nailed him. Way to go."

No. Instead, they started calling me Donkey Face. Not behind my back. Right in front of my face. Friends, band members, family. My own father called me Donkey Face.

Not all the time. Just most of the time.

CHICKEN PICCATA

After clothes shopping with a transvestite, there's nothing like a home-cooked meal. This dish is perfect after a long day at work.

I began with 3 large boneless, skinless chicken breasts that were a little too thick for this dish. So I cut them in half, and it worked out fine.

I have a friend who doesn't like garlic. It's okay, he's still my friend. This is one of the few dishes I cook that doesn't have any garlic. Or onions. So if you have any friends that don't like garlic or onions, this is the dish to cook.

INGREDIENTS

6 chicken cutlets, each about ½ inch thick

½ cup flour

Salt and pepper

2 tablespoons extra-virgin olive oil

2 tablespoons butter

¼ cup white wine

½ cup chicken broth

2 tablespoons capers

2 tablespoons fresh-squeezed lemon juice (remove the seeds)

A few sprigs of parsley for garnish

A few circular lemon slices for garnish

HERE WE GO!

SCAN THE QR CODE TO SEE THE YOUTUBE VIDEO

Heat your oven to warm (the lowest setting).

Rinse off your chicken breasts and pat dry with a paper towel.

Put the flour on a flat plate. Add a little salt and fresh-cracked black pepper.

Take a chicken cutlet, put it in the flour. Turn it over. Make sure both sides are lightly coated. Shake off any excess flour.

Repeat with all 6 pieces of chicken.

Put the oil and butter in a large sauté pan over medium heat. When the butter starts to bubble, put the chicken in the pan.

Cook for 3 minutes or until golden brown on the underside. Use your tongs and turn them over.

Cook for 3 minutes on the other side. Check for doneness. If done, place them on a plate and set them in a warm oven. If not, cook for another minute or so until done, then place them in the oven.

Turn the heat on the empty sauté pan to medium-high. Add the white wine and stir and scrape (deglaze the pan) for a minute or so.

Add the chicken broth and capers. Cook while stirring for a minute or so.

Add the lemon juice and cook and stir for a minute or so, and turn off the heat.

Take your breasts out of the warm oven. Place them on a nice platter. Pour a little sauce over each breast, garnish with lemon and parsley, and . . .

MANGIAMO!

LINGUINE and WHITE CLAM SAUCE

with Gary Puckett and the Union Gap

This dish was one of my uncle Oscar's favorites. He loved to cook this sauce, and his version was about as good as it gets. A few years ago, I was having brunch with Unc. He lived in a big house in this great section of Baltimore, Maryland, called Guilford.

As we were sitting on the outdoor patio, drinking Bloody Marys that sunny Sunday afternoon, I commented on the watch he was wearing. It was a Movado, the one with the plain black face and the big diamond at the top of the dial, where the "12" usually is. It was one good-looking watch, and I said so. He took it off his wrist and said, "I want you to have it." He gave it to me.

I told him that I didn't want it. Unc insisted. I resisted. This went back and forth for a few minutes, then he screamed, "Take the fuckin' watch!"

Oscar cursed a lot. So did my dad, his brother. Funny, it never sounded really vulgar coming from them. Just seemed kind of natural. They were tough guys, but well-educated and eloquent. They used the "F" word a lot.

I took the fucking watch. You don't say no to a guy like Unc—it could be lethal. I put it on my wrist. Wow. That was one beautiful watch. I figured I'd take the watch and give it back to Oscar the next day, after the Bloody Marys had worn off. It was way too expensive a watch to keep.

I had a date that night—a girl I'd had my eye on for quite some time. She worked in a club where my band played, and, for what seemed like years, I'd wanted to ask her out. I had a big crush. I finally got up the nerve to ask her out. I did. She said yes.

Now I had a new watch to wear on that first date.

I took this girl to my friend's restaurant—an elegant fine-dining place with a grand piano and a small dance floor. They had a guy who played piano and sang Sinatra, and you could wine, dine, and dance, Rat Pack style. The food was great, Italian stuff. The bar was cool. The lighting, the decor, and the ambiance were really kinda sexy. My uncle Oscar used to go there. So did a lot of successful Baltimore Italian guys, who looked like they were in the Mafia.

The waitresses—dressed in black bow ties, white shirts, and black vests—would stand inconspicuously in the shadows, hands clasped behind their backs, surveying the room like Secret Service agents. All someone had to do was make a hand gesture, and a waitress would be bounding across the room like an Olympic gymnast doing the floor routine. If you got up to go to the bathroom, or have a dance, when you came back, your napkin would be miraculously folded into some kind of Origami sculpture. That's the kind of place it was.

My date and I sat down at the bar and ordered drinks. We clinked glasses, she saw the watch and said, "That's a great watch." I thanked her, and then told her the story about Unc giving me the watch off his wrist. She seemed more impressed by the watch than by the fact that Oscar gave it to me right off his wrist. I changed the subject. I asked her what her favorite band was. She didn't hesitate, "Gary Puckett and the Union Gap."

Gary Puckett and the Union Gap? I knew who they were. I remembered their song, "Young Girl," whose first line is "Young Girl, get out of my mind, my love for you is way out of line," which is a line that if sung today, might get you thrown in jail, let alone be a big hit.

I had an ex who hated the word hate. She'd say "least favorite" instead. She turned out to be my least favorite ex.

Gary Puckett and the Union Gap are one of my least favorite bands. I mean, think of all the bands in the world—Led Zeppelin, the Beatles, the Stones, the Jimi Hendrix Experience, Sly and the Family Stone, U2—and you're going with Gary Puckett and the Union Gap? That's what was going through my mind as I sat there at the bar having a drink with this gorgeous girl who I had such a crush on.

"What time is it?" she asked.

I smiled and looked down at my watch with the big diamond and told her. She asked me again about five minutes later. I told her. Five minutes later, same thing. It was kind of cute—the first ten times she asked me what time it was.

We finally sat down for dinner. She asked me what time it was. Again. I smiled and looked down at my watch. The glass that covered the face was gone. The two hands were gone—the big one and the little one. The black face with the big diamond was gone. I was staring at a bunch of gears . . . that weren't moving.

I took the broken watch off my wrist and said, "Let's not worry about time. Let's just enjoy this moment." I put what was left of the watch in my jacket pocket. When my date excused herself to go to the bathroom, I dove underneath the table. The waitresses came bounding over, thinking I was having a seizure or choking to death. When I told them what happened, they helped me look. There were more lighters underneath that table than during a slow song at an Elton John concert. One of the waitresses alerted us that my date was on her way back from the bathroom, and they jumped back into position, and I got out from under the table.

The rest of the evening was nice if uneventful, except that every time my date would go to the bathroom, everyone from the busboys to the hostess was looking on the floor for the missing pieces of my watch. We had dinner, had a drink and a dance, and then I took her home.

We never went out again. I mean, she was a nice person, kind of sweet and funny. And gorgeous. I hate to admit it, but the Gary Puckett and the Union Gap thing bothered me. After I dropped her off, I went back to the restaurant. Nobody had found anything. I pulled the broken watch out of my jacket pocket and looked at it again. No glass. No hands. No face. No huge diamond.

I wasn't looking forward to telling my Uncle about the watch. He was a very understanding man, but he also had a temper. One time, Oscar got pissed off at his uncle, who had accused Oscar—who was a doctor—of not taking such great medical care of his wife. Oscar threw a glass at the guy.

Luckily, he missed. He hit the coffee table instead. Unc threw the glass so hard, that years later, when I was having the table refinished, the shards were so deeply embedded in the table top that they couldn't even sand them out.

And I was thinking about that glass when I called Oscar that morning. I told Unc that I had broken the incredibly expensive diamond Movado watch he'd so generously given me.

He started laughing. Really hard.

Then he told me that he'd bought the watch on the streets of New York City for ten bucks.

LINGUINE AND WHITE CLAM SAUCE

There's nothing like a little linguine with white clam sauce after your uncle has just played a huge joke on you.

Use the smallest clams you can find. Oscar sometimes used *vongole veraci*, tiny little clams from Italy the size of a thumbnail.

I used wild Manila clams, about the size of a quarter. A few months ago, I did a show at a club called Spaghettini, in Seal Beach, California. My brother and his wife had come in from Arizona for the concert. The day after the show, my brother wanted me to cook some clam sauce, so I searched and found fresh Manila clams in a seafood store deep in the heart of Cambodia Town, a neighborhood a few miles from Seal Beach. The clams were wild and fresh and looked and smelled wonderful.

Cleaning clams can be a pain. But that's one of the keys to this recipe—you have to clean your clams. Whatever clams you use, soak them in ice water for a few hours, or—even better—overnight. This is to get rid of the grit, to let the clams purge themselves of their sand.

After the clams have been soaking, pour the clams and the ice water they've been soaking in into a colander. Rinse the clams off and scrub each one with a vegetable brush. Repeat.

Whenever Oscar made clam sauce, he always mentioned the special ingredient my mom had told him about. Oscar loved my mom. It was my mom who suggested to Oscar that he put two anchovies in the sauce.

To some people, eating anchovies is like eating a sweaty eyebrow.

But when you add two anchovies in the beginning of this sauce, and mash them up, it really lends a great flavor. Just don't let anybody see you do it, and don't tell anybody about it. Like my dad used to say, "Nobody gets in trouble by keeping their mouth shut."

INGREDIENTS

6 dozen small clams, the smallest you can find

3 tablespoons extra-virgin olive oil

6 cloves garlic, thinly sliced (about 2 tablespoons)

Crushed red pepper (I start off with ¼ teaspoon)

2 anchovies

1 cup clam juice

¼ cup white wine

2 dozen or so grape tomatoes, yellow or red or both, cut in half, seeds squeezed out

A handful of fresh Italian flat-leaf parsley, chopped (¼ cup)

Kosher salt

HERE WE GO!

SCAN THE QR CODE TO SEE THE YOUTUBE VIDEO

Rinse the clams one final time in cold water and set aside.

Get a large pot, fill it with cold water and put it on the highest heat you got—this is for our pasta.

Let's make our sauce! Put the olive oil in a large pan. Put the heat on medium.

Add the crushed red pepper and the sliced garlic, and cook until the garlic is pale gold, a few minutes. Don't burn the garlic!

Add the anchovies and mash them with the back of a wooden spoon 'til they disintegrate.

Add the clam juice and the white wine. Turn the heat on high.

When the sauce comes to a boil, reduce it for a minute or so. Turn the heat to medium-low.

Add the clams to the sauce.

Then add the tomatoes and the parsley. Stir. Cover.

After a couple of minutes, take the cover off, stir, and put the cover back on.

Cook until the clams have opened up.

Throw out any unopened clams. This is important. Unopened clams are bad clams. No bad clams!

When your pasta water has boiled, toss in a few tablespoons of Kosher salt, and add a pound of linguine. Cook according to the instructions on the box. When it's supposed to be ready, taste the pasta. Take a piece, and bite through it. If it's chalky in the center it's not done. Check every 2 minutes, until the pasta is not chalky or chewy.

When the pasta is *al dente* (firm to the bite), drain and add it to the sauce. Drizzle with a touch of olive oil, and toss. Add about half of the clam sauce to the pasta and toss gently.

Dish it up! Put a small amount of pasta—about a handful—on a plate, and top off with a ladle of the clam sauce. Garnish with parsley, and serve it up.

MANGIAMO!

GRILLED SALMON MARSALA with GRILLED VEGETABLES

and Merci, Philippe!

Jacqueline

My dad told me that when his platoon was going across France behind General Patton in World War II, the towns they liberated were really grateful. How grateful?

In one town, as they went past an exuberant, cheering crowd, a woman grabbed my dad, dragged him into her bedroom and made love to him right then and there.

Now that's gratitude.

Before the war, my dad was drifting. He went to St. John's College in Annapolis, Maryland, but wasn't a good student; he was cutting classes and slacking off. In an effort to try and straighten him out, the school put him in charge of the café. One night, he took the money out of the cash register and lost it all in a late-night poker game; he had every intention of paying it back from his winnings, but it didn't work out as planned. They asked him to leave.

Soon after, he joined the Army and went to Europe to fight in World War II. It was a hellish and brutal experience that made my dad a man. His father, Romollo, died of a heart attack while my father was away at war. They were close, but he couldn't go back for the funeral. It was one of the loneliest times of my dad's life.

After the war, he went back to St. John's. He became a good student, graduated, and went on to law school. He became a lawyer. He did all of this with no money—he was the son of poor Italian immigrants.

He became a member of the U.S. Commission on Civil Rights. He helped start the Peace Corps. He wrote speeches for Vice President Hubert Humphrey. He became a professor of philosophy and literature.

World War II, the toughest time of his life, turned out to be his proudest moment—the turning point that changed his life in the best way possible.

My dad was in the Fifteenth Corps; they followed General Patton's Third Army through France, liberating town after town. One of the towns the Fifteenth Corps liberated was Lunéville, a small town in northeastern France, about fifty miles from the German border. Lunéville was still being bombed and strafed by the Germans. My dad was patrolling the streets one day, when he heard a German Stuka approaching. Stukas were small bombers, two-seaters that also had machine guns. My dad saw a one-armed Frenchman, frozen with fear.

My dad ran over, grabbed the Frenchman, and pushed him to the ground and covered him, bombs exploding, bullets flying. When the Stuka passed, the guy thanked my dad, and insisted he come to dinner. Fortunately, my dad spoke French; he had acted as an interpreter for the Army on quite a few occasions. He accepted the invitation. That night, my dad had dinner with the Frenchman and his wife in their modest home. They sat and drank plum brandy after dinner while the Frenchman, a former captain in the French Army in World War I, told stories. He was a decorated war hero who had lost his arm in World War I. The German army had recently ransacked his home, taking his car and guns and war medals.

Things got quiet when the captain started talking about his daughter, Jacqueline. He started crying as he explained that Jacqueline had been visiting a friend in a nearby town when the D-Day invasion took place, and all hell broke loose. He hadn't heard from her since. He feared the worse. He wanted to try to find his daughter, but the Germans had taken his car and guns. The Frenchman showed my dad a photo. She was beautiful. My dad offered to see what he could do to bring the daughter back. The Frenchman and his wife were ecstatic.

My dad left and went back to the makeshift barracks. He told the story of Jacqueline to his buddy Frank. He told Frank that he had offered to try and rescue Jacqueline. Frank thought my dad was crazy. Or drunk. Or both.

The next day, my dad dragged Frank to see the French captain. My dad told him they'd need a map, the address of the place Jacqueline had last visited, a letter from the captain so Jacqueline would know who they were, and the photo. The French captain gave them everything plus a 5,000-franc note for Jacqueline.

My dad and Frank left, and went back to the barracks. They were both on a two-day leave. Frank reluctantly agreed to help, but they didn't have a jeep. They went over to the nurses' quarters after sundown, figuring there might be a few male visitors who might have "borrowed" a jeep to get there.

Frank and my dad found a jeep and rolled it down the hill and started it. It had a mounted machine gun between the seats, the headlights had been blackened into little slits and were of little use. They drove in the night. It started to rain, the windshield had been removed, so visibility was low. There were small pockets of German soldiers still in the area, and there were rumors of German soldiers dressed as civilians.

My dad and Frank were trying to get to Heudicourt-sous-les-Cotes, a small town about sixty miles away, where Jacqueline had last visited. The rain and the lack of visibility slowed them down; they made it halfway there, soaked to the bone and dead-tired. They slept on the floor of a roadside house that belonged to a Frenchwoman who let them doze in front of her fireplace, so they could dry off and rest.

The next day they made it to Heudicourt. They went to the address and showed the woman the photo and the letter. She explained that Jacqueline had caught a ride a few days before to stay with an uncle in Verdun, a small town twenty-five miles to the north. She gave them the address, and my dad and Frank took off.

Verdun is close to the German border. It had recently been liberated by the Allies, but was still being attacked by the Nazis.

Frank and my dad made it to Verdun, and found Jacqueline at her uncle's house. My dad gave her the letter and the 5,000-franc note. She started crying. Then she packed a small bag, said goodbye to her uncle, and my dad put her in the back of the jeep and covered her with a blanket since there were still clusters of German soldiers roaming about. My dad and Frank took off, Frank driving, machine gun mounted between them, Jacqueline in the back, bouncing around under the blanket as the jeep flew down the small country roads.

They stopped at a town called Metz to gas up at an American motor pool. The MPs warned them about groups of German soldiers. As they were getting ready to take off, Jacqueline poked her head out. The MPs saw her. Before they could react, Frank floored the jeep and drove like mad to Lunéville. They got there at midnight; Frank dropped off my dad and Jacqueline at her house and took the jeep back.

Jacqueline ran inside, and there were tears and laughter, and hugs, and shrieks of joy. My dad stood in the doorway. The one-armed Frenchman kept pumping his one good arm in the air, crying and screaming, "Merci, Philippe! Merci, Philippe!"

GRILLED SALMON MARSALA with GRILLED VEGETABLES

I was at my dad's house when I concocted this recipe. It was Memorial Day weekend. He lives on top of a mountain, in the Catskills of New York. It's incredibly beautiful. It's also incredibly isolated—which can make you crazy after a while. Just look at me.

When my dad first got the place, he wanted it to be rustic. And that it was. It was just a square, cinderblock, two-story structure that looked more like a garage than a cabin. The ground floor was, well, it was the ground. It was dirt. The second floor was unpainted plywood, and there was a gas stove up there, and that's where I slept.

The stove is what we used for heat—for the whole place. Keep in mind, it gets down to below zero in the winter. There's snow on the ground from November until March. And there was no plumbing. None. There was an outhouse, and it was pretty scary; especially late at night, when you had to walk fifty yards through the snow to go to the bathroom. That's the way my dad wanted it. Rough. No frills. No phones. No TV.

That didn't last very long. The thought may have been romantic, but there's nothing romantic about getting up in the morning and walking across the frozen tundra to go to the bathroom in what is really just a hole in the ground. A stinking hole.

And now? My dad has three bathrooms, all indoors. The one on the second floor has a claw-foot bathtub with a view of the mountains. He has a big screen hi-definition TV, a satellite dish that gets a thousand channels, and the whole house has wireless internet. He has a phone. He even has a cell phone now. Now my dad is all plugged in, hooked up, and well connected, which is a good thing, especially during the brutal winter months.

Rat Tail Ridge is a great place to grill in the summer, when it's cool and breezy on top of that mountain. You've got a beautiful view, quite breathtaking. Batu loves it up there.

NOTES:
The salmon steaks I used were about an inch and a half thick. Keep in mind that thicker pieces of salmon take longer, and thinner pieces take less time. Also, some grills run really hot, some not-so-hot. No wonder it took me so long to get this recipe right. But I finally nailed it.

Also, trim your asparagus. Grab an asparagus spear. Hold the top end in between the forefinger and thumb of your left hand, and hold the bottom end with the thumb and forefinger of your right hand, and bend until it breaks. Throw away the stalk end.

There are two kinds of Marsala—sweet and dry. Sweet is the way to go. Sweet!

INGREDIENTS

For the sauce:

1 cup sweet Marsala (a wine from Sicily) or sweet vermouth

¼ cup extra-virgin olive oil

¼ cup fresh-squeezed lemon juice (use ripe, soft lemons, or Meyer lemons—remove the seeds)

1 tablespoon chopped fresh oregano, plus a couple sprigs for garnish (you can use a teaspoon of dried oregano if you can't find fresh)

2 cloves of garlic

For the salmon and vegetables:

4 salmon steaks

A dozen small potatoes cut in half (I used purple potatoes—found them in a local market)

A bunch of asparagus (16 or so), trimmed

6 Roma tomatoes cut in half length-wise

Extra-virgin olive oil

Kosher salt

Fresh-cracked black pepper

A small bunch of fresh chives

A handful of fresh basil leaves

1 tablespoon of balsamic vinegar

HERE WE GO!

Add all the sauce ingredients (except the garlic) in a small bowl. Mix. Put the garlic in a garlic press, and squeeze it into the sauce—you can also mince the garlic if you don't have a press. Put the sauce in a small pan over low heat, and let it reduce while you grill.

SCAN THE QR CODE TO SEE THE YOUTUBE VIDEO

Rinse off the salmon steaks, pat dry with paper towels, and drizzle both sides with olive oil. Then give a shake of salt and pepper on each side.

Keep your vegetables on separate plates. Take the potatoes, drizzle with olive oil, add salt and pepper, and make sure they're coated well. Do the same with the asparagus, and the tomatoes—but be gentle. Don't mangle your 'maters.

Heat your grill up! We want it to be medium heat; if it's too hot, things will burn.

The potatoes take the longest, about 20 minutes. Put them on first, cook for 10 minutes (depending on the heat of the grill) and then turn 'em over.

Put the asparagus and the salmon on the grill, and cook for about 5 minutes. After 5 minutes, turn over the asparagus and the salmon.

Add the Roma tomatoes to the grill, flat side down.

Cook the asparagus, salmon and tomatoes for 5 minutes. Don't turn over the tomatoes!

Remove everything to a gorgeous platter.

Use a scissors and snip some fresh chives on top of the potatoes.

Snip some fresh basil on the tomatoes.

Drizzle a little balsamic vinegar on the asparagus.

Dish it up! Put a salmon steak on a plate. Take the reduced Marsala sauce and drizzle some on top. Add some asparagus, potatoes, and tomatoes. Garnish with a fresh oregano sprig.

MANGIAMO!

CARROT and ONION SAUCE
at
The Funky Shack

(L-R) Howie (drums), Bob (guitar), Me, Tom (keyboards)

People use the word “literally” in the wrong way. For instance, my niece once said, “I literally puked my guts out,” which is so wrong on so many levels.

But way back when, when I was literally a starving musician, this was a sauce I loved to cook. I still do. Why? You can find the ingredients anywhere. It is quick, simple, healthy and delicious.

It is cheap to make. Pine nuts (pignoli) are a lot more expensive now than they were back then in 1492, but still, this dish doesn’t cost much to make. This was important back in the early days. We didn’t have much do-re-mi. I was in a band called BootCamp. We started off with a bang, had two of the first 100 videos ever played on MTV, and we were getting a lot of attention from folks in the music biz.

Our manager, Carl Griffin, called and asked if we wanted to spend the summer playing at a beach club in the Hamptons. On the beach. Long Island. New York. The Hamptons! It’s where all the rich and famous folk spend their summers.

We took the gig.

We packed up all our stuff, and headed up the New Jersey Turnpike. We were based out of Baltimore, Maryland; it was a five-hour drive to Long Island. The club had rented a house for us right across the street. We had visions of mansions, and pools, and tennis courts . . . and as we drove the final half hour to the club, we saw all of that. Every house we passed was fancier than the one before. Swimming pools. Fancy landscaping. Garages bigger than our houses.

But when we pulled up to the club, and saw the house right across the street, our hearts sank. It was a shack. Literally. We walked in. There were spaces between the boards of the walls that you could see through. There were mice camping out in the cracks of the walls, who later became our friends. There were a few really small rooms. The ceiling was maybe a little more than six feet high. I’m six feet two inches tall, and my head almost touched the sagging fiberboard panels that made up the ceiling. Literally. There was no heat. There was no air-conditioning. The only water that came out of the faucets, including the shower, was saltwater. The one and only bathroom was the size of a coffin.

We called it—the Funky Shack. This would be our home for four months. The glamorous life of show biz.

We went across the street to the club. They were still building it, and it looked like . . . a half-finished barn. There were construction materials all around. Workers were standing around looking confused. It was a mess. Literally. There was no way we were gonna play any music in that place anytime soon.

We walked to the beach. It was absolutely gorgeous. To the right was the private beach that belonged to the movie stars that lived on the ocean. To the left was a stretch of public beach, and then a canal. The only commercial zoning on the island was the little stretch of beach to the left. There were two nightclubs right on the ocean. Ours—the future Neptune Beach Club—was a rock club, and the one next door—Summer’s—was a disco. There was a small bar on the other side of the street, next to the Funky Shack. It was called Cat Ballou’s.

We went over there and had way too much to drink. Then we stumbled back to the Funky Shack.

It got really cold that first night, down to the low thirties. We were freezing. We hadn’t brought any heavy blankets, not thinking we’d need them, and we were close to frostbite. There was no heat in the Funky Shack. Being incredibly resourceful musicians, bolstered by booze, we walked across the street to the club, borrowed a bunch of two-by-fours, and started a fire in the shack’s small fireplace.

The next morning, some workers came over and asked us if we saw anybody taking any lumber, and we said, “No” as we were kicking the ends of the two-by-fours we’d pilfered back into the smoldering fireplace.

The Funky Shack was right on the bay. And when I say right on the bay, I mean it was literally on the bay. When the tide was high, the water came onto the back porch. I call it a back porch, but it was more like a small rotted wooden raft. It's not like the shack was on stilts, or had a pier. It sat flat on a marsh, and the bay was right out back. It was not really a bay, more like a big shallow body of swamp water.

Billy Joel stayed in that house. So did Leslie West. We heard more than one story about each of those guys living in the Funky Shack.

We tried to make it habitable. The guitar player, who was also a carpenter, made a screen door. He made a wooden platform for the shower; because it didn't drain, and the water would back up to your knees. When you took a shower, which was saltwater, you stood on the platform, and the spray literally hit you in the you-know-whats. I had to crouch over like the Hunchback of Notre Dame, because the ceiling was so low. If you wanted to wash your hair, you had to stand on your head.

That was how we showered for a little more than three months.

They eventually finished the club after a few weeks. After they did, we played six nights a week, seven hours a night, until 4:00 a.m., with double shifts on Saturday and Sunday.

And as crazy as it sounds—we were really happy.

And late at night, after the gig, if we wanted a dish of pasta, we'd walk across the street, sneak into the club, and fill our pasta pot with fresh water.

Then we'd go back to the Funky Shack and cook. Are you sure Billy Joel started off this way?

CARROT and ONION SAUCE

If you're sitting around the Funky Shack, and you want to feed your crew, carrot and onion sauce might be a good choice. It's inexpensive. Healthy. You can find the ingredients anywhere. Substitute the chicken broth with vegetable broth and it's vegan.

It's hard to screw up. Probably the worst thing you could do would be to burn the onions. But burnt onions taste pretty good. Burnt garlic? Not good.

That being said, try not to burn your onions. You want to cook them until they're soft and sweet and clear.

I made this dish the other day. I tasted a carrot before I started grating them all. It didn't taste right. I normally don't spit things out, but these carrots were no good. I took them back to the store, and bought a different batch. They tasted great.

So you might want to take a little taste of your ingredients when possible. Especially the main ones. Unless it's raw pork. That might not be a good idea.

I almost always cook a full pound of pasta. But I end up using about ¾ of a pound. I like a little more sauce these days, and a little less pasta. I save the rest of the pasta for a frittata or for the kids.

You know, the billy goats here at Slim's Shady Trailer Park.

INGREDIENTS

3 tablespoons of extra-virgin olive oil

1 cup minced onion

Crushed red pepper (I start off with ¼ teaspoon)

3 cups grated carrots

1½ cups chicken broth (or vegetable broth)

½ cup dry white wine

A handful of Italian flat-leaf parsley, chopped (about 2 to 3 tablespoons)

A handful (½ cup) of pine nuts (if you can't find pine nuts, you can use slivered almonds, as a substitute)

1 pound of pasta—*fusilli* is my favorite, but you can use *farfalle*, or *spaghetti*

Kosher salt to taste

HERE WE GO!

Put the olive oil in a large sauté pan over medium-low heat for 2 minutes.

Add the onion. Add some crushed red pepper to taste. Cook for 5 to 7 minutes until the onion is translucent.

Add the carrots, chicken broth and white wine.

Raise the heat to high.

When it comes to a boil, let it cook for 2 minutes.

Reduce the heat to medium-low. Taste for salt, add some if needed.

Simmer for 20 minutes or so, until the broth is nearly absorbed, and the carrots are tender but not mooshy. Stir often.

Just before the sauce is done, add the chopped parsley to the pan and stir.

Let's toast our nuts! Put the pine nuts (or slivered almonds) in a dry pan over medium heat. Cook and shake for a few minutes until golden brown. Don't burn your nuts!

You can use this sauce over rice, or on a bruschetta, or flatbread; but I put it over pasta.

Put a large pot of cold water on the highest heat you've got. When it comes to a full boil, add a few tablespoons of Kosher salt, and the pound of pasta.

Follow the cooking directions on the pasta box. When the time is up, taste the pasta. You want it to be *al dente*, which means "firm to the bite." Bite through a piece of pasta. If it is chalky in the center, it's not done. Cook it until it's not chalky or too chewy.

I cooked some *penne rigate* pasta the other night. It took 5 minutes longer than the instructions on the box. So keep on tasting the pasta as it cooks. You'll know when it's done.

When it is, drain the pasta in a colander and put it in a bowl. Drizzle with a tablespoon of olive oil and mix. Add most of the sauce to the pasta and mix 'em up.

Dish it up! Put some pasta on a plate. Add a little extra sauce on top, and top off with some toasted pine nuts. You can also add some grated Parmigiano-Reggiano cheese or even some Pecorino Romano, which is a little sharper and saltier.

MANGIAMO!

FRITTATAS

with Jimi Hendrix and Robert Plant

Spinach, mushrooms, and pancetta frittata

Smoked salmon, tomatoes, Spanish onion, and capers frittata

Leftover pasta frittata

I'd heard Hendrix was coming to town, so I bought two tickets. They were $6.50 apiece.

The show was at the Civic Center, right in the heart of downtown Baltimore. My friend, Jeffe, and I walked to the entrance. I wanted to be first in line. And I was. Jeffe and I waited until the doors opened, and I told him, "We're walking right on stage. Act like you own the place. If anybody asks, we're with the light crew."

I walked right up to the stage, strolled up the steps, and five seconds later, I'm backstage, standing next to Mitch Mitchell, Hendrix's drummer. He was trying to fix his bass drum pedal. He asked me if I'd hold the flashlight. There I was, holding a flashlight in my shaking hands, trying to help Mitch Mitchell fix his drums. He fixed his pedal, I gave him back the flashlight, and I went to the side of the stage and waited for the opening band to start. I felt like I was in some wonderful dream. It didn't seem real.

The first time I heard Jimi Hendrix was when Rob Grant brought the *Are You Experienced?* album down to my mom's house. We both lived on the same street, Rosebank Avenue. Rob played guitar, and he brought down this new album of this incredible guitar player, Jimi Hendrix.

I couldn't believe my ears. It sounded like music from Mars. I kept staring at the album cover. Hendrix looked like—well, like nobody I'd ever seen before, not just him but his whole band. I thought they were the coolest-looking, coolest-sounding band I'd ever seen or heard. His guitar playing was unbelievable. It was one of the reasons I took up the bass. When I heard Hendrix play guitar, I figured maybe I ought to play bass—there are less strings and, after all, how could I ever play like Hendrix?

Now here I was, backstage at the Baltimore Civic Center, waiting behind the huge red curtain for Hendrix to come out and play. A band called Cactus opened. Tim Bogert was on bass—he'd played with Vanilla Fudge. Carmine Appice played drums—he'd been with Jeff Beck. And the guitar player?

It was Jim McCarty, a blues guitarist who'd played with both Mitch Ryder and Buddy Miles. When Cactus started playing, I was behind the huge red velvet curtain; I was standing on one side of the stage, and Jeffe was standing on the other. We could see each other. The sold-out crowd couldn't see us, but we could see them. Cactus started playing. Then I felt a tap on my shoulder. I heard a voice say, "This guy's pretty good."

I turned my head. It was Jimi Hendrix. I was amazed. I was just hiding out on the side of the stage hoping security wouldn't take me away in handcuffs, and here I am, standing next to Hendrix. We stood shoulder to shoulder for twenty minutes, watching Jim McCarty play guitar with Cactus. I didn't say a word. I couldn't speak. Jeffe was on the other side of the stage, going nuts. Pointing his finger. Making animated faces. All I did was stand there, trying to be cool, with Hendrix at my side.

Cactus finished, and Hendrix went on stage. Billy Cox was on bass and Mitch Mitchell on drums. There is some footage on YouTube of the concert, and Hendrix's guitar-playing is jaw-dropping, show-stopping, some-kinda-wonderful.

The date was June 13, 1970. Hendrix played his heart out. I saw the whole show from ten yards away. It wasn't the first time I'd seen Jimi Hendrix. The first time was also at the Baltimore Civic Center; May 16, 1969. Noel Redding played bass, Mitch Mitchell played drums. That show was incredible, too. It was an amazing time for music.

How amazing? Nine days later, I went to Merriweather Post Pavilion, an outdoor venue outside of Baltimore. Merriweather was designed by Frank Gehry; it is a natural amphitheater, with a stage and seats at the bottom, and a large lawn up top, where you can lay on a blanket and watch the show down below. I had seen the Doors there. I had seen Frank Sinatra there. But on May 25, 1969, I was there to see Led Zeppelin.

They were opening for the Who. I loved both bands. It was the only time Led Zeppelin and the Who appeared on stage together. What an incredible evening, sitting on the lawn in late spring, listening to two bands that would make musical history.

Here's the crazy thing. Last year, I was at a funky little grocery store called "Bi-Rite" in a funky part of Nashville, and I saw Robert Plant, the lead singer for Led Zeppelin, in line. He had a twelve-pack of Miller High Life beer on the counter, although I'm not sure it was his. Nobody recognized him. I did. I had to say something. I walked up to him and said, "I saw you do a concert with the Who in Baltimore back in 1969."

Robert Plant looked at me and said, "I remember that show. I didn't want to do it."

"Why not?"

"I always thought we were better than they were."

"Well, I'm glad you did that show. It changed my life."

And then I snapped a photo.

FRITTATAS

If you ever want a wonderful breakfast after a big rock concert, don't ask me to cook. I'm not very good with breakfast. I've messed up simple fried eggs. I've mangled pancakes. I've even screwed up oatmeal. All on a regular basis. So you know what I eat almost every morning?

Fruit.

That's right, fruit. I try to eat nothing but fruit until noon. The key to this plan is simple. Sleep until twelve thirty.

But really, fruit is what I eat all morning. I like bananas. Old people with no teeth can eat bananas. Little kids with no teeth can eat bananas. They're easy on the stomach. They come with their own wrapper. You don't have to clean 'em. They don't have seeds. They're cheap. They're around all year. And they're almost always good. You can spot a bad banana a mile away.

If I have to cook breakfast, I'll make a frittata. I'm pretty good at making frittatas. A frittata is like an omelette, except it isn't folded. You can stick anything in a frittata, just like an omelette—onion, peppers, cheese—but you know what I like to do? I take leftovers and beat them in with the eggs.

Here is the key—if you use 8 eggs in your frittata, you'll need about 2 or 2½ cups of leftovers and 1 cup of grated Parmigiano-Reggiano cheese. I once used leftover asparagus and scalloped potatoes in a frittata. It was really good. In the video, I used some leftover *farfalle* pasta with cauliflower. It was *delizioso*. I recently made a frittata with leftover *fusilli* with spinach and grape tomato sauce that was also quite good.

I also like to make frittatas without leftovers. Yesterday, I made two frittatas. One had spinach, mushrooms, sun-dried tomatoes and pancetta (Italian bacon) and it was pretty good, if I may say so myself. The second frittata I made with smoked salmon, Spanish (purple) onions, grape tomatoes, and capers. Wow! It was delish.

Once again, for 8 eggs, you'll need no more than 2 or 2½ cups of extra ingredients and 1 cup of freshly grated Parmigiano-Reggiano cheese. Pre-grated cheese in a box is pretty nasty stuff. Avoid it if possible.

Frittatas need to be cooked low and slow on the stovetop for about 18 minutes. Then, you need to slip 'em under the broiler for a minute to make the top to golden brown.

It's best to use a pan that has an oven-proof handle, so it won't melt when you put the frittata under the broiler. You can also slide the frittata out of the pan onto an oven-proof plate, and broil it that way.

Either way, you want to broil your frittata for JUST A MINUTE OR TWO! Keep your eyes on these guys, you don't want to burn the top of the frittata. You want it to be firm and golden.

Serves 4 (unless you're living with teenagers, in which case this serves 1).

FRITTATA with LEFTOVER PASTA

INGREDIENTS

8 eggs

1 cup freshly grated Parmigiano-Reggiano cheese

2 cups of leftover pasta (I used 2 cups of leftover *fusilli* pasta with spinach and grape tomato sauce)

2 tablespoons butter

Fresh-cracked black pepper and Kosher salt to taste

HERE WE GO!

SCAN THE QR CODE TO SEE THE YOUTUBE VIDEO

Break the eggs in a large bowl. Add the cheese. Mix 'em up.

Add the leftover pasta, and mix 'em up. Add salt and pepper.

Put a large pan on medium heat. Add 2 tablespoons of butter.

When the butter melts, add the eggs/cheese/leftover mixture.

Smooth it out on top; you don't want a lumpy frittata! Let it set for a minute or so.

Turn the heat to low, and let it cook for about 15 to 18 minutes. The top might be a little jiggly, but the rest should be firm. If it isn't, cook it until it is.

Next, set the broiler on high, and put the frittata under the broiler for a minute or so. We want it to be golden on top. Keep your eyes on it!

Once golden, remove the pan from the broiler and let it cool for a minute or so.

Take a spatula, and loosen the sides of the frittata from the pan. Slide it onto a platter.

Dish it up!

MANGIAMO!

FRITTATA with SPINACH, MUSHROOMS, and PANCETTA

INGREDIENTS

8 eggs

1 cup freshly grated Parmigiano-Reggiano cheese

½ cup white mushrooms, cleaned and chopped

1½ cups fresh baby spinach, cleaned and cut into small pieces

2 tablespoons of sun-dried tomatoes, sliced (I use the ones in oil, drained)

½ cup chopped pancetta (I used a 4 ounce package of sliced Boars Head pancetta that worked nicely; you can also substitute bacon, or leave it out)

2 tablespoons of butter

1 clove of garlic, minced (a generous teaspoon)

Salt and pepper (to taste)

HERE WE GO!

Break the eggs in a bowl. Beat 'em up!

Add the cheese and mix.

Add the mushrooms, spinach and sun-dried tomatoes and mix.

Set aside.

Put the pancetta in a sauté pan with an oven-proof handle (I used a 10-inch pan) over medium heat.

Let the pancetta brown on one side for about 3 or 4 minutes. If it needs a little oil, give it a splash.

Give it a turn, and let's brown the other side for 3 or 4 minutes. We want it brown, not burnt!

When the pancetta is brown, remove it with a slotted spoon to a small plate that has a paper towel on the bottom.

There might be a little pancetta drippings in the bottom of the pan. I leave them in. If this grosses you out, wipe the pan.

Turn the heat to medium-low.

Add 2 tablespoons of butter.

Add the garlic.

Sauté and stir for 2 minutes or so.

As the garlic sautés, add the pancetta to the bowl with the eggs and the other ingredients.

Add a little salt and pepper. Mix 'em up!

When the garlic has cooked for 2 minutes, pour the eggs and everything in the bowl into the pan with the sautéed garlic. Smooth it out. Let it set for a minute or so.

Turn the heat down to low.

Cook for about 15 to 18 minutes until firm. Don't stir. After about 15 minutes, the top will probably be a bit jiggly, but the rest should be firm. If it ain't, cook it until it is.

Put your broiler on high.

If you have cooked your frittata in an oven-proof pan, put it under the broiler for a minute. If not, slide the frittata out of the pan and onto an oven-proof dish and broil for a minute or so.

When the top is firm and golden, remove from the broiler.

Dish it up.

MANGIAMO!

FRITTATA with SMOKED SALMON, TOMATOES, SPANISH ONION, and CAPERS

INGREDIENTS

8 eggs

1 cup freshly grated Parmigiano-Reggiano cheese

1¼ cup smoked salmon, cut into small pieces

¾ cup grape tomatoes, halved, with the seeds squeezed out

2 tablespoons minced Spanish (purple) onion

2 tablespoons capers

Salt and pepper (to taste)

2 tablespoons of butter

HERE WE GO!

Break the eggs into a bowl. Mix 'em up.

Add the smoked salmon, the tomatoes, the onion, and the capers and mix 'em up!

Add a little salt and pepper.

Put a sauté pan (I used a 10-inch pan with an oven-proof handle) over medium heat.

Add the butter.

When the butter melts, add the egg mixture. Smooth it out on top. You don't want no lumpy frittata!

Let it set for a minute or so.

Then turn down the heat to low and let it cook without stirring for about 15 to 18 minutes. We want the top to be a little jiggly, but the rest of the frittata to be firm. Cook it until it is.

Turn your broiler to high.

If you have used an oven-proof pan, put it under the broiler. If not, slide the frittata out of the pan and onto an oven-proof dish.

Broil for a minute or so until the top of the frittata is golden and firm.

Remove from the broiler, and dish it up.

MANGIAMO!

CHICKEN MILANESE
and Taking a Toilet to the Turk

Paps

I was in a hotshot, up-and-coming rock band called BootCamp. We had two of the first 100 videos on MTV. Record companies were calling. Managers were courting us. We got an offer from a beachfront club in the Hamptons (Long Island, New York), an offer to play all summer long. We didn't have to think too long. We took the gig.

It was the summer of 1980. It was the wildest summer of our lives. We lived in a funky little shack right across the road from the club, a place called Neptune Beach Club. BootCamp did really well that first summer. So well, in fact, that they asked us back to play the following summer—the whole summer—six nights a week and twice on Saturdays and Sundays.

I told my dad about it. BootCamp is heading back to the Hamptons.

He called me the next day. Get this—he wanted me to go to my uncle's house (his brother, Oscar), pick up a toilet, and take it to my dad's girlfriend's house in Long Island. Why? I don't know. It's not that toilets are expensive or rare. You can find them just about anywhere. And just why am I taking this toilet to my dad's girlfriend's house anyway? Was my dad trying to impress her? "Hey, honey, I'm getting you a new toilet for your birthday. My kid's gonna hand deliver it."

I thought at first my dad was screwing with me. But when I called Oscar, he confirmed the story. He told me he had the toilet—a new one he had left over from his new house—and I was supposed to pick up this toilet at his house in Baltimore, Maryland, drive it up the New Jersey Turnpike, and drop it off in Long Island at my dad's girlfriend's house on the way to my big gig in the Hamptons.

And the kicker? My dad wasn't going to be there. Neither was his girlfriend. His girlfriend's Turkish father was supposed to be there. And? Her father didn't speak English. Not a word.

The BootCamp Boys packed up the old Chrysler station wagon that belonged to our keyboard player's dad. We packed for the whole summer. We had a ton of suitcases, keyboards, and guitars—everything we'd need for four months away from home. After we packed, we went to my uncle's house and picked up the toilet. We put it on top of all our stuff. Four rock stars with a toilet in the back of an old beat-up station wagon, and the toilet was clearly visible for all passing motorists to see. We headed up the New Jersey Turnpike.

We decided to have some fun.

Whenever we'd stop at a rest area, we'd take the toilet out of the car and carry it into the men's room. And then carry it back out to the car. Like it was the normal thing to do. It was the beginning of summer. The rest areas were crowded with folks heading to the beaches. And these folks were staring at us. Four crazy musicians, with 1980s hairdos that looked like several small animals had perched on top of our heads, carrying a toilet in and out of the men's room; then packing it into an old Chrysler, and driving off.

When we got to my dad's girlfriend's house in Long Island, I took the toilet out of the car, carried it to the house, and rang the bell. A short man with wavy hair opened the door. He took a look at me, and then at the toilet. He obviously had no idea who I was, or why I was there.

So, I'm standing there holding a toilet in my arms, trying to explain who I was and why I was there. The guy understood nothing. Not a word. I kept saying, "Toilet! Toilet for you!" I started yelling, as if by saying it louder, maybe he'd understand what I was saying. "TOILET! TOILET FOR YOU!"

He looked at me like I was from another planet. I finally just left the toilet on the porch and walked away. I waved goodbye as we pulled out of the driveway.

Come to think of it, I hope I had the right house.

CHICKEN MILANESE

After hauling toilets up and down the east coast, there's nothing like a nice dish of chicken Milanese.

Chicken Milanese is pretty much the same as chicken cutlets, except you slice your breasts thinner, and you put them in flour first; then you dip them in the egg, then the breadcrumbs. You don't usually add any sauce or cheese to chicken Milanese. They are *molto delicato*. You eat them plain.

They're that good! Some folks pound their breasts to make them really thin. I just slice them into ¼ inch cutlets.

I cook the cutlets in equal amounts of olive oil and butter. Some folks use just butter, but I had to Slimmify it a bit.

Always be careful when handling raw chicken; clean every surface and utensil, and clean your hands while you're at it. You know those suits that beekeepers wear? You could put one of those on when you're handling raw chicken.

I'm not into making my own breadcrumbs. But the other day I was getting ready to make chicken Milanese, and I had about 2 tablespoons of minced macadamia nuts that were leftover from a salad. I also had about ½ cup of Parmigiano-Reggiano cheese leftover.

I took a cup and a half of plain panko breadcrumbs (I think they were Kikkoman brand) and put them in a bowl. I added the macadamia nuts and the Parmigiano. Then I added a teaspoon of oregano and a tablespoon of dried basil and mixed it all together and . . . man, they were really good. And it didn't take much time at all.

SLIM'S QUICK BREADCRUMBS:

1½ cups plain panko breadcrumbs

2 tablespoons minced macadamia nuts (or chopped, toasted pine nuts)

½ cup freshly grated Parmigiano-Reggiano cheese

1 teaspoon of dried oregano

1 tablespoon dried basil

Mix all the ingredients together. That's it!

If you don't want to go through all that, I recommend Progresso Panko Italian Style breadcrumbs, or a 50/50 mix of Italian style and plain.

I don't get any money from Progresso. But if they offer, I'm taking.

INGREDIENTS

6 thin chicken breast cutlets (¼ inch thick), boneless, skinless

½ cup flour

2 eggs

Salt and fresh-cracked black pepper

Breadcrumbs (2 cups—you might not use them all)

2 tablespoons butter

2 tablespoons olive oil

A few sprigs of fresh Italian flat-leaf parsley for garnish

A few circular slices of lemon for garnish

HERE WE GO!

SCAN THE QR CODE TO SEE THE YOUTUBE VIDEO

Rinse off your breasts and pat them dry with paper towels. Do the same with the chicken breasts.

Put your flour on a flat plate.

Put 2 eggs in a bowl, add a little salt and fresh-cracked black pepper, and beat 'em!

Put your breadcrumbs on another plate.

Take a chicken cutlet, press it into the flour, turn it over, do the same on the other side.

Dip it in the egg, both sides.

Put the cutlet on the breadcrumbs, and press. Do the same with the other side of the cutlet.

Put the breaded cutlet on a plate.

Do this with all 6 breasts.

Get a large sauté pan. Put it on medium-high heat. Add the butter and the olive oil.

When the butter starts to brown, add the breasts to the pan. Cook for 3 minutes until golden brown.

Turn over, and do the same on the other side.

Remove to a warm platter.

Garnish with a few sprigs of Italian flat-leaf parsley, maybe a couple of circular lemon slices. These cutlets would go real well with pasta and tomato sauce . . .

MANGIAMO!

CRAB SOUP
and
How Destiny Found Me

stevenschuman.com

The day I turned fourteen, I got my worker's permit. I've been working ever since. I've worked myself up from nothing to a case of extreme poverty.

Soon after I got my worker's permit, I got a job at my grandmother's office as an office boy. At that time, she was Vice President of the International Ladies' Garment Workers Union.

Angela was an incredible woman, a poor Italian immigrant who worked in a garment sweatshop in New York City. Disgusted with the working conditions, she became an organizer, was assigned to the Delaware, Maryland, and Virginia region, and helped start the International Ladies' Garment Workers Union (ILGWU).

The ILGWU offices were in Baltimore, Maryland, on the corner of Howard and Baltimore Streets—right across the street from the Civic Center, which was where I saw Hendrix, the Doors, Led Zeppelin, and a ton of other bands.

My mom didn't drive, and my dad moved back to New York when they got divorced. This meant when I needed to get around, I took the bus. In the morning, I'd walk to the bus stop and take the bus to school. After school, I'd take the bus home and have lunch. Then I'd catch a bus downtown, and work at Angela's office until it closed. Then I'd catch the bus back home, have some dinner, do my homework, and go to sleep.

One cold winter day, I was waiting outside the Civic Center to catch the bus home from work. It was downright frosty. I noticed a kid about my age, no coat on, no winter clothes, standing there shivering. I went over and asked him if he was okay.

He told me he had run away from home, had just arrived from Florida—no money, no clothes, no job, no nothin'. I invited him to the house for some dinner.

We got on the bus and rode to my neighborhood. The bus stop was about a half-mile from my house on Rosebank Avenue. When I walked in, I started to introduce this kid to my mom, but I didn't know his name. When I asked him, he told us his name was—

Destiny.

He had long, blond, scraggly hair. He was short and slight and skinny as could be. He was shaking from the cold. About the only thing he had to his name besides the clothes on his back was his harmonica. I asked my mom if he could stay for dinner. She said yes. Destiny ended up staying with us for about a year.

My mom was the sweetest woman in the world. She was so wonderful in so many ways that it could fill a whole book or two. She brought out the best in people; everybody shined a little brighter in her presence. She took Destiny under her wing.

Destiny immediately went to look for a job. About the only thing he could find was a job at a car wash. In the winter. I gave him some of my clothes, but he was a lot shorter than I was, so he looked kinda funny. We went to an Army surplus store, and got him a military coat, and some other things.

Destiny would come home from the car wash, and he would be frozen, his shoes soaked with water. My mom would feed us dinner, and Destiny and I would go upstairs. I'd do homework. Then, I'd play guitar and Destiny would play his harmonica.

He used to sing this song that he wrote . . .

"The River of Love is soft and free."

Then he'd play a little harmonica riff.

"The River of Love was meant to be."

Then he'd play another riff.

What he lacked in talent, he made up for with enthusiasm. It was a catchy little tune. We became really good friends. He also became pretty good on harmonica.

My mom loved him.

Destiny was an incredibly polite and positive kid. I never heard him say a bad word about anybody or anything. I never heard him complain. He had a funny laugh, like he was almost embarrassed for chuckling.

My mom was a great cook. She cooked all kinds of different stuff—Italian, French, Indian, Mexican. Destiny had never eaten food like that. He ate a lot of grilled cheese sandwiches and Campbell's tomato soup out of a can. When my mom would cook some exotic foods, Destiny would get this look of apprehension on his face.

One time my mom cooked crab soup. Her recipe was amazing. She would not only use crabmeat, she used other parts of the crab as well, mostly the claws. When she served you a bowl, there would be a vicious-looking crab claw peeking out at you.

The first time my mom served Destiny a bowl of crab soup, he saw that crab claw, and had no idea what to do. We showed him how to crack it, and eat it. Destiny was clearly not used to anything like that. He took one look at that crab claw, and you could see the trepidation in his eyes. He was way too polite to do anything but try to figure out how to eat it. After he finished, I could tell he was trying to say something sweet to my mom. He looked at her and said,

"Thank you very much, Miss C.; it's been a long time since I had a meal like that."

One Friday night, there was a knock at the front door. I opened it up. A young kid asked me if Destiny was around, and I showed him upstairs. The two kids hugged. Destiny introduced the other kid. His name was—

Joker.

I'm not joking. Joker was Destiny's younger brother. The two of them left Rosebank shortly thereafter, and I didn't hear from Destiny for years and years.

I got an email from Destiny a couple years ago. He told me how he'd moved to Florida, and then to Georgia, and had a kid. Destiny was so grateful for what we'd done, he named his son after me. Not Slim, my real name. Scrappy.

Destiny told me that he had taken up painting. Not houses, but artwork. He sent me one of his paintings. It was really cool. I was flattered.

The painting was called—LOVE.

It's all about LOVE.

CRAB SOUP

My mom loved steamed crabs. In Baltimore they use blue crabs; they catch them in the Chesapeake Bay and the surrounding rivers in the summer and import them from the Gulf of Mexico in the winter. The fine people of B-Mo steam the crabs in beer, vinegar and Old Bay. Old Bay is a seasoning with salt, pepper, paprika and other spices. It was created in Baltimore; they used to make it at a factory on the water by the Inner Harbor. In the summertime, downtown Bawlmer smelled a bit . . . spicy.

Every once in a while, my mom would get a couple dozen steamed crabs from a place called Bo Brooks and bring them home. We'd cover the table in newspapers, grab some wooden mallets, and have a little crab feast as we listened to the Baltimore Orioles baseball game on the radio. It's a Bawlmer tradition, Hon!

When we were done, my mom would pick through the leftover crabs, and use the meat and some of the claws to make crab soup. But unless you're in Baltimore in the summertime, you're going to most likely use a pound of crabmeat for crab soup rather than fresh-picked steamed crabs.

Jumbo lump crabmeat comes from the top of the hind leg; it's really good but expensive. You can also get lump crabmeat, which comes from the top of the other legs, and is less expensive but really good. You can also buy claw meat, which is the least expensive and not as quite as moist or tasty as the others. But still pretty good. You can use a combination of these crabmeats; just make sure you end up with a pound.

If you're using a pound of unseasoned crabmeat, you'll need to add Old Bay seasoning to the soup. I use 2 generous tablespoons. If you're not into spicy food, start off with 1 tablespoon, give the soup a taste halfway through. If it needs a little more spice, add another tablespoon of Old Bay.

If you're using leftover crabs, they'll have some Old Bay on them, so you might not need any additional seasoning. Give the soup a taste halfway through the process, and if it needs more spice, add some Old Bay, a teaspoon at a time.

INGREDIENTS

3 tablespoons extra-virgin olive oil

½ cup each—chopped celery, carrot, and onion

4 or 5 celery tops (the leaves at the top of the stalks)

2 cups water

2 cups beef broth (you can use vegetable, chicken or seafood—in Maryland we use beef)

1 cup each—lima beans, sweet corn (fresh, canned, or frozen), string beans—ends trimmed and broken into bite-size pieces

1 (28-ounce) can of Italian tomatoes, smooshed by hand into small pieces

2 tablespoons Old Bay seasoning

1 pound of jumbo lump crab meat

OPTIONAL: 8 steamed crab claws, don't rinse off the Old Bay!

HERE WE GO!

Get a large heavy soup pot or Dutch oven and put the heat on medium.

Add the olive oil and let it heat up for 2 minutes.

SCAN THE QR CODE TO SEE THE YOUTUBE VIDEO

Add the celery, carrots, and onion. Add the celery leaves. Cook for 5 to 7 minutes, until soft. Stir, stir, stir.

Add the water, the broth, the lima beans, corn, and string beans.

Add the tomatoes.

Add the Old Bay seasoning.

Cover, turn the heat on high.

When it comes to a boil, reduce to a simmer, and cook—covered—until the vegetables are tender, about 10 minutes. Stir every couple of minutes.

As the soup simmers, put the crabmeat in a bowl.

Gently feel for any crab shell or cartilage.

Be careful! You don't want to break up the lumps.

Discard any shell or cartilage.

After the soup has simmered 10 minutes, and the vegetables are tender, add the crabmeat to the soup, along with any leftover steamed crab claws—if you got 'em.

Let the soup simmer—uncovered—for 10 minutes. Keep in mind, the crab claws and the crabmeat are already cooked, you're just heating them up—don't overcook, and don't stir too often. You don't want to break up the lumps of crab.

Taste for Old Bay seasoning, and add another tablespoon if needed.

Taste for salt, and add if needed.

Dish it up! Get a large soup bowl, ladle in some soup, place a claw on the side of the plate to give it that dangerous look, maybe sprinkle a dusting of Old Bay on top, and . . .

MANGIAMO!

GRILLED SHRIMP and SCALLOP KABOBS with SHERRY SAUCE

at Mack and Myer's

Might have fun, might not.

That was the sign outside Mack and Myer's nightclub in Essex, Maryland. My band, BootCamp, was the house band at Mack and Myer's. In the music binniz, that means we played there almost every night. It was the '80s. The 1980s, not the 1880s.

Essex is a town outside Baltimore with a bad reputation; I've always liked the place. It has a singular charm. People in Baltimore make fun of people in Essex. Why? Maybe it's because it's on a river that has two, well, poop-processing plants right in the middle of the water. They look like two huge silver breasts, side by side, floating in the water, pointing to the sky.

They let off a stench that is hard to ignore. A HazMat suit or a gas mask might be in order while near that body of water. The river is named Back River. There is a bridge over those troubled waters, and right across that bridge was a club called Mack and Myer's.

The club was owned by Dave Hutchinson. Dave was a cool guy; smart, funny, and hip. He was one of those guys who was in the know, but a little offbeat. Dave embraced Essex and all its lowdown uniqueness. His brother was an elected official, an important executive for Baltimore County. My guess is that Dave was the black sheep.

When you walked inside Mack and Myer's, there were all kinds of strange things hanging from the ceiling. Old wooden chairs. Trombones. Guitars. Old street signs. All kinds of junk was suspended by wires and string, hanging from the ceiling—which was only a few feet overhead. Mismatched Christmas lights were strung everywhere.

There was a jukebox in the corner. A real old-time jukebox. Dave had it stocked with every funny crazy old single ever released. "Yakkity Yak (Don't Talk Back)," "Along Came John," "Sixteen Tons,"—

I loved the jukebox. I loved Mack and Myer's. I loved Dave. And I loved Sophie.

Sophie was a divorced cocktail waitress who lived down the street. She had a bee-hive hairdo of red hair that was so thick and lacquered with Aqua Net that you could have bounced bowling balls off her hair without so much as a dent. She had a thick Baltimore accent and called everybody "Hon."

Her favorite song was "Do You Think I'm Sexy" by Rod Stewart, so the BootCamp Boys learned the song. Whenever we did the song, Sophie would get up on stage and dance the hootchie-cootchie dance and sing off-key.

It was precious. She was precious. There was a band room in the back. One night, before a show, Sophie ran her hands through my hair as I sat in a chair in front of her; the guys in the band were getting ready to go on. Sophie said, in that lovely Baltimore accent, "Your hair is just like the hair on my *****, Hon! If I didn't trim it, it would grow down to my knees!"

Forgive the language, but that's the way she talked. That was so Sophie.

Mack and Myer's was funky. It was eclectic. It was a crazy mixture of people—black, white, rich, poor, gay, straight, intellectuals, blue-collars—who were all in on what seemed like an inside joke. It was a three-ring circus. Dave was Ringmaster. He called me "Boot" as in BootCamp.

"Hey, Boot!" he'd scream across the club. BootCamp started getting popular. Mack and Myer's was packed every night. It went on like that for months and months. Then we got an offer to spend the summer as a house band in a club that was on the beach—IN THE HAMPTONS. New York. Long Island. Movie stars. Seaside mansions.

In the spring, we left Mack and Myer's. We left Essex, Maryland. We left Back River and the Poop Processors. We left Dave. We left Sophie. We bought an old beat-up, yellow bread truck. No radio, no AC. We filled it with all our suitcases and equipment, and we drove up the Jersey Turnpike to the Hamptons. It turned out to be the craziest summer of my life. Everyone has one. That was mine.

The club was called Neptune Beach Club. We played six nights a week until 4:00 a.m. and did double shifts on Saturdays and Sundays. After all those hours on stage, BootCamp was getting pretty good. When the summer ended, we drove back down the Jersey Turnpike in our yellow, beat-up bread truck; tanned, trim, and dead-tired. A peculiar stench told us we were getting close to Back River. We crossed the bridge and saw the Mack and Myer's "Might Have Fun, Might Not" sign. The Boys Are Back!

Dave was outside waiting, beaming like a proud papa.

We got out of the bread truck, and Dave led us inside. He had us close our eyes. When we opened our eyes, we saw a huge sign, about six feet tall and twelve feet long, with big black letters on a white background. The sign took up the whole wall. It said:

NEW YORK CITY

Dave looked at us and said, "Whaddya think?"

We had no idea what the sign was about. That's when Dave told us he'd re-named the band. Instead of being called "BootCamp," we were now—

"NEW YORK CITY."

We explained to Dave: we'd been playing all summer in New York as BootCamp, we had videos on MTV, labels were interested, managers were calling, and a name change might not be the best idea in the world. We kept our name. Dave kept the sign up anyway. We kept playing Mack and Myer's but not quite as often as we used to. It was still packed whenever we played; but we were starting to get lots of other gigs.

We were opening for Split Enz, Squeeze, and the B-52s. We started playing other clubs, drawing 500 people on Monday and Tuesday nights. We were doing showcases in Manhattan for major labels. It was time to move on. Dave knew it. We knew it. We said a sad goodbye to Sophie, Dave, Mack and Myer's, Back River, and the Poop Processors. We crossed that bridge and took off for the Big Time.

A few years later, I was at the airport in Baltimore. I had just flown in from a Slim Man gig. Things were going well. It was late at night, and there weren't a lot of folks around. I was facing the baggage carousel when somebody tackled me from behind. We fell to the ground. The guy had me in a bear hug. We started rolling around.

"Boot!"

Dave. Scared the shit out of me. We got up, and Dave smiled at me. He was a tall, burly guy with a beard, curly, sandy hair, laughing eyes, and a distinguished voice. He thanked me. He thanked me for the good times. He thanked me for the money I'd made him. He told me Mack and Myer's did so well while BootCamp was there, that he was able to relax for quite a while. Then he gave me a hug.

Might Have Fun, Might Not.

We had fun.

A ton of fun.

GRILLED SHRIMP AND SCALLOP KABOBS WITH SHERRY SAUCE

When you make this dish, make sure your scallops and shrimp are not from Back River.

I love grillin'. I love chillin'. This is one of my favorite grill dishes because there's not a lot of fuss. You know what I don't like about grillin'? When the food you're grillin' falls through the grill and onto the charcoals. That's why I like kabobs. When you put your food on skewers, not only do you keep things from falling onto the charcoal, but they're a lot easier to turn over.

If you're using bamboo skewers, soak them for in water for 30 minutes or more. If you don't, they'll catch fire and burn down the trailer park.

I skewered the vegetables on one set of skewers and the seafood kabobs on another. Why? Because the vegetables take longer. Also, when grilling, a little non-stick cooking spray (or olive oil spray) helps a lot. Spray your kabobs lightly before grilling—but don't spray directly into the fire!

Note for my peeps—there are two kinds of sea scallops, dry and wet. Use dry scallops. Wet scallops are soaked in who-knows-what, and throw off a lot of liquid when cooking. Ask your fish dude; he'll know whether the scallops are wet or dry. Make sure you remove the small side muscle from the scallops. It's about the size of a postage stamp. Just peel the side muscle off; it should come off easily.

INGREDIENTS

8 large shrimp, de-shelled and de-veined

8 sea scallops

¾ cup cream sherry (you can use sweet Marsala or port as a substitute)

¼ cup extra-virgin olive oil

1 tablespoon each of freshly grated ginger, freshly minced garlic, freshly chopped thyme (or dried thyme)

Some hot sauce, baby this evening

½ Spanish onion

1 yellow bell pepper

8 cherry tomatoes

Salt and pepper

HERE WE GO!

Rinse off the shrimp and pat dry with paper towels. Rinse off the scallops and pat dry with paper towels until the towels no longer get damp.

SCAN THE QR CODE TO SEE THE YOUTUBE VIDEO

For the marinade:
Combine the sherry, the olive oil, the ginger, garlic, thyme and hot sauce (to taste). Add salt and pepper to taste and mix 'em up. Let it sit for a while.

For the vegetable kabobs:
Cut the Spanish onion and the yellow bell pepper (remove the stems and seeds) into pieces that are about the same size as your cherry tomatoes.

Take a piece of onion, put it on the skewer, followed by a cherry tomato and a piece of yellow bell pepper. Then add another piece of onion, a tomato, a piece of pepper. Your skewer should be full. Make 4 skewers.

For the seafood kabobs:

Take a shrimp. Pierce it with a skewer, going through the bottom of the shrimp, and then through the top. Then add a scallop—pierce it through the side. Add another shrimp. Then a scallop. That's 1 skewer—2 shrimp and 2 scallops.

Make 4 skewers. Put the seafood and vegetable skewers in a large baking dish, and drizzle the marinade over them. Refrigerate for an hour or so.

Heat up the grill! Set the heat to medium, and when the grill is nice and warm, add the 4 vegetable kabobs. Cook for 5 to 7 minutes, and then turn over.

Put the seafood kabobs on the grill.

Now, while the seafood kabobs cook, pour the leftover marinade from the baking dish into a small sauté pan over high heat. Let it come to a full boil, and cook for a few minutes. Then reduce the heat to low and let the sauce simmer.

When the seafood kabobs have cooked for 3 to 4 minutes, turn over. Cook for another 3 or 4 more minutes, until done. The seafood and the vegetable kabobs should be done around the same time. Remove to a platter, drizzle with a little reduced marinade, and . . .

MANGIAMO!

ANGELA'S CHICKEN STEW

and Eat That Spaghetti or I'll Shove it Down Your Throat

Almost every Sunday, we'd go to my grandmother's house and have a big Italian dinner. The usual suspects would be there; my mom and dad, and us three kids, and my uncle Oscar, and his wife and three kids. The kids would play in the backyard, wrestle on the living-room floor, and jump on the beds in the basement. Angela would cook, and when the pasta was ready, she'd serve us kids at the kitchen table and say . . .

"Eat that spaghetti, or I'll shove it down your throat."

Which we kids thought was ridiculously hilarious.

Angela was my grandmother. She was an Italian immigrant, who came from Italy to New York City as a child. The family lived in Harlem. As a teenager, Angela and her sister, Marie, started working in a garment sweatshop—like so many other Italian immigrant women—seven days a week, all day long, for next to nothing. Disgusted with the working conditions, she and Marie helped organize the first dressmakers strike for the fledgling International Ladies' Garment Workers Union.

Their mother, Giuseppina, accompanied her daughters on the strike, brandishing a rolling pin, telling anybody within earshot that if anybody messed with her girls, they'd have to go through her first. Angela and Marie continued to organize, with Giuseppina following them with her rolling pin.

Angela was very effective; she was an eloquent, persuasive, and fearless organizer. She was eventually offered a chance to organize and manage the Delaware, Maryland, and Virginia area (later known as the Upper South Department of the ILGWU), and she accepted the challenge. So she gathered up her two sons, and moved to Baltimore, Maryland.

Angela started by going to small towns on the Eastern Shore of Maryland. She didn't drive; the ILGWU eventually found her a driver, a one-eyed African-American named Jesse. I can only imagine what it must have been like, going to these tiny towns in the not-so-deep south, an Italian woman and her black driver, trying to convince people to join the union.

Organizing was a tough business in those days. Factory owners didn't want anything to do with unions—it would obviously cost them money to pay a decent wage and provide benefits. A lot of those factory owners ran their towns. They had the politicians and police in their pockets.

My grandmother was thrown down a flight of steps when she tried to organize one shop. She was thrown in jail after trying to organize another. She was beaten more than once, but she persisted. Why? Because it pissed her off the way the workers were treated; women were locked in factories for hours at a time. One hundred and forty-six garment workers died in a fire at the Triangle Shirtwaist factory in New York because the owners had locked the doors to keep the workers from taking any breaks. Workers made very little money, they had no rights or benefits. Women were sexually abused; Angela wanted to change all that.

And she did; she took her region of the Ladies' Garment Workers Union from nothing to about 16,000 members by the time she retired in 1972. She was the first woman vice president of a major union, she substantially raised the standard of living for thousands and thousands of people, and she did it without expecting anything in return. She told me more than once . . .

"When you give, you give with no strings attached."

Everybody loved her, including the bosses she fought with; they respected her.

Angela made some tough choices when she started organizing in New York; her marriage suffered. Her husband, Romollo, was an Italian from Rome; Angela's father had arranged the marriage. Romollo, who was old-fashioned and older than Angela, didn't approve of her radicalism, and they filed for divorce. During the divorce, their children—my father Philip and my uncle Oscar—were put in an orphanage while Angela and Romollo fought for custody.

Romollo was a waiter at a fancy hotel. Angela was a radical union organizer who'd been thrown in jail. Romollo used that evidence against Angela and won custody; a crushing blow to Angela. She was furious with Romollo; she started using her maiden name, Bambace.

Angela wanted to stay close to her kids; Giuseppina bought a house in Queens near Romollo's, and she and Angela watched over the two boys. As soon as she could, Angela moved the family to Baltimore; she helped put Oscar through medical school and Philip through law school.

Angela was amazing—feisty, strong-willed, and courageous. Philip called her strength "soothing and comforting." She drank (bourbon Manhattans or Chianti), she smoked (Larks), and she cared more about people than anyone I have ever known.

Angela used to wait in the alley in her housecoat during Christmas to tip the garbage men. Homeless guys would come to the back door; she'd make them a sandwich, and then pay them to do yard work. All this from a woman who was invited to John F. Kennedy's inauguration and had U.S. Senators sending her Christmas cards. Mayors and governors would stop by the house during holidays.

One day, she was in the hospital for a surgery when Hubert Humphrey, the vice president of the United States, called. They were friends. The nurse handed the phone to Angela, but she thought it was her son, Philip, playing a joke. So she hung up, saying she wasn't in the mood for any of his "crap."

A few moments later the phone rang again. The nurse told Angela it was the vice president. Again. She took the call.

Angela would cuss on occasion. I remember one night she took us kids to a restaurant, and she told the Baltimore City Comptroller, Hyman Pressman, that he was "full of shit" after he recited an impromptu poem about my sister. Everyone laughed, including Hyman, who knew my grandmother well and loved her. The politicians admired Angela because she was honest, uncompromising, and she couldn't be bought or influenced. She fought for what she believed in; she was a hero to the workers she represented—people who were really struggling to make ends meet.

Angela was modest, in every sense of the word. She never bragged about her accomplishments, she lived in a modest house, and she didn't wear diamonds or fancy jewelry. Oscar once bought her a fur coat; she didn't feel comfortable wearing it, because she thought it would be hypocritical to be fighting for the causes of working people while waltzing around in a mink coat.

My family lived with Angela from the time I was born until I was six. I lived with Angela again when I was a teenager. I used to do her shopping; I'd drive (in the used American Motors Rambler she bought me) to a little store behind the Lexington Market in downtown Baltimore called DiMarco's. They used to sell Italian meats, cheeses, and wines.

I used to buy her Chianti—in the small straw bottles—that didn't cost more than two or three dollars. Angela and I would have dinner, have a glass of Chianti, and she'd tell me stories about her life. I was fascinated. Crazy how some kids get so attached to their grandparents. I was really attached to Angela.

One night, Oscar walked in with a suitcase and a case of wine; he told us he had just left his wife. I guess Oscar's wife wasn't too happy about it, because the reason he brought the case of wine was he didn't want her pouring his ridiculously expensive vintage vino down the sink after he left.

Oscar moved in, and the two of us shared my bedroom in Angela's club basement.

Angela and I were having dinner one night when Oscar told us he was going out. He left, and we finished our dinner and our glass of Chianti. When she asked me for another glass, I told her there was no more. She asked about Oscar's wine. I told Angela that all we had was Oscar's special wine. She looked at me and said,

"Who more special than we?"

Angela told me to go get a bottle, so I pulled a bottle from Oscar's case, and poured us each a glass. Angela took a sip and started laughing—the wine was incredible. After we finished our glass of wine, she wanted to go to sleep. I asked her what to do with the wine; she said to stick a cork in it and put it in the fridge. I did and went to bed.

A little after midnight, I woke up when I heard Oscar yelling my name. He walked down into the basement bedroom. He wasn't too happy about finding his fine wine in the fridge with a cork jammed in it. "What the fuck were you thinking?" is what he said. Then I told him the story.

When I got to the "Who more special than we?" part, he started laughing.

Then he explained to me, as he was getting ready for bed, that the bottle I had opened was a 1954 Chateau Mouton Rothschild. Every year, the Rothschild's had a different famous artist design the label—Salvador Dali, Picasso, Miro. When he told me what the bottle was worth, I couldn't sleep.

For three years.

ANGELA'S CHICKEN STEW

We called Angela "Nanny," which is a screwed up version of *nonna*, which is what most Italian kids call their grandmothers. Angela didn't seem to love cooking, and who could blame her? She worked long hours and was frequently out of town. We ate out a lot. She loved Chinese food; we used to go to a place on Charles Street in Baltimore called Jimmy Wu's. She ate lunch almost every workday in a basement restaurant called Oyster Bay in downtown Baltimore, right around the corner from her office. Pete was her waiter; Angela loved steak tartare, and French onion soup.

When Angela cooked, she had a rotation of three dishes for our big Sunday Italian dinners.

Pasta *piselli* was a spaghetti dish she made with peas and onions. She also made the classic Italian meat sauce—sausages, meatballs, and pork in a tomato sauce that cooked all day long. And she made an Italian chicken stew, which I recently tried to recreate with the few remaining brain cells that I have left. The stew was *delizioso*. Most chicken recipes call for chicken breasts. I love chicken breasts. I'm a big fan. Yes, breasts are sexy. A lot of attention gets paid to the breast, and rightfully so. But what about the much overlooked chicken thigh?

It's an underdog. It's neglected. It needs someone to champion its cause. If Angela were alive today, she'd be singing the praises of the delicious dark meat, fighting for its rightful place in the culinary catalogue.

So in Angela's chicken stew, I use chicken thighs. Hail to the thigh!

I admire the thigh. It's juicy. It starts at the knee and goes all the way up to the hip—which is really close to some sexy stuff. I think thighs are sexy. And I'm bringing sexy back.

Notes:

When you brown your chicken thighs, you want the heat high enough to make them brown, but not so high that they burn or stick to the bottom of the pan. It should take about 4 minutes or so per side. If it takes longer, the heat ain't high enough. Don't move 'em around, let 'em brown.

Pancetta is Italian bacon. Cook it like bacon; get it brown on one side, and then try and get the other side brown. You can substitute regular bacon if you can't find pancetta. Or you can leave it out.

Dutch ovens work well for a dish like this.

Stoves vary in temperature—on my stove at Slim's Shady Trailer Park, the temperature varies FROM BURNER TO BURNER! It's enough to drive you crazy.

Well, I was a little crazy to begin with.

Fresh peas are best. If you're using frozen green peas, measure out a cup-and-a-half and let them sit. You don't have to defrost them. By the time they're ready to go in the stew, they'll be defrosted. If you don't like peas, you can substitute asparagus tips.

Finally, when I was at the grocery store, I was waiting in line to buy a whole piece of pancetta, which I was going to chop into small pieces for this stew. But the line at the deli was real long, so I picked up a package of Boar's Head pancetta, four ounces, thinly sliced. I chopped it up into smaller pieces, and it came to a generous cup.

It browned really well, and got deliciously flaky and crisp. I'll probably use it again in the future. It was *delizioso*.

When working with raw chicken, wash your cutting boards, your knives, your hands. Power wash the kitchen.

Serves 6 adults, or maybe 2 teenage boys.

INGREDIENTS

2 pounds boneless, skinless chicken thighs (about 6–8 thighs)

Kosher salt and fresh-cracked black pepper

4 ounces pancetta cut in small pieces (1 generous cup)

1 cup each—chopped onions and celery

1½ cups chopped carrots

Celery tops—those leafy green things? Save 4 or 5 leaves!

3 cloves minced garlic (about 1 tablespoon)

½ teaspoon dried oregano

1 cup white wine

4 cups chicken broth

2 tablespoons of flour

4 small red potatoes, skin on, cut into pieces about the size of a ping-pong ball (you'll need about 2½ cups)

2 tablespoons medium sherry (or sweet vermouth, or sweet Marsala)

1½ cups green peas (fresh are best, frozen are okay; you can substitute asparagus tips if you like)

Extra-virgin olive oil (optional)

HERE WE GO!

SCAN THE QR CODE TO SEE THE YOUTUBE VIDEO

Rinse the chicken and pat dry with paper towels. Salt and pepper both sides, I use Kosher salt and fresh-cracked black pepper. Rub it in. Rub-a-dub-dub.

Heat a large heavy pot, like a Dutch oven, over medium heat for 2 minutes.

Add the pancetta, let it cook for 4 minutes, or until brown. Try and turn the pancetta over and let the other side brown for 4 more minutes or so. The objective here is to try and get all sides of the pancetta pieces golden brown. If the pan gets dry, drizzle a little olive oil in it.

When the pancetta has browned, remove with a slotted spoon to a small bowl.

There should be some drippings in the bottom of the pot/Dutch oven. We need just enough to coat the bottom of the pan—about 1 tablespoon.

If there is not enough, add a drizzle of olive oil until there is. If there's too much oil, the chicken won't brown. If there's too little oil, the chicken will stick to the bottom of the pot. You're smart. You can do this.

Turn the heat to medium-high for 1 minute.

Add the chicken and let it brown for 4 or 5 minutes. Don't move it around! Let it brown.

When it's brown, use some tongs and turn each piece over. Let them brown on the other side for 4 or 5 minutes, until golden. Keep in mind, the chicken is gonna cook in the stew for another 30 minutes or so.

Remove the chicken thighs to a platter, and let 'em cool, baby.

Turn the heat down to medium. There should be enough juicy stuff in the bottom of the pan. We'll need about 2 tablespoons. If there's not enough liquid/oil in the bottom of the pan, add a little olive oil.

Add the onion, celery—both the chopped celery and the tops—carrots, garlic, and oregano to the pot. Cook for 5 to 6 minutes, until the onions are translucent. Stir frequently.

Put the heat on high. Add the cup of white wine. When it starts to bubble, let it cook off for 1 minute.

Reduce the heat to medium, and cook for 5 minutes, stirring often.

Add the chicken broth, and turn the heat to high.

Whisk in the flour, 1 tablespoon at a time, until it's smooth and all the lumps are gone. When both tablespoons have been whisked in, and it's all smoovy-smoov . . .

Add the potatoes. When the broth comes to a boil, let the potatoes cook for 3 minutes, while boiling.

Reduce the heat to medium. Add the 2 tablespoons of sherry or sweet vermouth.

Cook for 15 minutes.

The chicken should be cool by now. Cut each chicken thigh into smaller pieces, about the size of a strawberry.

Put the chicken in the pot. Reduce the heat to low. Cook for 15 minutes.

Don't stir! This is a stew. Let it sit and stew for a while. You keep stirring this thing and the potatoes are gonna break up, and the chicken is gonna break down.

After 15 minutes, give it a stir.

Then cook for another 15 minutes.

Add the peas and the cooked pancetta. Cook for 10 minutes.

Scrape the sides of the pot, right above the stew-line. Scrape it right into the stew, this is some flavorful stuff! Give the stew a gentle stir, taste for salt and pepper and adjust.

Stab a potato with a folk—it should be tender. Take a bite of the chicken—it should be firm and just a bit flaky—like me.

Dish it up, and . . .

MANGIAMO!

CIPPOLINI and RED BELL PEPPER SAUCE over SOLE

with B.B. King

Baked salmon

Sautéed sole

I saw a tour bus driving north on Route 29 and started following it. I had just come from the recording studio in Washington, DC. It was the early 1990s, I had written a song for a singer named Brian Jack. Brian was the former lead singer in a Baltimore band named Child's Play. He had a great voice, big charisma, and I took him into the studio to do some songs I'd written. We hit it off.

The two of us lived in a house on Sue Creek in a town outside Baltimore called Essex. The house we shared was incredible. It was right on the water. We had windsurfers, Sea-Doos, all these great water toys. None of them were ours—people parked their things at our pier, and they'd let us use them in return. I got a golden retriever, named her Jessie, and she loved the place.

The previous tenant had been hauled off to jail for insurance fraud. I remember the first time I met him—he was standing in the huge living room. It had cathedral ceilings, a big fireplace, and massive floor-to-ceiling glass doors that overlooked the deck, the pier, and the river. I'll never forget what the guy said—

"I laid a lot of pipe in this house."

I thought maybe the guy was a plumber. Then it hit me—he wasn't talking about those kind of pipes. Brian and I moved in soon after the guy was taken off to prison. I wrote songs for Brian, he sang 'em. Things were starting to take off; he was getting airplay and packing the clubs.

Brian and I were heading home from the studio when we saw the tour bus and started following it; I had this intuitive feeling that we should tag along behind the bus. A couple minutes later, it pulled over to the side of the highway onto the shoulder, and I pulled right behind it. The driver got out of the bus, came over, and asked me if I knew the way to Merriweather Post Pavilion.

As a matter of fact, I did. I told him to follow me.

I saw the Doors at Merriweather Post Pavilion on their first tour. I saw Led Zeppelin at Merriweather when they opened for the Who back in 1969—the only time that ever happened. Procol Harum, Paul Simon, Frank Sinatra; I'd seen them all there. I'd even played on that stage before, so I knew where the backstage entrance was. The big-ass tour bus followed me in my little blue Honda station wagon.

We reached the security gate, and I told them what was going on, and they waved us through. They didn't even ask any questions; I'm guessing they were well aware that whoever was on that tour bus was running late. The tour bus followed me on the small, winding road through the woods to the backstage area. When we got there, the bus driver parked, got out, and thanked me a million times. And then guess who stepped off the bus?

B.B. King.

When I was a kid, my mom had brought home an album of his called *Indianola Mississippi Seeds*. Man, did I love that record. I must have played it a million times. "Chains and Things," "Nobody Loves Me But My Mother," "Hummingbird"—which was written by Leon Russell—I loved those songs. Joe Walsh played guitar on that album, Carole King played some keyboards. B.B. King called it ". . . the best album I've done, artistically." It was my favorite B.B. King record.

And there he was, standing right in front of me. He thanked me and then asked Brian and me if we'd like to stay and see the show. He walked us to the side of the stage, and dropped us off, right behind the curtain. We waited in the wings; I looked out at the crowd. It was buzzing.

A few moments later, B.B. King's band took the stage and played one song. Then B.B. King came out, and played and sang his heart out, all night long. Brian and I watched the whole concert from the side of the stage, a couple yards away. It was an amazing show.

After the show, B.B. King invited us back to his dressing room. He signed autographs for everybody waiting in line. He told stories; he was charming, laid-back, and as gracious as could be. B.B. signed a photo for me.

A crazy coincidence . . .

The guy who signed me to Motown way back when was Carl Griffin. Carl had produced a CD for B.B. King called *Live at the Apollo*. It won a Grammy in 1992 for both B.B. and Carl. When I mentioned to B.B. King that night that Carl was one of my best friends, B.B. smiled and said, "Carl's a good man."

Yes, he is!

Want to hear the rest of the story about the Grammy Award-winning *Live at the Apollo* CD?

Ray Charles was scheduled to do the concert that night at the Apollo Theater with B.B. King. But right before the show, Ray Charles demanded to be paid an additional fifty grand—in advance—to be included in the live recording. Nobody had that kind of cash lying around on short notice. So Carl decided to go ahead with the show. Ray Charles played the concert, but was not included on the CD.

CIPPOLINI AND RED BELL PEPPER SAUCE OVER SOLE

After a night of singing the blues, this is a dish that will make you happy.

The first time I made this sauce, I used maple syrup. Not pancake syrup, maple syrup. Big difference!

My dad lived on top of a mountain in upstate New York. It was really isolated, hardly any people, but there were lots of trees. Maple syrup was everywhere—you could see taps on maple trees with buckets underneath all over the place. Real maple syrup is really good, especially up there. One time, I ran out of sugar for my coffee. Getting to the grocery store from my dad's house was an ordeal, so if you ran out of something, you had to spend a good hour driving to and from town to get what you needed.

So I put some maple syrup in my coffee instead of sugar and loved it. It's still my preferred coffee sweetener. Another time, I ran out of honey; I was going to use it in a sauce for grilled salmon. I used maple syrup instead—just a little—and loved it.

I know some real good cooks who look down on this kind of thing. One of them suggested I try a medium sherry instead, and I did. I cooked the sauce both ways, with sherry and with maple syrup.

I did a taste test at Slim's Shady Trailer Park. Everybody loved the sauce with the maple syrup much better than the one with the sherry. But what the hell do those people know?

If you want to substitute sherry for maple syrup, use a cream/sweet sherry.

I use this cippolini sauce over fish. I cook the fish one of three ways; I bake it, sear it, or sauté it.

Bake:

Thick, firm fish works best for baking—salmon or halibut works well. To bake a piece of fish, heat your oven to 400 degrees. Rub your fish all over with a little olive oil, and then sprinkle a little salt and pepper on top. Put it in a glass or ceramic baking dish and bake for 10 minutes. Check it with a fork. The top should be flaky, the center should be firm. I baked a piece of salmon this way, and drizzled some cippolini sauce over it at the end, and it was delish.

Sear:

Ahi tuna and mahi are fish that sear well. Almost any fish sears well. I sear salmon all the time. Thick pieces take longer than thin pieces. To sear a piece of fish . . . get a medium sauté pan. Put it over medium-high heat. Add a tablespoon of butter, and a tablespoon of olive oil. Salt and pepper one side of your fish, then sprinkle a LITTLE brown sugar (or turbinado sugar, or regular sugar in a pinch) on top.

When the butter starts to bubble, put the fish in the pan—salted/peppered/sugared side down first—and sear for 2 or 3 minutes, depending on the thickness. As the underside sears, sprinkle the top with a little salt, pepper, and brown sugar. You can put a piece of aluminum foil over top of the pan—LOOSELY—if you want to cut down on the splattering.

Then, lift the fish out of the pan with tongs, swirl the butter and oil around in the bottom of the pan so you're not putting the fish on any dry spots, and turn the fish over and sear the other side for a couple minutes. Drizzle a little sauce over it, and there ya go!

Sauté:

If you want to sauté a piece of fish, I recommend filet of sole or flounder. It's not expensive, it cooks quickly, and it's *delizioso*. Sole filets are thin and don't take long. You want them crispy and brown on the outside, but not burnt. Dust both sides of the sole filets with some flour. Add some salt and pepper. Put a sauté pan over medium-high heat, add a tablespoon of olive oil and a tablespoon of butter. When the butter starts to bubble, add the sole. Cook for a quick minute or so. Flip it over—GENTLY—and cook on the other side for a minute or so.

Whatever fish you cook, however you cook it, when it's cooked to your liking, drizzle a little cippolini sauce on top.

You don't need a lot of sauce. This is powerful stuff!

Notes:

Cippolini onions are small onions, a little sweeter and milder than regular onions. You can find them in most grocery stores. If you can't, use shallots instead.

Meyer lemons are my favorites; they're sweeter and milder than regular lemons. I'm into sweet and mild these days, I guess. If you can't find Meyer lemons, use a ripe, soft lemon.

You can use red bell pepper, or a combination of red and yellow bell peppers. Whatever combination you use, you'll only need a tablespoon or so of sauce for each piece of fish.

INGREDIENTS

For the Cippolini Sauce:

2 tablespoons olive oil

1 tablespoon butter

2 tablespoons peeled, chopped cippolini onions

1 tablespoon minced red bell pepper (or half and half red and yellow bell pepper)

1 tablespoon maple syrup

¼ cup dry white wine

1 tablespoon fresh-squeezed lemon juice (remove any seeds)

1 tablespoon chopped fresh Italian flat-leaf parsley

Kosher salt

Fresh-cracked black pepper to taste

HERE WE GO!

Put the olive oil and butter in a small sauté pan over medium-high heat for 2 or 3 minutes—don't let the butter burn!

When the butter starts to bubble, add the onions and red bell peppers and cook for 2 minutes while stirring and swirling. This is how you swirl . . . remove the pan from the heat for about 10 seconds, and swirl everything all around. Put the pan back on the heat for 30 seconds and repeat.

Add the maple syrup and cook for 2 minutes, swirl and stir.

Add the wine and cook for 1 minute. Shall we swirl and stir?

Add the lemon juice. Cook for 2 minutes.

Add the parsley; add Kosher salt and some fresh-cracked black pepper to taste.

That's the sauce! You are now The Boss of the Sauce—use it over seared mahi, or baked salmon, or sautéed sole, and . . .

MANGIAMO!

SAUTÉED SPINACH with TOASTED ALMONDS and GOLDEN RAISINS

and The Bride of Baltimore

On the Love Boat

A lot of people ask me to sing at their weddings. My answer is usually,

"Yes. Yes I can."

I love singing at weddings, it's such a happy time. When I'm singing at a wedding where I hardly know anyone, that's a lot of fun; watching strangers go nuts at a wedding is a blast. Watching people you know and love go nuts at a wedding is enough to make you want to grab a dart gun and shoot somebody in the neck.

A couple years ago, a young gal from Baltimore asked me to sing "End of the Rainbow" at her wedding. She had no budget. I told her, "I can do it. But if Taylor Swift asks me to open up for her that day, or if Jimmy Kimmel calls me at the last minute, I won't be able to. If you can live with that, yes. Yes I can."

The week before her wedding, as hard as it is to believe, Taylor Swift did not call; Jimmy Kimmel did not appear on my doorstep. I told her yes. She was so ecstatic. Ever since she saw me sit down at the piano and sing "End of the Rainbow" at a concert in Annapolis at the Rams Head Tavern, it had been her wish for me to sing that song at her wedding. I was flattered. Really. When she asked me to sing, I was thinking—I could walk in, sing "End of the Rainbow" and then get back to packing.

Packing? Yes. I was moving. The day after her wedding, I was leaving Baltimore to move to Nashville. A permanent move, a big move. The wedding was on a Saturday, and I was leaving Sunday. I didn't mention My Big Move to the bride to be—I figured she had enough on her mind. A couple days before the wedding, we were talking on the phone about details when she said,

"You need to be on the boat by 11:00 a.m."

Boat? Pardon me . . . did you say "boat"? Yes. The wedding was a cruise around Baltimore—for five hours. We would be out to sea the whole time, and there was no getting off the boat. What I thought might take a couple hours at most, was now gonna take all day. Thoughts that were running through my mind—maybe I could have someone pick me up on a Jet Ski after my song; maybe I could have a helicopter drop a ladder, or I could jump on a passing barge.

But *una promessa é un debito*—"A promise is a debt." That's what my uncle used to say. I told the Bride of Baltimore that I'd be on the Love Boat bright and early.

That Saturday, I jumped in the Slim Vehicle, and drove to the Inner Harbor of Baltimore, parked my car and walked a few blocks down to the water. I saw some folks boarding a small cruise ship—it held maybe 200 people. I got on the boat at 11:00 a.m.

The Love Boat was all decked out in flowers and ribbons; it was a beautiful spring day, the sun was out, it was warm—but not too—and there was a slight breeze as the boat slowly headed out into the Chesapeake Bay. They had the ceremony on the top deck, they exchanged their vows, and everybody walked downstairs to the middle deck. And there I was, sitting at the piano. I sang "End of the Rainbow" for the bride and groom and their guests.

After I finished, people were crying.

They were crying, "Don't give up your day job, Donkey Face!"

After I sang, I guess people needed alcohol—my music usually drives people to drink. I know it drives me to drink. Folks were lining up at the bar; I was in line to get a festive beverage when I saw a friend named Annabelle. I've known her for years, Annabelle is a joy to be around.

Annabelle and I used to work together at a dive bar in Fells Point called the Horse You Came In On. She tended bar, I sang the blues. My band was called the Scrappy Harris Blues Band. I would write songs on the spot, and one night, I wrote a song about Annabelle.

"Annabelle . . . my sweet Annabelle, I'm going down to the wishing well . . . wish for a girl like Annabelle."

Annabelle and I had a blast at the wedding. After dinner, a band played; the guitar player was amazing, in a Stevie Ray Vaughan kinda way. I got up and sang some blues. The band was good. Real good. At the end of the shindig, Rob Fahey got up and sang "Raised on the Radio." Rob was in a great Baltimore band called the Ravyns, "Raised on the Radio" was a big hit for them. It was used in the movie *Fast Times at Ridgemont High* with Sean Penn.

Rob sang his heart out. What a way to end the wedding.

The Love Boat pulled up to the Inner Harbor; it docked right by the food pavilions. The Baltimore skyline was shining in the setting sun. I said my goodbyes, and started walking from the Inner Harbor to the parking lot.

I went home, changed, and walked Batu, then I went to sleep. The next day, Slim Drummer John E Coale came over in his SUV. We packed up everything into our two cars, and drove 700 miles to Nashville. Batu was in the back of the car, his dog bed piled on top of all the boxes, his head poking between the front seats.

Goodbye, Baltimore. Hello, Nashville.

But wait! There's more!

I got an email the other day, "Can you sing "End of the Rainbow" as we walk down the aisle for our wedding? That song has been our song ever since we met."

He told me he was getting married Labor Day in Palm Springs. I'd already been staying in Palm Springs for a few months. I wrote back and told him the same thing I told the Bride of Baltimore—if Taylor Swift calls at the last minute, I'll have to bow out. If you can live with that, yes. Yes I can.

He was so excited. He wrote me back and told me he was going to keep it a secret—he wanted it to be a surprise for his partner, Jack.

SAUTÉED SPINACH WITH TOASTED ALMONDS AND GOLDEN RAISINS

If you need some fortification before a Big Day, like a wedding day, why not make some spinach? It worked for Popeye!

A few things about this dish . . .

I used multi-colored, organic, grape tomatoes. Why?

I saw them in the grocery store; they looked real cool and colorful, and they were inexpensive.

You can buy almonds already toasted, but I like to toast my own nuts. I use raw slivered almonds, and toast them in a dry pan over medium-high heat. Do not leave your nuts unattended. Nothing worse than burnt nuts.

I only cook the tomatoes for a couple minutes; you don't want them to lose their shape or their skin.

And only cook the spinach for a couple minutes, just enough to wilt it.

Add the toasted almonds and raisins last, because you don't want your nuts getting soggy, and you don't want the raisins to absorb all the sauce.

Golden raisins look and taste great in this dish. You can also use brown raisins.

Serves 2.

INGREDIENTS

8 ounces of baby spinach (I use organic)

2 tablespoons raw almonds, chopped or slivered

2 tablespoons extra-virgin olive oil

2 tablespoons chopped shallots

Crushed red pepper (I start off with about ¼ teaspoon)

⅓ cup white wine

1 cup grape tomatoes, cut in half, seeds squeezed out

1 tablespoon raisins (golden are best, but brown are fine)

Salt to taste

HERE WE GO!

Rinse off the spinach and spin dry—unless it's the kind that has been triple-washed. Make sure it's clean, SlimNation.

SCAN THE QR CODE TO SEE THE YOUTUBE VIDEO

And now, let's toast our nuts. "Here's to you, you nuts!"

Get a small sauté pan.

Put the heat on medium-high.

Grab your nuts, put them in the dry pan.

Shake your nuts around until they're golden brown.

Put your toasted almonds on a plate. Let 'em cool.

Put the 2 tablespoons of olive oil in a large sauté pan over medium heat.

Add the 2 tablespoons shallots.

Add the crushed red pepper.

Cook for 2 minutes or so, stir every now and then.

When the shallots are almost clear, add the white wine, turn the heat to high, and let it cook off for 1 minute or so.

Turn the heat to medium-low, add the tomatoes, and cook for 2 minutes, stirring every now and then.

Add the spinach, cook and stir for 2 minutes—or until it wilts.

Add the toasted almonds.

Add the raisins.

Give it a stir.

Dish it up! This would make a great side dish for any of the Slim Fish Dishes.

MANGIAMO!

ITALIAN CHICKEN SOUP

on Valentine's Day

My dad (I called him Paps) had eyebrows that looked like two small porcupines had perched above his eyes. His eyebrows were so wild and wooly he could have combed them straight back and it would have looked like he had a full head of hair.

Paps was bald—maybe that's why he wouldn't let anybody trim his eyebrows. It was the last patch of thick hair he had on his head. You would have needed a weed-whacker to trim them, anyway. We kids would beg my dad to trim the shrubbery, but he wouldn't; the barber would offer to clip the hedges, and my dad would refuse.

His eyebrows were a topic of conversation among the family. They were hard to ignore. They'd enter the room a few minutes before he would. If you got too close to him, they'd poke your eyes out. My dad had some real serious eyebrows that he never trimmed. Except once.

My dad had come down to Baltimore to fix up his Mom's house. Angela had died a few months prior—April, 1975. I was living with her when she passed away. It was a horrible time; I was really close to my grandmother. She was so sick and in so much pain. After she died, I continued to stay in her house, which was near Pimlico Racetrack, a horse-racing track where they hold the Preakness Stakes.

I idolized Angela. She was tough but sensitive; she was passionate and compassionate. She was a woman of conviction, and she was such a comfort to be around. When she died, I was heartbroken; I wanted to keep on living in the house, but my dad and his only brother, Oscar, wanted to sell the place. So my dad came down from New York to get the house ready to put on the market.

The first day was the hardest. We worked all day getting the outside ready to be painted; trimming bushes, cleaning cobwebs, patching things up. That night, my dad and I were sitting at the kitchen table; he wanted to cook something in the oven. It was one of those old gas stoves that you had to light by hand. Paps turned the gas on. I explained to him that you had to light the stove by hand, so he bent over, opened the oven door, and struck a match. Before I could stop him, a blast of flame knocked him flat on his ass. I thought for sure that his face was fried, but it wasn't. He was sitting on the kitchen floor, facial hair smoldering. I helped him up and sat him in a chair.

His eyebrows were trimmed at last. As a matter of fact, I think they might have saved his life. The flame probably had a hard time burning through the shrubbery that was his eyebrows, which probably saved his face from getting flame-broiled. His eyebrows looked normal for once. That was the one and only time my dad's eyebrows got trimmed.

We worked on the house just about every day, cleaning, painting and fixing everything up. I was really struggling with the loss of Angela. One day, when I was feeling low, my dad took me to the racetrack. He thought it might take my mind off things, so we walked up the street to Pimlico.

On the way, Paps found a wallet in the bushes stuffed with cash—hundreds of dollars. Paps looked at the address on the driver's license, and we walked to the house. Paps walked up and knocked on the door. A guy answered, and my dad handed him the wallet. I'll never forget the look of relief and gratitude on the guy's face. He offered my dad some money. My dad raised his hands in the air in refusal. He didn't take it.

Paps and I walked the rest of the way to Pimlico. When we got there, he explained to me how to bet, how to pick horses. I lost every race. I was more depressed than ever! When the last race came around, Paps explained that it was a trifecta, which means, if you pick all three of the winning horses in order, you win big. I picked the #2 horse to come in first, the #1 horse to come in second, and the #4 horse to come in third.

2-1-4. It was Angela's birthday—February 14th—Valentine's Day.

The horses took off out of the starting gate. For the whole race, the #2 horse was in front, the #1 horse was second and the #4 horse was third. When they crossed the finish line, the #5 horse beat out the #4 horse for third place. The final order was 2-1-5. I was a big loser.

I showed my dad my ticket, and then threw it on the ground. He picked it up, gave it back to me and told me that the race wasn't official yet. He explained that the race wasn't official until they had a chance to review the race, which took a couple minutes. A voice came over the PA system. There was an objection against the #5 horse—he had bumped into the #4 horse right before the end of the race.

The officials then disqualified the #5 horse, and the final, official result was 2-1-4.

I won $899 on that race!

We went back to the house, and the next day, started working again. We eventually got the place all fixed up. It didn't take long to sell Angela's house; it was a great place, with an apartment on the second floor that had a big balcony off the main bedroom. I hated to see the place go.

My dad took the money from the sale of Angela's house and bought a place in upstate New York. It was called Rat Tail Ridge. Forty acres on top of a mountain with a view that was breathtaking.

ITALIAN CHICKEN SOUP

The toughest thing about making Italian chicken soup is finding an Italian chicken. They're usually the ones in the corner of the coop, drinking wine and arguing.

My dad loved soup. He was a soup guy. Maybe it was because he lived on Top of Old Smokey, where winters were so cold that bears knocked on the front door looking for a place to hibernate. Hot soup works wonders when you come in from the cold.

I roasted a chicken the other day and used my mom's recipe, which is basically sticking a whole lemon inside a chicken and baking it. The next day was a cold and rainy winter day, so I made some soup from the chicken.

If you have leftover chicken (turkey works, too), here's what you do—pick the meat off the bones and the carcass. I usually end up with about three cups of chicken meat. Throw away the stuff you don't like—fat, skin, small bones and such.

I broke the carcass into two pieces. I used those and a couple leg and wing bones in the soup—they add great flavor—just make sure you remove all the bones and stuff before you serve the soup. Take a slotted spoon and go fishing for bones or skin and remove them—you don't want any of your guests breaking a bicuspid on a chicken bone.

After you've made the soup, if there is any fat on top, skim it off.

You can serve this soup as is, or you can add some pasta or rice.

I like using small pasta, like *ditalini*. I cook the pasta separately, and put some in each individual bowl. I used to put it right in the soup and let it cook in there, but the pasta absorbs too much broth, and gets soggy.

I also like using rice; but I cook it separately and add it to each individual bowl right before serving.

You'll need to smoosh the Italian tomatoes before you add them to the soup. Open the can, pour them in a bowl, and dig in with your mitts and smoosh 'em up! Remove the small yellow core from each tomato, and any skin or stems.

Or you can use already crushed Italian tomatoes.

INGREDIENTS

¼ cup of extra-virgin olive oil

1 cup each—chopped celery, carrots, and onion

4 garlic cloves, minced

2 cups cabbage, sliced into small pieces (I used Napa, you can also use regular cabbage)

8 cups chicken broth

Chicken or turkey carcass and bones

2 cups water

1 bay leaf

1 (28-ounce) can whole, peeled Italian tomatoes, smooshed up by hand

2 tablespoons fresh oregano (or 1 tablespoon dried)

3 cups of chicken or turkey meat, white and dark

1 cup of corn—fresh, canned, or frozen

½ pound of pasta (*ditalini* works well, as does elbow macaroni)

Salt and pepper

HERE WE GO!

Put a large pot on medium heat.

Add the olive oil; let it heat up for 2 minutes.

Add the celery, carrots, onion and garlic.

Let it cook for about 7 minutes, stirring every so often.

Add the cabbage.

Cook for 5 minutes.

Add the chicken broth.

Put the chicken/turkey carcass and bones in the pot.

Add the water.

Add the bay leaf.

Add the tomatoes.

Add the oregano.

Turn the heat on high and bring to a boil.

Then lower the heat to medium-low, cook for about 30 minutes, stirring occasionally.

Remove the carcass pieces and bones

Pick off any remaining meat from the carcass and bones that you've just removed, and add the meat to the soup. Discard the bones and carcass.

Add the 3 cups of chicken or turkey meat to the soup.

Add the corn.

Cook for 10 minutes.

Take the soup off the heat.

Check it for bones, skin and any other funky stuff.

If you want to add some pasta . . .

Get a pot, fill it with cold water, and put it on high heat.

When it comes to a boil, add a couple tablespoons Kosher salt.

Add the pasta.

When it is VERY FIRM, drain it.

Dish it up! Ladle some soup into bowl.

Add a little pasta. Give it a stir.

You could also add cooked rice, instead of pasta. Either way, she's a-delish!

Serve with some crusty bread, and . . .

MANGIAMO!

EGGPLANT PARMIGIANO
and
I've Heard Enough

My old apartment had three bowling alleys in it; they were built in the 1930s and were a bit dilapidated. The balls and pins were made of wood, and they weren't in the best of shape, but you could play a game if you didn't mind setting up the pins after each shot.

There were two grass tennis courts out back, and they, too, were dilapidated and overgrown. You could play a set if you brought a machete. The house was huge; it had a fireplace on the first floor that could hold a Volkswagen.

The house belonged to Peggy; she was outspoken, feisty, cynical, and almost a hundred years old. Peggy lived upstairs, and I lived downstairs with my girlfriend and my dog, Batu. Peggy was hard-of-hearing. On her hundredth birthday, her son gave her a present, they were on the screened-in porch upstairs; I was on the patio beneath them. I could hear her son yelling,

"Mom! I got you a present!"

Silence.

"Mom! Open it up!"

Silence. Then I could hear her opening the wrapping paper.

"Mom! It's a hearing aid!"

Silence.

"Mom! What do you think? IT'S A HEARING AID!"

Silence. And then Peggy spoke softly,

"I'm a hundred years old. I've heard enough."

The house used to be a country club called Stoney Run Club. Peggy and her husband bought it, and did some minor renovations—like adding bedrooms—but it still felt and looked like a small old country club. The apartment downstairs must have been an old clubroom. There were the bowling alleys on the side, a large main room with a fireplace, and a huge patio that overlooked the overgrown tennis courts. You entered the apartment through a big screen door in the kitchen. The kitchen was great: lots of large windows, a big antique sink, and old wood countertops. It had a small four-burner stove in the corner that worked like a charm.

Batu and I started making cooking videos in that little kitchen, I'd whip up a dish, shoot video, take photos, and write down the recipe. I'd take Peggy a plate every so often; I'd go up the ancient wooden staircase, past the moldy bookcases, take her a plate, and have a chat and a chew.

Roland Park is a wonderful neighborhood; the grocery store, Eddie's, has been there for seventy years; it's an old family store that has a guy who opens the door for you when you walk in and out. The hardware store, Schneider's, has been there for more than a hundred years, and the pharmacy, Tuxedo, has been there more than seventy-five years.

It's that kind of neighborhood, big old Victorian houses, big old trees, and it's right in the middle of Baltimore City. I went to school in Roland Park, I've always loved the neighborhood. I loved that apartment, so did Batu. And I adored Peggy.

She helped create senior centers and infant centers to help the young and the old. She fought for women's rights and civil rights. She once got pissed off that a big department store in downtown Baltimore wouldn't allow black people to try clothes on, so Peggy took a black friend shopping there, and they tried on clothes. She was one of the most powerful women in Baltimore, and she used that power to help people who were less fortunate.

At a hundred years old, Peggy got around pretty well—she used a walker, but she got around. Whenever she had a problem, she'd bang her cane on the floor, and I'd come up and help.

Once a year, in late September, I'd grab Batu, and we'd head to Ocean City, Maryland. My uncle Oscar had a small apartment at the end of the boardwalk overlooking the Atlantic Ocean; he'd let the family use it for vacations. September is a great time of year to go—no crowds, no traffic, the weather and the water still warm.

I'd hang out for a week or so; bodysurf, fly my kites, cook, eat, drink, write, play guitar. And then I'd lock up the joint and head back to Baltimore. I was driving home from the beach one early evening, Batu was in the back, and I was listening to the Orioles and Yankees baseball game on the AM radio. I stopped at a roadside stand and picked out a couple ripe and lovely homegrown tomatoes and some eggplant. I drove home, crossing the Bay Bridge as the sun went down.

When I got back to Roland Park, I found out that Peggy had passed away, she was 103. I was shaken and sad; I was gonna miss Peggy. I needed to cook something; I was having a hard time wrapping my head around what had just happened. I looked at the tomatoes and eggplant that I had picked up from the produce stand on the way home from Ocean City and made some eggplant Parmigiano.

A couple weeks later, her son sold the house. He didn't give us much notice; we had to move in a hurry, in the dead of winter, right after Christmas. As I was going through my stuff, I came across a card Peggy had given me for my birthday.

"Eat, drink and be merry, for tomorrow you may die."

Love, Peggy.

EGGPLANT PARMIGIANO

If I have some amazing homegrown tomatoes, I'll use them to make a sauce. I chop 'em up, and remove any stems or blemishes and cook 'em up. But I usually use Italian tomatoes in a can. San Marzano tomatoes are best. Most cans are 28 ounces, which is usually about 3 or 4 cups. I open the can, put the tomatoes in a bowl, and smoosh 'em up by hand, removing any stems, cores, or blemishes.

You'll need 3 generous cups of tomato sauce for this eggplant Parmigiano.

Some folks fry the eggplant slices first, some folks bake 'em. I've done it both ways. In the video, I fry the eggplant, but baking is now by far my favorite; it makes the dish much lighter. Eggplant throws off a lot of liquid. But when you bake it, the liquid evaporates.

INGREDIENTS

For the tomato sauce:

3 tablespoons extra-virgin olive oil

6 cloves of garlic, sliced thin (about 2 tablespoons)

Crushed red pepper (I start off with ¼ teaspoon)

4 cups of tomatoes, fresh or canned

Fresh basil leaves (about ½ cup)

Kosher salt

HERE WE GO!

The Sauce:

SCAN THE QR CODE TO SEE THE YOUTUBE VIDEO

Put a large sauté pan over medium-low heat.

Add the olive oil, the sliced garlic and the crushed red pepper.

Cook until the garlic is pale gold, 3 to 5 minutes. Stir often.

Add the 4 cups of tomatoes—canned or fresh.

Add some salt, and stir.

Put the heat on high.

When the sauce comes to a boil, reduce the heat to a simmer.

Take half the basil leaves, and tear or snip them with scissors into the sauce. Stir.

Cook for 20 minutes, stir often.

Then, taste for salt and red pepper and adjust.

Take the rest of the basil leaves, and snip them into the sauce.

Remove from heat. You should have about 3 cups of tomato sauce.

INGREDIENTS

For the Eggplant Parmigiano:

3 small eggplant

3 eggs

3 cups panko breadcrumbs, or whatever breadcrumbs you like

OPTIONAL: ¼ cup olive oil (if you're frying, rather than baking)

3 cups of tomato sauce

A handful of fresh basil (¾ cup)

1 pound of mozzarella (two large balls sliced into ¼ inch circular slices)

1 generous cup Parmigiano-Reggiano cheese, freshly grated, plus some for sprinkling

Kosher salt

Fresh-cracked black pepper

HERE WE GO!

Slice off the ends of the eggplant, and cut the eggplant into circular slices, about ½ inch thick.

Take the eggs, beat 'em in a bowl, add salt and pepper.

Take your breadcrumbs, put 'em on a flat plate.

Dip an eggplant slice in the beaten egg, let the excess drip off.

Dip it in the breadcrumbs. Coat both sides. Do all the eggplant slices the same way.

If you're baking, put them in a non-stick baking pan, and stick 'em in the oven at 375 degrees until golden brown, about 12 to 15 minutes or so. Then, flip them over and bake for another 12 to 15 minutes until golden brown.

If you're frying, put the olive oil over medium heat, and fry on both sides until golden, about 4 minutes a side, then put the slices on paper towels when done.

In the bottom of a baking dish (I used a 9 by 13-inch glass baking dish), add a layer of baked/fried eggplant. Then add a cup of tomato sauce, spreading it out evenly. Then add some basil, about ¼ cup—snip the leaves with a scissors or tear them with your fingers.

Then take a ⅓ cup of freshly grated Parmigiano-Reggiano cheese, and spread it on top. Add a layer of sliced mozzarella, about a third of what you have (⅓ pound).

Go back, Jack, do it again—a layer of eggplant, a layer of sauce, a layer of basil, a layer of Parmigiano, and a layer of mozzarella.

Do three layers. Sprinkle the top of the final layer of mozzarella with grated Parmigiano and a few breadcrumbs.

Put the eggplant Parmigiano in the oven. Let it cook for about 25 minutes.

Then, put the broiler on high, and put the baking dish underneath the broiler for just a quick minute, to brown the top. Keep a close eye on this! When the top browns, take out the dish.

If there is any excess liquid in the bottom of the pan, use a turkey baster to remove it.

Let the eggplant sit for a couple minutes. Then . . .

Dish it up! Make it look nice, put some freshly torn basil leaves on top, add some freshly grated Parmigiano, and . . .

MANGIAMO!

CRAB CAKES
with Stevie Wonder in the Bronx

I always wanted to be a songwriter. There was a time when I thought I wanted to be an artist, to be in the spotlight; but the more I thought about it, the more I wanted to be behind the curtain, not in front of it. I wanted to write songs and have other people record them.

I figured if you're a songwriter, you could lose your teeth, lose your hair, gain 100 pounds and nobody would care. Most people know the latest smash hit single, but chances are they don't know who wrote it. You could be a hit songwriter and walk into the 7-11 in your bathrobe with no drawers on and nobody would even know who you are.

That's who I wanted to be—not the guy in the 7-11 in his bathrobe with no drawers on—the guy who wrote the songs. The behind-the-scenes guy. So I studied. I learned. My dad got me the Cole Porter songbook. I bought the Motown songbook. I got all kinds of songbooks; I analyzed all those songs; I learned every hit I could get my hands on.

Stevie Wonder was one of my favorite songwriters. *Talking Book*, *Innervisions*, *Songs in the Key of Life*—those were the albums that inspired me. I loved that style of songwriting. It was jazz; it was pop; it was soul. I wanted to write songs like those.

I wrote and recorded some of my own songs at a studio in Baltimore, Maryland, named Flite III and started shopping them around. After a dismal meeting in New York with a big publisher, I knocked on Motown's door on 57th Street in Manhattan, right across the street from Carnegie Hall. The VP of Motown at the time was a guy named Carl Griffin, he liked my songs and signed me as a songwriter.

I had been writing songs for years, and now, all of a sudden, I was writing songs for Motown. One of the first songs I wrote for Motown was included on Angela Bofill's debut CD, *Angie*. The CD did much better than expected; it got rave reviews in the *New York Times* and the *Los Angeles Times*; it was selling like crazy.

That's when Motown offered me a recording contract. I was a little bit conflicted—on the one hand, I was having a blast writing songs for other people. Who needs to be an artist? But, on the other hand, how many times in your life are you going to get offered a recording contract with Motown? Without even asking?

So I signed with Motown as a recording artist, and they gave me a small advance. What did this Baltimore Boy spend his first advance on? Tickets to see the Baltimore Orioles play the Pittsburgh Pirates in the World Series; it was the only extravagance I afforded myself all year. The rest of the time I was working on my Big Debut CD, I did most of my writing and recording in Baltimore.

I was living at my mom's. We were sitting around the dinner table one night, and the phone rang. My sister answered it, and told me it was for me. I talked for a while, and then came back to the table. My sister asked me who it was.

"Stevie Wonder."

I was working on a song for my Motown album and needed to know the name of a percussion instrument Stevie had used on one of his songs. Stevie called me and told me. It was a "cuica."

My sister freaked out, she couldn't believe it was Stevie. I had asked Carl to see if he could find out what the instrument was, but I wasn't expecting Stevie Wonder to call me—but it was mighty nice of him to do so.

It took me a year to finish the Motown album. I wrote string charts, I wrote horn charts and chord charts. I practiced bass and piano until I couldn't practice anymore; I worked as hard as I've ever worked. I hired some guys from the Baltimore Symphony to play strings; I conducted. I hired the percussionist from the O'Jays to play bongos. Hit Man Howie Z played drums.

It took me a while, but I finally got the music to the point where it sounded just right. I was finished. Carl and I mixed the album in Baltimore. Motown chose two songs to be the first singles, and they flew me out to L.A. to mix them in their brand new, state-of-the-art recording studio. They put me up in Hollywood at the legendary Chateau Marmont hotel in a private bungalow. Not too shabby. It was so big, I could have played Frisbee in the living room. When we finished mixing the singles, Motown flew me back to the east coast.

I was waiting for a release date for my Big Debut when I got invited to a party in New York City at the Bronx Botanical Gardens. Stevie Wonder was having a release party for his *Secret Life of Plants* album; his label was distributed by Motown, and they threw him a lavish fiesta. The party was amazing—the food, the wine, the flowers, the music, the decorations—I'd never seen anything like that. I was hanging out at this wonderful party, with Stevie and other Motowners, and having a blast. I was in heaven.

I went to the bathroom, and one of the Motown executives was washing his hands, looking at me in the mirror, and said,

"Sorry to hear about your album."

I asked him what he meant. That's when he told me that my album had been put on the shelf, the VP in charge of my record had been fired, and all the projects he'd been working on had been put on ice, including mine. That's the way I found out about it.

It wasn't the happiest day of my life.

My album is still sitting in a vault somewhere at Motown; it never saw the light of day. I don't even have a copy. And here's the thing, Motown didn't want to release the CD, but they also didn't want to release me from my contract; they didn't want anybody else picking me up and possibly making them look bad. I was handcuffed.

I was doing the same kind of music at Motown as I'm doing now, a combination of pop, soul, and jazz. It was like early Slim Man. Slim Boy, if you will.

I started writing really loud and angry rock songs, songs with titles like "Gimme a Break" and "I'm a Victim." Instead of singing in my normal range, I was screaming at the top of my lungs. I was trying to do anything to get out of my Motown contract. It worked; Motown eventually released me.

The guy downstairs from the Motown office in New York heard these rock songs I wrote and he loved them. He had a punk rock record company called STIFF Records. Their motto—which was on their T-shirts, merchandise, and their front door—was,

If It Ain't STIFF, It Ain't Worth A F**K.

They had Ian Dury and the Blockheads, Lena Lovitch, and Elvis Costello. I loved the music they put out. Ian Dury is still one of my favorites. Reasons to Be Cheerful, Part Three!

The guy at STIFF Records asked me the name of my band. I told him I didn't have one. He suggested the name BootCamp.

CRAB CAKES

When you're feeling crabby after getting dropped from your record label, do what I did. Make crab cakes.

Crab cakes are to Baltimore what barbecue is to Kansas City and what gumbo is to New Orleans. Ask a thousand people in Baltimore how they make crab cakes and you'll get a thousand different recipes.

The thing to remember when making crab cakes is that the crabmeat is the King. You don't want too much other stuff going on in there. Also, keep in mind that the crabmeat has already been cooked—you're just heating it up, basically. So you don't want to cook them too long, they'll dry out.

The most expensive and delicious kind of crabmeat is jumbo lump, which comes from a section of the crab that's right above the back leg. There is also lump crabmeat—from the tops of the other legs—which is less expensive and still pretty good. Then there's the claw meat, which is a lot less expensive and not nearly as good.

Some people fry their crab cakes, some people broil them. Broiling is my favorite; it's quick, healthy, and *delizioso*. Hit Man Howie Z is the Crab Cake King. He doesn't always eat crab cakes, but when he does, he prefers them broiled.

Makes 6 crab cakes.

INGREDIENTS

1 pound jumbo lump crabmeat

1 egg

¼ cup plain breadcrumbs, or plain panko breadcrumbs

2 tablespoons of mayonnaise

1 tablespoon Worcestershire sauce

1 teaspoon Old Bay seasoning (more if you like it spicy!)

1 teaspoon dry mustard

1 tablespoon chopped fresh Italian flat-leaf parsley

Extra-virgin olive oil

1 tablespoon butter (if frying)

HERE WE GO!

SCAN THE QR CODE TO SEE THE YOUTUBE VIDEO

Put your crabmeat in a bowl, check it for shells, but be gentle! You don't want to break up the lumps. Add all the ingredients except the olive oil and butter. Moosh gently until it looks and feels right—not too dry and not too soggy. If it's too soggy, add a bit more breadcrumbs. If it's too dry, add a little more mayonnaise.

Take some crabmeat mixture in the palm of your hand, about the size of a tangerine, and roll it into a ball. Then flatten it a bit. Repeat the procedure until you have about 6 crab cakes.

Turn on your broiler. Get a baking pan, rub just a little olive oil on the bottom. Put the crab cakes on the pan, make sure they're not all crowded together.

When the broiler gets hot, broil for 3 to 5 minutes until golden brown on top, then flip them over and broil on the other side for 3 to 5 minutes, until the tops are golden.

Keep in mind every oven, every stove is different, cooking times may vary. Wildly!

If you're frying, put a large sauté pan over medium-high heat. Put just enough olive oil in the pan to cover the bottom, about a tablespoon, then add a tablespoon of butter. When the butter melts, fry the crab cakes for 3 to 5 minutes. Flip 'em over. Fry for 3 to 5 minutes on the other side. You want the tops to be golden brown.

However you cook your crab cakes, make 'em look nice! Dish 'em up. Garnish with a sprig of parsley, maybe a slice of lemon. You can eat 'em plain, or you can serve them with cocktail sauce, tartar sauce, or wet mustard. You can make a sandwich, maybe add a little lettuce, tomato and mayo and . . .

MANGIAMO!

LUIGI'S CHICKEN with RED WINE

and My Grandfather the Anarchist

Luigi was my grandfather. Luigi Quintiliano. Grandpa Luke is what I called him; he was quite a character, a tough guy, an Italian immigrant. He left Italy, came to New York City, got his start as a tailor in a sweatshop, and then got involved in the labor unions.

Luigi was an anarchist. Just so you don't have to look it up, an anarchist is someone who doesn't believe in government, who believes in the absolute freedom of the individual. Luigi was a political activist; he helped edit the anti-Fascist Italian newspaper *Il Martello*, which was started by labor organizer Carlo Tresca. Tresca survived an assassination attempt by Fascists, but was later gunned down by the Mafia because he insulted a mob boss.

Luigi was also secretary of the Italian Committee for Political Victims, which raised money to defend Italians who had been imprisoned because of their political beliefs. Luigi helped raise funds for Sacco and Vanzetti, two Italian anarchists who had been accused of murder and robbery. Most folks conclude that they were railroaded. Luigi testified at their trial. Sacco and Vanzetti were convicted of murder in 1921; the case was appealed, and for the next six years, the Sacco and Vanzetti case got worldwide attention. Protests were held in most major cities in the world.

Luigi helped raise money for the appeals process to try to get them acquitted, but in 1927, the verdict was upheld, and Sacco and Vanzetti were executed. Most scholars agree that they were convicted because of their anarchist beliefs, not because they were guilty of murder.

Luigi was handsome, well-dressed, articulate, and elegant. He was also an anarchist, a radical, an activist, and carried a gun—a .32 automatic. But to me, he was Grandpa Luke; the gentle guy who gave me silver dollars and said "Donna tella nobody." He was always so sweet to me.

I didn't find out until I was older that Luigi wasn't my real grandfather. My real grandfather died before I was born. Luigi was my grandmother Angela's . . . boyfriend? That sounds weird. Lover? Even weirder, especially for a grandson. They were in love, Angela and Luigi—that's for sure.

Even though they never married, a lot of folks knew them as husband and wife. In the U.S. census in 1940, they were listed as Luigi and Angela Quintiliano; back in those days, two people in love didn't just shack up, they usually got married if they wanted to live together. But Luigi, being an anarchist and all, didn't believe in marriage. Even though Angela and Luigi never got married, I know they loved each other.

Luigi had a sister, Estherina, who was a nun. She was in a convent in Italy, and then later was assigned to a convent in New Jersey. Estherina wasn't too happy about her situation in Jersey. Apparently, the convent in Italy was a lot more respectful of the nuns than the convent in Jersey. I imagine the food in the Italian convent was a little bit better than the one in Jersey.

Estherina was miserable.

Luigi was more than happy to help Estherina leave the convent. Luigi told Estherina that his friend, Joe, had agreed to marry her, so she could stay in this country. Luigi arranged for my uncle Oscar—Angela's oldest son—to get her out of the convent.

Oscar and a friend drove to the convent in New Jersey, snuck Estherina out of a window, over a wall, and then drove her to Baltimore. Luigi introduced Estherina to his friend Joe, and they got married. Luigi wanted Estherina to get married in order to become a U.S. citizen, but he didn't want her to stay married. But something crazy happened . . . Estherina and Joe fell in love. They moved up to Flushing, Queens, and lived happily ever after in New York.

Luigi continued his anti-marriage crusade. When Oscar was getting ready to get married, Luigi was against it. Oscar's fiancé's family was against it as well—they didn't want their daughter marrying an Italian. They offered Oscar money not to get married; Luigi got offended. On one hand, he was against marriage, but on the other hand, Luigi was pissed off that they thought Oscar wasn't good enough to marry their daughter. Harsh words were exchanged.

Oscar's fiancé's family threatened Luigi with a gun. Luigi said, "You better not miss, because I never do."

There was a lot of animosity between the families, but never any gunfire; Oscar got married anyway.

When my dad fell in love with my mom and wanted to get married, he brought her to meet Angela and Luigi. Luigi made a feast; he made antipasti, pasta, cutlets, sauces, meats, and he kept serving my mom. My mom, being ever so gracious, ate what was served. Luigi was amazed that she hung in there like a real Italian—it was like he was testing her, and she passed with flying colors. Luigi developed a soft spot in his heart for my mom, you could see he loved her.

Still, Luigi was against marriage, so I guess that's why my mom and dad eloped—they got married in New Orleans.

Luigi and Angela eventually broke up; I guess a girl can only take not being married for so long. Angela broke it off, somewhat reluctantly. I have letters from Angela to Luigi, and they are so sad. Angela really loved Luigi, but he couldn't commit, couldn't let himself go.

What a shame.

When Angela died, I was going through her stuff, and found Luigi's gun at the bottom of a trunk. I still have it. It's the only thing of Luigi's I have, besides a few letters and this recipe. . . .

LUIGI'S CHICKEN WITH RED WINE

Luigi used to make this dish with rabbit. I don't know if it's because I love Bugs Bunny so much, but I'm not crazy about eating rabbit. I don't wake up in the middle of the night and say "Damn! I wish I had me some rabbit to nibble on."

When I cook this dish, I use chicken. Most times, I use organic, free-range chicken, although in all the western movies I've seen, and in all my travels, I've never seen herds of wild chickens roaming the free range. I've seen buffalo roaming. I've seen horses. But never chickens.

When I first cooked this dish, I used chicken on the bone; I had my butcher-dude chop each breast into three or four pieces, and each thigh into two pieces.

When I cooked this recently for a lovely lady friend of mine, she mentioned that chicken cut like that would never fly in a restaurant—people might choke on the bones. She told me I should use boneless chicken instead.

I felt like grabbing Luigi's gun and firing a couple of rounds in the ceiling, but I didn't. I just agreed.

You know what? She's right. You don't want Grandpa Luke choking on a chicken bone!

So the next time I made Luigi's chicken, I used boneless, skinless chicken breasts and thighs. It was real good, but I thought that it could be even a bit mo' better with just chicken thighs. Boneless, skinless chicken breasts don't hold up well in a dish like this; they tend to get a little dry.

So last night, I cooked this dish with boneless, skinless chicken thighs. And it tasted really good. Moist and *delizioso*! I dig the dark meat; it really made this dish sing.

I used about two pounds of chicken thighs. You need to cut them into thick pieces, about the size and shape of a flattened egg. Or a big chicken McNugget.

The chicken needs to brown; that means the oil has to be hot enough so the chicken sears, but not too hot that it burns and sticks to the bottom of the pot. The chicken should sizzle when you first put it in. Don't stir it around; let it sit and brown. Each piece has to brown on each side. This is important; browning sears in the juices so the chicken doesn't dry out. Browning also gives the stew a nice color.

If the chicken thighs take longer than five minutes to brown on one side, your heat ain't high enough.

Dutch ovens are good for searing, and then making a stew like this. I used a 7-quart (12-inch diameter) Dutch oven. You can use any big, heavy pot.

You'll need to peel the pearl onions. It's easy. Drop them (with the skin on) in boiling water for a few minutes. Remove, and cut off the tip of the root end. Grab the pearl onion by the top, and squeeze the onion out of the skin.

In the video, I cook the pearl onions and the chicken together. I was using a really big Dutch oven, and everything fit easily. If you're using a smaller, 7-quart Dutch oven, brown the chicken first, take it out, and then brown the pearl onions.

And please be careful when you light the Cognac on fire. Stand back! It's explosive. Have the water pistol loaded and ready.

When handling raw chicken, clean every surface it touches really well.

INGREDIENTS

8 boneless, skinless chicken thighs, about 2 pounds, cut into large cubes

Flour (½ cup should do) plus 1 tablespoon

Kosher salt

Fresh-cracked black pepper

5 tablespoons extra-virgin olive oil

3 dozen or so pearl onions peeled (about 2 cups)

2 ounces of Cognac (about ¼ cup)

3 cups sliced white mushrooms

1½ cups of chopped celery

5 garlic cloves, chopped fine (about 2 tablespoons)

2½ cups chicken stock

1 cup dry red wine

1 tablespoon chopped fresh rosemary

HERE WE GO!

Rinse your chicken pieces in cold water.

Pat dry with paper towels.

Take some flour, put it on a plate.

Take each piece of chicken, and roll it in the flour, coating all sides lightly.

SCAN THE QR CODE TO SEE THE YOUTUBE VIDEO

Do this with all the chicken. Salt and pepper the tops of the floured chicken pieces.

Put some olive oil, a generous 3 tablespoons, in the bottom of a large pan or Dutch oven over medium heat.

Let the pan heat for 2 minutes, and then add the chicken; salted/peppered side down.

Add a little salt and pepper to the tops of the chicken pieces as the underside cooks.

Don't stir; let the chicken brown for 4 or 5 minutes. The chicken needs to be BROWN, Slim People.

Flip the pieces over and brown on the other side—still no stirring—for 4 or 5 minutes.

Remove the chicken from the pan, and put on a plate.

Put the onions in the pan and let them brown for about 3 minutes.

Give them a stir, and let them brown on the other side for about 3 minutes.

Add the Cognac to the onions.

Be careful! Get a lighter with a long handle, and stand back as you light the Cognac on fire—it's gonna explode!

When the flames die down, and your wig has stopped burning, add the mushrooms and celery. Add a tablespoon of olive oil.

Give 'em a stir. Scrape the delicious bits off the bottom of the pan.

Let the celery and mushrooms cook for 5 minutes, stir often.

Add the garlic, cook for 3 minutes.

Now, put the chicken back in the pan.

Add 2 cups of the chicken stock.

Add the cup of red wine.

Add the rosemary.

Turn the heat on high.

When it comes to a boil, let it boil for a few minutes, then reduce the heat to medium-low, and cook, uncovered, for 10 minutes.

Take a tablespoon of flour, whisk it in the remaining half-cup of chicken broth, and stir it into the sauce. The sauce needs to be thick, like gravy.

Turn the heat to simmer, partially cover and cook for about 30 minutes, until the chicken is tender, and the gravy is gravylicious! Stir every so often.

Taste the sauce for salt and pepper and adjust.

You can serve it as is, with some crusty bread. Or you can serve it over egg noodles—I use a half pound of *pappardelle*. You might want to cook them first.

Cook the pasta according to the instructions. Drain, put in a bowl and drizzle with the final tablespoon of olive oil.

Pour some of Luigi's chicken over the egg noodles, make it look nice, and . . .

MANGIAMO!

ROASTED POTATOES and VARIOUS VEGETABLES

with Ronnie Dunn and Slim Chance

Roasted sweet potatoes

Red and yellow beets

Roasted potatoes with rosemary and shallots

Roasted red beets with goat cheese and chives

Back in the mid-1980s, a good friend of mine asked me to help him organize a country music talent contest. Nationwide.

The friend was Carl Griffin—the guy who signed me to Motown; we were both "in between engagements" at the time, which is a polite way of saying "out-of-work" in showbiz. My band, BootCamp, had just broken up. My girlfriend and I had just broken up, too. I was all broked up. And broke.

Carl had Marlboro as a sponsor. Marlboro wanted us to find the next big country music star; they didn't want to just run a contest—they wanted whoever won to be HUGE. Marlboro wanted to be a leading force in the country music scene. They sank a ton of dough into sponsoring concert tours and talent contests.

Carl wasn't a big country music fan. I liked it enough. But when Carl told me how much Marlboro was paying, I started liking country music a whole lot more. Carl ran the talent contest out of New York City. He asked me to organize the contestants, which I did for the first two tours. For my third Marlboro tour? Carl asked me to MC and host the shows. A promotion.

Marlboro wanted me to have an assistant, someone to do my old job—organize the bands. The first call I made was to Hit Man Howie Z. Howie was the drummer in my band, BootCamp; he was in between engagements, too. Howie signed on and we hit the road, two city boys heading out into the Wild Wild West. Marlboro chose a bunch of markets—mostly small southern towns—all across the USA. Bands would submit their music to the NYC office, and the New Yorkers would choose thirty bands for each town. Ten bands a night, three nights in a row, all in the same club.

In each town, we had a panel of judges—local music biz folks—who would choose one band to represent their town at the finals in Nashville. The contests were held in what I affectionately call honkytonk hellholes—rough and tumble small clubs on the outskirts of a town.

The grand prize was substantial—a $50,000 production deal with Barry Beckett, who had produced Hank Williams, Jr. and Bob Dylan, among others. Each band had fifteen minutes on stage. If you went over your fifteen minutes, big points were deducted, that was a strict rule.

Let me set the stage . . . a small Southern town, a small club, packed with country music fans, smoking the free Marlboros they'd been given. The lights go dim and Lee Greenwood's "God Bless the USA" blasts out of the speakers. The song finishes, a spotlight cuts a beam through the fog of cigarette smoke and lands on a microphone stand, center stage. . . .

The very first time I walked on stage and looked over the audience, I could feel the apprehension. It got mighty quiet. I could almost hear the whispers, "Where is this boy from? New York City?"

I introduced myself to the crowd. My real name is real long, real complicated, and real Italian. Silence. I looked totally out-of-place, like Joe Pesci in *My Cousin Vinny*. People didn't throw stuff at me, but I did see some folks looking around for a piece of rope and checking their guns for ammo.

I didn't get killed that first night, but I decided I needed a stage name, something to lighten things up. The next day, I came up with a nickname—Slim Chance. Slim, because I thought it was a good countrified name. And Chance, because it was a talent contest, after all. From then on I introduced myself as Slim Chance; it didn't get a ton of laughs, but at least it kept the cowboys from pulling out their six-guns.

"Good evening cowboys and cowgirls! My name is Slim . . . Slim Chance. Welcome to the Marlboro Country Music Talent Roundup!"

One day, Howie and I pulled into Tulsa, Oklahoma. The contest was at a place called Tulsa City Limits. We got the club ready for the big show; we made sure the Marlboro signs were hung, we made sure the sound company was good to go, and that the judges were ready to judge.

The bands showed up for their sound checks. There were some good bands that day, but nothing really knocked us out until the last band started their sound check. That's when the whole club went silent. They were incredible, the drummer was amazing, and the singer was even more amazing. He had a great voice. I looked at Howie and said,

"Here's our big winner. This Guy's going all the way."

They went on first that night, and they killed. Killed. But going on first in a talent contest that's being judged by judges and not the audience is tough. The judges have nobody to compare you to, so they tend to score the first band low, rather than high.

The local favorite that night happened to be a gal named Suzie Brandt. She packed the place with her fans. Towards the end of her fifteen minutes, she started yodeling, the way some country singers do on occasion. Then she started yodeling faster. And faster. And higher. And higher. I thought her head was gonna explode. Suzie kept on yodeling; she was going so fast it sounded like she was speaking in tongues, like Robert DeNiro at the end of *Cape Fear*.

Suzie went into overtime. She finally stopped and the crowd went wild. I went out to the microphone, told everybody to sit tight and that I'd be back with our big winner. I went into the back room with the judges and we totaled up their score sheets. Suzie had won, but when we deducted the penalty points for the overtime yodeling, she came in second.

Who came in first?

The Guy. The Guy went on to win the national finals in Nashville. My psychic prediction came true. Marlboro started grooming this guy for success, Barry Beckett produced some songs, Scott Hendricks engineered the session, and everything was going great, when suddenly . . .

Nothing happened. The Guy couldn't get a record deal—not a bite, not a nibble. A few years later, the engineer—Scott Hendricks—was in a meeting with a record executive who mentioned that he was looking for a country music duo. The executive already had one-half of the duo—a guy named Kix Brooks—and needed the second half. Scott Hendricks just happened to have the Barry Beckett demo of The Guy with him. He played the demo, the executive liked it, put the two halves together and they became . . .

Brooks and Dunn. Ronnie Dunn was the Guy who sang at Tulsa City Limits. His drummer, Jamie Oldaker, who had played with Eric Clapton a few years before, had entered Ronnie Dunn in the contest. Brooks and Dunn went on to become one of the most successful country music duos ever. Their debut CD sold well over six million copies.

A few years ago, I was playing a small jazz club in Fresno, California. I walked outside the hotel and took a jog. On the way back, I noticed a bunch of 18-wheelers, painted black, parked outside the big auditorium downtown. The fleet of trucks had the Brooks and Dunn steer horns logo on the side. I finished my jog and walked inside the hotel, and who was walking out? Ronnie Dunn. He said,

"Slim! Man! How are ya?"

Slim. Man. It had a nice ring to it. . . .

ROASTED POTATOES AND VARIOUS VEGETABLES

After a long night of honky-tonking, ain't nothin' like some roasted vegetables to soak up the booze and ease the joints. Here at Slim's Shady Trailer Park, I roast vegetables a lot. Why? It's easy—you chop 'em up, add a little olive and salt and pepper and stick them in the oven.

Another reason? Roasted vegetables are real healthy.

The most important reason? They are *molto delizioso*. That's Italian Cowboy talk for, "These vittles are lip-smackin' good!"

The other night, I decided to make dinner. The first thing I did was peel and chop up some red beets, I then added a little olive oil and salt and pepper. Then I stuck them in the oven while I prepared some salmon with my incredibly incredible cippolini and bell pepper sauce.

I roasted the beets for 20 minutes at 400 degrees. Then I gave them a stir and put them back in the oven. I checked them every 10 minutes, stuck them with a fork. It took about an hour, total. They were delicious.

The next time I cooked beets, it took about 40 minutes, total. I used the same oven, the same baking dish, but it took 20 minutes less. Why?

Who the hell knows?

The important thing to remember is . . . give the vegetables a stir after 20 minutes, and stab 'em with a fork. If it goes in easily, the vegetables are done. Most likely, they're not. Put them back in the oven, and check every 10 minutes or so. Average cooking time is about 40 minutes for beets, carrots, potatoes, things like that.

When they're done, take them out of the oven and let them cool for a couple of minutes. You don't want to be burning the roof of your mouth!

That's my basic roasting method. Olive oil and salt and pepper, roasted in a 400-degree oven for 40 minutes to an hour.

A FEW IMPORTANT THINGS . . .

Use a metal pan if you want your vegetables to be crispy on the outside. When I cook potatoes or sweet potatoes, I use a metal pan, because I want the outsides to be crunchy.

I use a glass baking dish when cooking beets and carrots, because they roast better that way.

When roasting vegetables, it's important to remember to roast vegetables that are similar.

For instance, sometimes I roast red beets and carrots together. They both take about the same amount of time, about 50 minutes, usually.

Zucchini and summer squash roast together quite nicely, they only take about 15 or 20 minutes.

I like roasting potatoes. I use red potatoes, or Yukon gold. I also roast sweet potatoes. Sweet!

There are so many variations. Here is the basic roasted beets recipe, followed by some delectable variations.

Makes 4 side servings, perfect with just about any Slim Dish.

INGREDIENTS

Roasted Red Beets:

4 cups of red beets

1½ tablespoons of extra-virgin olive oil

Salt and pepper to taste

OPTIONAL: 1 tablespoon balsamic vinegar

HERE WE GO!

Preheat your oven to 400 degrees.

SCAN THE QR CODE TO SEE THE YOUTUBE VIDEO

Wash and peel the beets. Cut the smaller beets in quarters, cut the larger beets in eighths. The larger the pieces, the longer they take to cook. They should be about the size of a small egg.

Put the beets in a glass baking dish. I used an 8 by 11-inch dish, and 4 cups fit perfectly.

Drizzle with the olive oil and mix. Make sure they are coated with oil, but not swimming in it!

Add the salt and pepper. I start off with about a ½ teaspoon of Kosher salt, and about 6 turns of the peppermill.

Mix, make sure all the beets have a bit of salt and pepper on them.

Put them in the oven.

After 20 minutes, give the beets a good stir. Then, stick a fork in one. If it goes in easily, they are done. My average cooking time for roasted beets is about 50 minutes.

Check every 10 minutes or so. When the fork goes in easily, they are done.

When the beets are done, take them out of the oven, and let them cool for a few minutes.

If you want, you can add a tablespoon of balsamic vinegar.

Toss gently and serve.

That's it!

MANGIAMO!

BEET VARIATIONS

Roasted Red and Yellow Beets:

Use 2 cups of red beets and 2 cups of yellow beets, and follow the instructions above.

Roasted Red Beets and Carrots:

Use 2 cups of red beets and 2 cups of baby carrots and follow the directions above.

Roasted Red Beets with Goat Cheese and Chives and Balsamic Vinegar:

Follow the instructions above. When the beets are done, pull them out of the oven. Add a tablespoon of balsamic vinegar and stir. Crumble 3 or 4 ounces of goat cheese over top of the warm beets. Top off with about a tablespoon of snipped chives (I use a scissors).

Roasted Potatoes with Rosemary and Shallots:

Preheat your oven to 400 degrees.

Use red potatoes or Yukon gold potatoes. Scrub the potatoes. Leave the skin on! Cut them in quarters.

INGREDIENTS

4 cups red or Yukon gold potatoes, scrubbed, skin on, and quartered

1½ tablespoons olive oil

1 tablespoon chopped fresh rosemary

1 tablespoon chopped fresh shallots (you can substitute garlic if you like)

Salt and pepper

HERE WE GO!

Put the potatoes on a metal baking pan. You can line it with aluminum foil beforehand if you like.

Drizzle the olive oil on the potatoes and mix. Make sure each one is coated.

Add the rosemary, shallots and salt and pepper. Mix. Make sure each tater gets some love!

Put the taters in the oven.

After 20 minutes, give them a turn. Only stir once! We want each side of the potatoes to get nice and brown.

Cook for another 20 minutes. Stick a fork in a piece of tater. If it goes in easily, it's done.

My average cooking time is about 50 minutes.

When the potatoes are done, take them out of the oven and . . .

MANGIAMO!

Roasted Sweet Potatoes:

Two sweet potatoes should give you about 4 cups, depending on the size. Scrub your sweet potatoes. Leave the skin on. Cut them into small wedges.

INGREDIENTS

4 cups of sweet potatoes, cut into small wedges

1½ tablespoons of extra-virgin olive oil

Salt and pepper

HERE WE GO!

Put the sweet potatoes on a metal baking pan. Line with aluminum foil, if you like.

Drizzle the olive oil over the taters and mix. Make sure each wedge is coated!

Add the salt and pepper and stir. I usually use about ½ teaspoon of Kosher salt and 6 twists of the peppermill.

Mix the sweet taters again.

Put them in the oven.

After 20 minutes, turn them over. We want each side to get toasty brown.

Let them cook for another 20 minutes.

Then, stick a fork in one. If the fork goes in easily, they're done.

Dish 'em up!

MANGIAMO!

Roasted Zucchini and Summer Squash with Oregano and Garlic:

One medium zucchini should yield about 2 cups sliced. Same with the summer squash. You'll need 2 cups of each.

Fresh oregano is milder than dried. If you use fresh oregano, you'll need a tablespoon, chopped. If you're using dried, a generous teaspoon should do it. I prefer dried for this dish.

Scrub your zucchini and summer squash. Slice in circular slices.

Peel 4 cloves of garlic, and smash each one with the flat side of a knife.

INGREDIENTS

2 cups of zucchini, cut in circular slices

2 cups of summer squash, cut in circular slices

4 cloves of garlic, peeled and smashed

1½ tablespoons of extra-virgin olive oil

Salt and pepper

1 teaspoon of oregano (I use dried, you can use either dried or fresh)

OPTIONAL: ¼ cup or so of freshly grated Parmigiano-Reggiano cheese

HERE WE GO!

Put the zucchini, squash and garlic in a glass baking dish.

Drizzle the olive oil over the vegetables and mix gently. Make sure each piece is coated with olive oil, but not swimming in it. Start off with 1½ tablespoons of olive oil. You can add more if you need to.

Add the salt, pepper, and oregano and give it a gentle stir.

Put it in the oven.

After 10 minutes, check your vegetables! Take a stab at a piece of zucchini. If the fork goes in easily, it's done. Most likely, it ain't. No need to stir or flip the vegetables.

Cook for another 10 minutes and check.

They should take about 20 minutes to be done.

Take them out of the oven. You can sprinkle a little freshly grated Parmigiano-Reggiano cheese on top, if you like.

Dish it up!

MANGIAMO!

SEARED SCALLOPS with ROSEMARY and PROSCIUTTO

and Tarzan

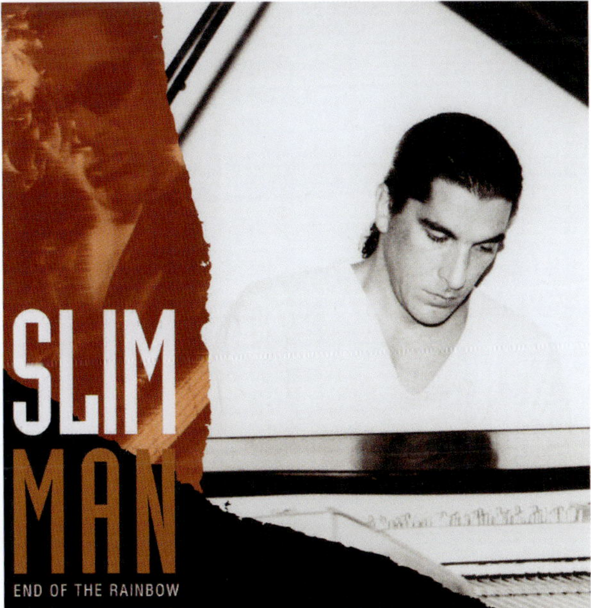

After BootCamp broke up, I decided to circle the wagons, so I gathered up the mules and the Conestogas, and sat by the campfire for a while, trying to figure out my next move. One night, after getting kicked in the head by one of the jackasses, I came to the realization that I needed to go back into the studio and start writing and recording again. So that's what I did. Monday through Thursday, from 10:00 a.m. until 3:00 p.m., I wrote songs. The studio was owned by Rick O'Rick, AKA Cowboy Pickles; it was right outside of Washington, DC.

I'd leave Baltimore at 9:00 a.m., drive an hour to the studio, write and record for five hours, then drive back.

At night, I was singing in piano bars. I had decided to learn all my favorite songs, to find out what made them work; I thought it might help my own songwriting. From Sinatra to Elvis to Motown, I studied and learned every hit song I ever loved; I would sing these songs and play piano at restaurants in and around Baltimore, Maryland. I also had a blues band—the Scrappy Harris Blues Band. We played every Wednesday night at a dive bar called The Horse You Came In On.

That was My Life After BootCamp. I played piano bar, I played the blues, and I wrote songs—all kinds of songs.

I wrote a rock song and needed a singer for the demo. Someone had mentioned the name Brian Jack, so I looked him up. He was in a band called Child's Play; they had released an album on a major label, and had just broken up after being dropped. I reached out to Brian and asked him to sing one of my songs.

I picked him up—he didn't have a car—and drove him to the studio. He walked in, opened his mouth, and sang that song like he'd sung it a hundred times. It was nothing short of magic. Everyone who heard the song loved it, and loved his voice—he sounded like a young Rod Stewart.

I continued writing songs with Brian in mind. I'd write a song, all the words and music. I'd get everything recorded—the guitars, keyboards, bass, backing vocals, horns, everything—and then I'd go pick up Brian and drive him to the studio. I'd give him the lyric sheet, and he'd sing, as I guided him along. It took us an hour a song, at most, to do the vocals. That's the way it got started. We became the best of friends.

I wrote. I produced. Brian sang. He had an amazing voice.

After about a year, when I had twelve songs finished, I suggested we put out a CD. I borrowed some money to get the CDs made. Rick O'Rick and I took care of the studio bill. Brian did the artwork. He sent it off to the manufacturer. When we got the CDs back, I was pretty surprised when I read the back cover . . .

All songs written by Brian Jack and Tim Camp.

When I asked him why he listed himself as songwriter on the credits, he told me, "I always wanted to be known as a songwriter."

I suggested that he might start by writing his own songs, not by putting his name on mine. I let it go. I already had the songs copyrighted.

The CD took off like a rocket, and we started getting lots of airplay on the big rock station in Baltimore. Brian put together a band and asked me to play keyboards. I didn't want to—I had just finished the BootCamp saga, and I was in no hurry to play in a rock band again. But Jackson—that's what I called him—insisted, so I started playing keyboards in his live show.

He was packing 1,000 seat clubs. Jackson put together an incredible show; at one club called Hammerjacks, he hung a rope from the ceiling, which was twenty feet high. He would swing from the stage up into the balcony, hold the railing, sing a few notes, and then swing back on stage. He was like Tarzan; bare-foot and bare-chested, swinging from the rafters, screaming at the top of his lungs. He was selling out wherever he went; he had a great voice along with charm, looks, charisma, and stage presence.

And he had incredible hair, which is the most important thing in the music binniz.

I started calling some folks I knew in the music business. I hooked Brian up with my attorney—who's also my close friend—who hooked Brian up with a manager, Dee Anthony. Dee Anthony started off as a road manager for Tony Bennett. Dee went on to manage Peter Frampton, J. Geils, Devo, and Basia, among others. His daughter, Michelle, was a bigwig at SONY/Epic.

Dee came out to a show and loved it. Brian signed with Dee, and Dee signed Brian to SONY/Epic. Frankie LaRocca was hired to produce—he had just come off a big hit with the Spin Doctors. The future looked mighty bright.

When it came time for Brian to record his CD for Epic, I found out that none of my songs would be included. Dee then set Brian up to write all new songs with some big-name writers. I was out. Like Tom Hagen in *The Godfather*, I was out.

I went back into the studio by myself and started writing again. I wasn't writing for anybody but me this time. I just wrote whatever came to mind. After a few months, I put all of these songs together and decided to do a CD of my own. I had a working title; *End of the Rainbow*. I needed a CD cover, so a friend arranged for a photographer to shoot some photos of my donkey face. I sat at the piano, and he took pictures. After the photo shoot, I made dinner, and as we were eating, I asked the photographer what kind of stuff he liked to photograph. He told me he was a forensic photographer for the Baltimore Police Department.

He took photos of dead bodies.

SEARED SCALLOPS WITH ROSEMARY AND PROSCIUTTO

I have a great friend named Clubby Clubb, who lives in Ocean City, Maryland. Clubby Clubb has an incredible wine store and deli a block from the beach. He lives a charmed life; he only works six months a year, April to September. The rest of the year?

Mostly, he goes fishing, and he plays with his kids.

One day, when I told him I wanted some fresh scallops, he told me about a bayside fish store where the boats bring everything in fresh each morning to service the resort restaurants.

I went there one morning, and they had these incredible scallops. I love scallops, and I created a way of searing them that is so quick, so simple, and so delicious that you are going to send me a million dollars after you try these.

Make all checks out to Mr. Man.

Scallops are expensive—I've seen them as high as $36 a pound. I found them for $20 a pound recently, and bought a pound. There were 10 big scallops, which I seared. They were *delizioso*!

One last note—make sure you buy dry scallops. This is very important. Your fish guy should know. Wet scallops are injected with chemicals and crap and are impossible to sear.

Buy dry scallops, and gently rinse them, then gently pat them dry with paper towels. Keep patting them dry until the paper towels are no longer damp. Even dry scallops retain a bit of water. Water ain't good for the searing process! *Capisce*?

And finally, if you don't like prosciutto, just leave it out. You can still pierce the scallops with the rosemary—without the prosciutto.

INGREDIENTS

10 dry sea scallops, about one pound

10 slices of prosciutto, sliced thin, fat trimmed off

10 thin rosemary sprigs, each at least 4 inches long

A little brown sugar or turbinado sugar (you can use regular sugar in a pinch)

Salt (I use Kosher salt)

Fresh-cracked black pepper

1 tablespoon butter

1 tablespoon extra-virgin olive oil

HERE WE GO!

SCAN THE QR CODE TO SEE THE YOUTUBE VIDEO

Rinse off the scallops and pat dry with paper towels. Remove the small side muscle from each scallop, and discard the muscle—not the scallop! Place the scallops on a plate.

Take a slice of prosciutto, and trim it so it's about the same size as the scallop. Remove some of the fat if you like. Wrap the prosciutto around the sides of the scallop. I wrap the prosciutto around once, and slice off the remaining prosciutto.

Take a sprig of rosemary, about 4 inches long, and strip off about an inch of the leaves from the bottom of the sprig. Take the bottom end of the rosemary sprig, and pierce it through the side of the scallop, to hold the prosciutto in place.

The end without the leaves should be poking out of one side of the scallop, and the other end—the top of the sprig—should be poking out of the other side of the scallop.

Do this with all 10 scallops.

Add a sprinkle of brown sugar, salt, and pepper to the top of all 10 scallops.

Put a large sauté pan over medium-high heat. Add 1 tablespoon of butter and 1 tablespoon of olive oil. When the butter starts to bubble and turn brown, place the scallops in the pan, salted/peppered/sugared side down.

Cook for 90 seconds, 2 minutes maximum. As they cook, add a LITTLE salt, pepper, and brown sugar on top of each scallop.

Use some tongs to lift each scallop out of the pan. Before you set each scallop back in the pan, swirl the butter and olive oil around in the pan, so you're not placing the scallop in a dry pan.

Turn the scallop over, and cook for 90 seconds—2 minutes maximum—on the other side.

Remove the scallops with some tongs. Make sure the scallops are done. Cooking times can vary according to the heat of your stove and the thickness of the scallops.

Dish it up! You can serve these over some wild greens, with some tomatoes on the side. Or eat them all by themselves.

MANGIAMO!

ITALIAN KALE with DRIED CRANBERRIES and PORT

and Cowboy Pickles

Roger Eddy, sax

We left Ellicott City, Maryland, in an Isuzu Rodeo, a small SUV. It was me, drummer John E Coale, and keyboardist Rick O'Rick, AKA Cowboy Pickles.

All three of us, our luggage, and all the gear—drums, keyboards, bass amp, CDs—were crammed into the car. It was tight; you had to allow an extra fifty yards when you hit the brakes, otherwise, a snare drum might smack you in the back of your cranium.

It was our first Slim Man tour—the year was 1995. Our Big Debut CD, *End of the Rainbow*, was starting to sell, and the first single, "Faith in Us," was getting a lot of airplay all around the U.S.

Our first gig was in Cleveland, Ohio. Hello, Cleveland! It was a club called Peabody's Down Under. Why Down Under? Because we played in the basement, it was just us down there, us and the bathrooms. People stood around a circular balcony on the first floor, and looked down at us, playing in the basement. We had to look up to see the crowd.

There were about twenty-five people there, and after the show, a large and lovely woman came up to me and said,

"You're like Fabio . . . but you can sing!"

We packed up the Rodeo after the show that night and drove all the way to San Francisco—2,500 miles. It took us a couple days, and when we got to San Francisco, I dropped John E and Cowboy Pickles at the hotel. I was driving the Rodeo to the parking garage when I heard "Faith in Us" come on the radio. It was the first time I'd ever heard one of my songs on the radio. I was so excited, I almost drove off the road.

The next day, we pulled up to the Great American Music Hall for sound check, I walked up to the front door, and there was a line around the block. I asked some guy waiting in line who the line was for. He said,

"Slim Man."

Wow. I looked at the line and thought . . . all these people are coming to see me? It didn't make me nervous—quite the opposite. I couldn't wait to play, I was pumped up. I'm rarely nervous on stage—I'm nervous the other twenty-three hours of the day.

We played that night to hundreds of people—it was crazy. When we played "Faith in Us" the crowd went wild. We signed autographs afterward for what seemed like hours, and sold a ton of CDs. I hate to admit it, but it felt pretty damn good. It was okay wallowing in obscurity for all those years, but not as nice as wallowing in a brief moment of minor celebrity.

We had a sax player sit in with us in San Francisco that night. We had never played with him before. We didn't even rehearse; we didn't have time. He showed up at sound check, we introduced ourselves, and then did the show. But that's the way we rolled on that first tour; we traveled as a trio. We had to—we couldn't fit anybody else in the car. We would pick up a soloist whenever we got to town—a sax player, trumpeter, anybody. And the sax guy in San Francisco that night at the Great American Music Hall was pretty good.

Two nights later we played in San Jose at the Ajax Lounge, and everyone in the audience bought a CD. There were only six people there. Seriously. That was it. I remember counting them—it didn't take long. It didn't bother me; I was just glad to be out playing and touring.

Next it was off to Monterey. We played outside on a deck, overlooking the bay. A guy named Roger Eddy played sax—like most of the soloists who joined us on the road, it was the first time we'd ever met him. The place was small, but packed.

We left Monterey and headed south. As we were driving down the Pacific Coast Highway, Rick O'Rick suddenly got violently ill, disgusting stuff was coming out of every hole in his body. We had to stop a lot. We eventually made it to Viejas, a brand new Indian Casino outside of San Diego. It was so new, they were still hammering nails into the floor as we were loading in. Literally.

The concert hall must have held at least a thousand people. It was beautiful—a gorgeous stage, with a big red velvet curtain, a brand new PA, and new lights. We did our sound check, and then they closed the curtains. We stayed backstage with Rick right up until showtime.

We had a percussionist sitting in named Michael Kelleher. We had not met Michael until that night, and I'm sure he was a bit apprehensive when he saw Rick O'Rick looking like the Alien might burst out of his chest at any second. When showtime came around, we got Cowboy Pickles propped up behind his keyboards. We all waited quietly behind the closed red curtain.

They announced our name over the PA—"Ladies and Gentlemen, Slim Man!" The curtains slowly parted, and . . .

There were two people there—in a place that held a thousand. There was the promo gal from the local radio station, Janet, and there was a guy standing at the bar—that was about it. Seriously. But we played our hearts out—we always do, I'm proud to say. Both people seemed to really like the show.

After the show, the guy at the bar introduced himself. Art Good. He asked us to play the Catalina Jazz Festival. That was one good thing that happened that night. The other good thing was Rick O'Rick was feeling better. Thank God, because we had to drive all the way to Kansas City the next day. Fifteen hundred miles. We made it in two days. We're going to Kansas City, Kansas City here we come!

The show was at a place called America's Pub. We drove up, unloaded the Rodeo, did our sound check, and went to the hotel room to shower and change. When we walked into America's Pub in KCMO that night, the applause was deafening. It was packed to the rafters. Sold-out. Standing room only. SRO. It was one of the most amazing responses we've ever had. The crowd was screaming.

I couldn't tell exactly what it was they were screaming, but it seemed really positive. We had a sax guy sit in that night, and of course, we had never heard him play before. He was really good, brought some of that bluesy and soulful Kansas City style to the Slim Men.

It was the loudest crowd I'd ever heard in my life; the whole band was on cloud nine.

The next day, we drove to St. Louis—the last gig of the first Slim Tour. We pulled up to a place called Brown's Pub, and an old, white guy came up to us. I have nothing against old, white guys. Some of my best friends are old, white guys. This old, white guy was dressed like he was getting ready to play golf—with the Three Stooges in 1955. He had on knickers, a wild shirt, and a crazy hat, all in bright colors and patterns. I dug it. It was certainly colorful. He said,

"My name is Chops. I'll be your trombone player tonight."

Okay, Chops. We walked inside the club; the place only held about seventy-five people. A gorgeous gal introduced us to the crowd; she was a DJ from the St. Louis station, KNJZ, that was playing our music. The response from the crowd was like the applause you hear at a golf course. Polite. Apprehensive. Right before we started, I leaned over to Chops and said,

"I'll cue you for your solos. Don't play over the vocals."

John E Coale counted off the first song—and Chops played non-stop from beginning to end. His trombone playing was like Dixieland meets Bugs Bunny. Chops could play, the only problem was . . . he never stopped playing. We finished the song, and the crowd was giving us funny looks. I leaned over to Chops and whispered,

"Chops! Don't play while I'm singing!"

John E counted off the second song. Chops started playing from the first beat and didn't stop until the end of the song—the man didn't take a breath. The crowd was looking at their watches and checking the exits. Even though we'd only been playing about ten minutes, I told the crowd we were taking a break. I walked the band outside and told Chops that it wasn't working out. I paid him in full, and he left. We went back in and continued as a trio. As we were playing, I spotted a guy in the back of the pub with a trumpet case slung over his shoulder. I called out to him, over the PA,

"Hey! Can you play that thing?"

The crowd turned around and looked at the guy. He came up and started playing. I've always loved the trumpet. He was really good, had a Latin vibe that really fit well. His name was Alex Galvez, I really liked his style, and so did the crowd. The rest of the night was really cool, and that trumpeter really blew, so to speak.

The next morning, John E, Cowboy Pickles, and I packed up the Rodeo, and drove the 800 miles back to Baltimore.

ITALIAN KALE WITH DRIED CRANBERRIES AND PORT

When I'm out on tour, and there's a lot of road ahead of me, I'll get a bag of sunflower seeds in the shell and eat 'em and drive. One time, on the way back from a Slim Show in Santa Rosa, California, I stopped at a roadside fruit and nuts stand. I was thinking I might run into some of my nutty and fruity relatives there.

The Slim Family wasn't there, but there were bags of salted, roasted sunflower seeds, without the shell. I bought one. They were delish. I even saved some.

I've been noticing a lot of Italian kale in the grocery stores these days, and not just the ridiculously expensive Whole Foods-type stores. Most normal grocery stores have Italian kale, it's called *lacinato* kale, most of it is organic, and it's ridiculously inexpensive. How inexpensive? A buck a bunch at my local grocer. One dollar! I bought some and took it back to Slim's Shady Trailer Park in Palm Springs, California.

Kale is so good for you. The only problem is it tastes like old hedge-clippings.

I cooked it in some olive oil and garlic, just to see what it tasted like. It was not as bitter as normal kale, but it needed a little something. I tried cooking the *lacinato* kale different ways. With tomatoes, with red bell peppers, with white wine. . . . Nothing was working.

One night, I decided to cook it with some port wine. Why? It was all I had! I took a sip, the port tasted great, so I added a ¼ cup to the kale. The sweetness of the port cut the bitterness of the kale.

It needed a little saltiness, so I added some salted sunflower seeds from the roadside stand. I also added some dried cranberries, and it gave it some color and a nice texture.

It was good. It was real good!

NOTES:

If you don't have any port, any sweet wine will do. Sweet vermouth would work, so would Marsala, or sweet sherry.

If you can't find *lacinato* kale, you can use regular kale. Either way, you'll need to clean the kale. Here's how to do it: start at the top of the leaf. Start tearing the leaves by hand into strips, about 1 to 2 inches wide.

When the center stalk starts getting tough—about ⅓ of the way down the kale leaf—start pulling the leaves from the side of the stalk, and throw away the stalk.

Clean the leaves with cold water and spin dry. You'll need 4 cups.

And finally, add the sunflower seeds and dried cranberries last. You don't want your nuts to get soggy or the cranberries soaking up the port.

Serves 2.

INGREDIENTS

1 bunch of Italian kale, also known as *lacinato* kale, 4 cups cleaned and dried

3 tablespoons extra-virgin olive oil

2 tablespoons chopped shallot

Crushed red pepper to taste (I start off with ¼ teaspoon)

¼ cup of port (or any sweet dark wine—sweet Marsala, sweet vermouth)

¼ cup dried cranberries

2 tablespoons salted roasted sunflower seeds

Salt (I use Kosher—*mazel tov*!)

HERE WE GO!

Put your *lacinato* kale in a bowl.

SCAN THE QR CODE TO SEE THE YOUTUBE VIDEO

Put the olive oil in a large sauté pan over medium-high heat, and let it heat up for 2 minutes.

Add the 2 tablespoons of chopped shallots, and crushed red pepper to taste, and cook for a couple minutes, until the edges of the shallot start to turn golden brown.

Add the port, or whatever wine you're using. Turn the heat to high, and let it cook off for a minute or so.

Reduce the heat to medium. Add half of the kale.

Cook and stir until the kale wilts, a couple minutes.

Add the rest of the kale. Cook and stir until the kale wilts, a couple minutes. Add a sprinkle of Kosher salt, stir.

Add the dried cranberries and stir.

Add the sunflower seeds and stir.

Taste for salt and adjust.

Dish it up!

This is a great side dish, I made it with chicken Piccata the other night, and it was a-delish.

MANGIAMO!

CHICKEN MARSALA
at
Graceland

I was in Memphis in the late 1980s organizing a country music talent contest with my friend Michael Elder.

Michael is black. I'm white. Well, Italian.

Marlboro sponsored the contest. Why they picked a black guy and a white guy—two city slickers, no less—to do a country music talent contest, is still puzzling. It's not puzzling why Michael and I did the contest—they paid us a lot of money, and they paid all our expenses. Carl Griffin was the Big Boss; he ran the contest out of New York City. I ended up doing four tours for Marlboro. The one with Michael was my first.

Michael and I traveled around the U.S. looking for the next big country music star. We went to more honkytonk hell-holes than most cowboys. We'd roll into a town like Memphis, find a club, organize the bands, and do the contest.

I was in charge of the bands; I made sure all the musicians knew where to go, what to bring, and what to do. Michael was the MC. When Michael appeared on stage, and introduced himself to the primarily white, all-country crowd, there was a little apprehension—on both sides of the microphone. He'd come out and say,

"Ladies and Gentlemen, welcome to the Marlboro Country Music Talent Roundup."

That's when the crowd got a little quiet. Michael was from New York City, and he sounded like it. He'd continue,

"I know I don't look like the Marlboro Man, and I don't sound like the Marlboro Man, but tonight . . ."

He'd reach down and put on his white, ten-gallon, Hoss Cartwright, cowboy hat and continue—

"I am the Marlboro Man."

Michael always got a laugh when he smiled and put the huge white hat on. He had a singular charm.

Marlboro tossed a lot of money at this thing. We had all kinds of great merchandise—denim jackets, satin jackets, duffle bags, playing cards, T-shirts, polo shirts, denim shirts, and posters. And they gave away free cigarettes at every show. All you could smoke. The smoke was so thick in those clubs, you couldn't see your hand in front of your face.

Here's how we ran the contest—we had ten bands a night, three nights in a row. Each band got fifteen minutes on stage. Judges picked the winners—not the audience. We'd find judges—usually three—from the local talent pool; DJs, producers, managers, agents. One band from each town would go on to the finals in Nashville, where they would compete with the other finalists for the grand prize; $50,000 of studio time with a Big Name Producer.

Before we got to Memphis, Michael and I got a call from Carl. He told us to be careful. It was the 20th anniversary of Martin Luther King's assassination in Memphis. And then Carl told us that the club owner was rumored to have ties to the KKK. The club was called The Vapors, a country music honky-tonk in the middle of Memphis. Michael and I pulled up to the club in our rental car, walked inside, and met the owner. He was friendly and as nice and helpful as could be.

Michael and I got set up for the show that night; we had to hang all the Marlboro Country Music Roundup signs around the club, we had to make sure the sound company was good to go, the bands ready to play, and the judges ready to judge.

We finished sound check and had a few hours before showtime. Michael had a friend who had a limo and tour bus company based in Memphis; she rented these things out to bands and rock stars. She invited us for a limo ride to Graceland and a private tour—she was a friend of Elvis Presley's Mom. Graceland is the house that Elvis built, it's now a museum.

Michael and I drove over to his friend's house; she had all these limos and tour buses parked all around her property. She got behind the wheel of one of the big black limos, and Michael and I got in back. She put the limo in reverse and floored it. BANG! She rammed it into the side of one of her tour buses that was parked right behind. We got out and surveyed the damage. It was substantial—to both the limo and the tour bus.

She left the smashed-up limo right there, got into another one, and drove us over to Graceland, where she gave us a private tour. We saw the Graceland that not many people get to see. It was surprisingly small and had a sixties vibe to it—lots of yellow vinyl and white shag carpets and mirrored walls. Elvis must have loved TV, there were TVs everywhere. He had quite a collection of cars, all kinds of exotic sports cars. Elvis also had two luxury jets parked right across the street from Graceland.

After the Graceland tour, Michael and I went to visit the Lorraine Motel, where Martin Luther King, Jr. was assassinated. There were TV news crews doing interviews about the 20th anniversary, and one of them came up to Michael and interviewed him. It was eerie. Michael and I went back to our hotel—a Holiday Inn. We decided to take a jog before the big show that night, so we put on our running shoes and started jogging down the streets of Memphis, side-by-side. On our way back, we heard someone shout from a car—you'll have to excuse the language, but this is the way it went down.

"Hey nigguh boy! Hey hippie fag!"

True story. That's exactly what was said. I couldn't believe my ears. Then I heard it again.

"Hey nigguh boy! Hey hippie fag!"

Oh, shit, I thought. Here we go. A black guy and a longhaired white guy, running down the streets of Memphis. I stopped and looked to where the voice was coming from. It was the owner of the Vapors. He was laughing, hanging out the window of his car, smacking his hand on the door.

"I got you! I got you goin'! See you fellas at the club later! Have a nice run!"

He smiled and waved and drove off, laughing. He got us, all right.

We did the contest that night at The Vapors. The owner couldn't have been nicer, the crowd was as cool as could be, and the show went as smooth as glass.

CHICKEN MARSALA

I love Memphis—Sun Studio, Graceland, Beale Street—and any city with a restaurant named Automatic Slim's is okay in my book. They didn't have chicken Marsala, but my version would look mighty good on their menu.

I came up with this dish a few weeks ago. I used porcini mushrooms and the water they soak in. It was amazing, if I may say so myself.

The next night I cooked it for a very beautiful woman of excellent taste, and it was just okay. I overcooked the chicken, and it was a bit dry and tough; so don't overcook your chicken.

I like to serve this sauce over egg noodles—not a lot, just a little bit underneath each serving.

I used three boneless, skinless chicken breasts. They were real thick, so I cut each of them in half. I had six cutlets, each was about ¼ inch thick.

Marsala is a wine from Marsala, Sicily. There are basically two kinds; dry and sweet. I used sweet Marsala.

Be careful when handling raw chicken—put on the HazMat suit and clean every surface it touches. Or slip into your SCUBA gear and get out the power washer.

INGREDIENTS

6 chicken breast cutlets, about ¼ inch thick

½ ounce dried porcini mushrooms (soaked in 1 cup of water for a minimum of 20 minutes—don't throw out the water!)

2 tablespoons butter (1 for the sauce, 1 for the chicken)

2 tablespoons extra-virgin olive oil (1 for the sauce, 1 for the chicken)

½ shallot, chopped fine, about 2 tablespoons

3 garlic cloves, sliced thin, about 1 tablespoon

¾ cup sweet Marsala

1 cup of water

1 tablespoon fresh rosemary, chopped

½ pound of egg noodles—*pappardelle* work well

Kosher salt and pepper to taste

HERE WE GO!

Rinse off your chicken breasts and pat them dry with paper towels.

Remove the porcini mushrooms from the cup of water with a slotted spoon.

Take the remaining porcini water and strain through cheesecloth—I used a coffee filter, by the way. I've even used paper towels as strainers. Whatever you use, save the water—you'll use a half cup for the sauce and a half cup in the pasta water—if you want to put the sauce over pasta.

Rinse off the mushrooms and pat dry. Chop into small pieces.

Grab your breasts. Then grab your chicken breasts. Notice the difference. Salt and pepper the top of the chicken breasts. Fresh-cracked black pepper is the way to go. Salt and pepper just one side of the chicken breasts.

LET'S MAKE THE SAUCE FIRST.

Put a small sauté pan over medium heat.

Add 1 tablespoon of butter, and 1 tablespoon of olive oil.

When the butter starts to bubble, add the shallots.

Cook and stir for 2 minutes, until the shallots just start to brown.

Add the garlic, cook for 2 minutes. Give it a stir.

Add the Marsala.

Add ½ cup of porcini water.

Turn the heat to high and let it cook for 2 minutes.

Turn the heat to medium-low, and add the porcini mushrooms.

Cook for 2 minutes while stirring.

Add the rosemary. Cook and stir for 2 minutes.

Remove from heat. Sauce is done!

Let's do the chicken.

Get a large sauté pan (I used a 12-inch skillet). Put it over medium-high heat.

Add 1 tablespoon of butter and 1 tablespoon of olive oil.

When the butter starts to bubble, add the chicken breasts, salted/peppered side down.

Cook for 2 or 3 minutes until golden.

Flip 'em over.

Cook for 2 or 3 minutes on the other side until golden. Don't be afraid to give a cutlet a slice, to make sure it's done.

Pour most of the Marsala/porcini sauce over the breasts.

Remove from heat!

Plate 'em up! You can eat 'em as is, or you can put this sauce over egg noodles.

I like to use an Italian egg noodle called *pappardelle*. It comes from the word "*pappare*" which means "to gobble." I use a half pound.

Get a large pot, fill it with cold water. Add the remaining ½ cup of porcini water to the pasta water. When it all comes to a boil, add 2 tablespoons of Kosher salt.

Add the *pappardelle*, cook until *al dente* (firm to the bite), drain and drizzle with a tablespoon of olive oil. Stir.

Put a SMALL PORTION of egg noodles on a plate. Put some Marsala sauce over the noodles, put a chicken breast on top, spoon some sauce and juice and mushrooms on top and . . .

MANGIAMO!

RED WINE SAUCE with AHI TUNA

and

The Baltimore Colts

Front and center

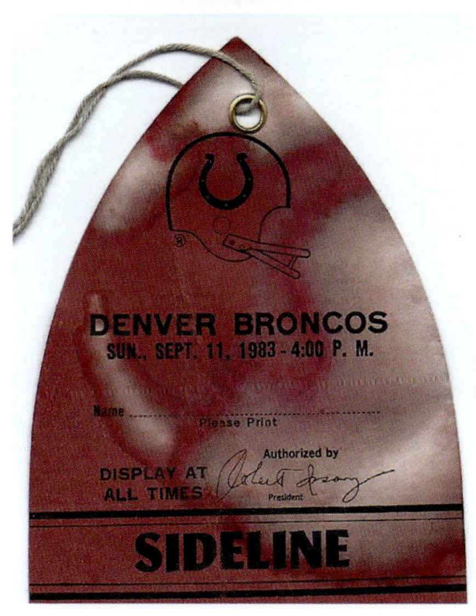

Why don't cannibals eat divorced people?

They're bitter.

September 11, 1983. The Baltimore Colts football team was scheduled to play the Denver Broncos. The year before, 1982, the Colts had not won a game, and because they stunk so bad, they got the first pick in the NFL draft the following year.

The Colts chose quarterback John Elway, from Stanford University. Elway refused to play for the Colts; he was even considering joining the New York Yankees baseball team rather than play football for the Colts. So the Colts traded Elway to the Denver Broncos, and in the second game of the 1983 season, the Broncos came to Baltimore to play the Colts at Memorial Stadium.

I had been a Baltimore Colts fan since I was a kid. My uncle Oscar had season tickets from their very first game—the seats were in the mezzanine, right next to the press box. Oscar played football in high school and was good enough to be offered a full scholarship to college, but chose medicine instead. When the Colts came to Baltimore, Oscar bought the best seats; I went with him to as many games as I could. I knew all the players, their numbers, their statistics, and their nicknames.

Lenny Moore, #24. Gino Marchetti, #89. Artie Donovan, #70. Johnny Unitas, #19. Raymond Berry, #82. I loved football. When I was a kid, I played football in little league; I wasn't offered any scholarships, but I loved playing, and I loved the Colts.

You can imagine how thrilled I was when the Colts called and asked my band to sing the national anthem for Elway's first appearance in Baltimore. The band was BootCamp; we'd been making a name for ourselves in the music biz. We had worked up a great acapella version of the "Star-Spangled Banner." It was a show-stoppa. At parties, shows, concerts, weddings, funerals—all of a sudden, out of the blue we'd burst into the national anthem. It was a cheap way to get a standing ovation, but our four-part harmony rendition was quite stirring, if I may say so myself. We sounded like a rock and roll barbershop quartet.

When we got to Memorial Stadium that Sunday, we were escorted through the Colts locker room, and into an underground tunnel that led to the field. As we were coming to the end of the tunnel, we heard this rumbling . . .

The players, all suited up and breathing fire, were coming down the tunnel right behind us. We stood up against the wall and let them pass. They were big, and they had a look in their eyes that was fierce, like gladiators getting ready to enter the Coliseum. When they passed, we followed them out onto the field. We walked up to the microphone; the announcer asked everyone to stand and remove their hats. Memorial Stadium got dead quiet. Then he introduced us, "Ladies and Gentlemen, Baltimore's own BootCamp!"

We sang our hearts out. Fifty-thousand people standing on their feet, cheering. A standing ovation! Of course, they had to stand because it was the national anthem; but I'm marking it down in my bio as "a standing ovation before a sellout crowd of 50,000."

When we finished, we walked to the sidelines, and stood among the Colt players. The Colts' front office had given us field passes—I'm sure when they gave them to us they weren't thinking we'd stay on the field for the whole game, but there we were, standing on the sidelines with the players and coaches. All the players and coaches were giving us funny looks. I can't blame them. We were dressed like . . . well, it was the 1980s. We looked like a cross between Duran Duran and Devo; we had on as much eyeshadow over our eyes as the Colts did under theirs.

On the opening kick-off, I couldn't see what was going on, but I could hear it. The two teams charging down the field sounded like a stampede of wild horses, and when they hit each other, you could hear the crack of the helmets, the grunts and groans of the players. When the special teams unit came over to the sidelines after the kick-off, it was something I'd never witnessed before. The players were out of breath, wheezing, and panting—fingers were broken, uniforms were muddy, noses were bloody. Right then I realized . . . playing football is a brutal sport.

Playing music is not. Musicians don't encounter a lot of violence. Unless, they're really, really bad.

The Baltimore fans were booing Elway mercilessly that day. People from B-Mo were pissed off, and they weren't afraid show it. John Elway had said he'd play anywhere but Baltimore, and we Baltimorons took it personally. It would have been nice if the Colts had won, but the Colts were pretty bad that day. They lost, 17-10.

Six months later, on March 29, 1984, at 2:00 a.m., fifteen Mayflower moving trucks arrived at the Baltimore Colts training complex. Eight hours later, they were loaded up and heading to Indianapolis. They took everything—the Colts' name, the trophies, the memorabilia, the mascot, the uniforms. All gone to Indianapolis. The mayor of Indy had offered the owner of the Baltimore Colts a $12 million loan, a $4 million training complex, and a new $77 million stadium.

When I heard the news about the Colts leaving town, I was pissed off; so much so, that I didn't go to a football game, or follow the NFL for years. It was a nasty divorce. I was bitter. Lots of folks in Baltimore were.

More than ten years later, when the Baltimore Ravens came to town, Oscar got season tickets—great seats in the club section. I resisted at first, but after a couple years, I gave in; I went to my first Ravens game. The guy sang the national anthem, and it sent chills up and down my spine. The crowd cheered; jets roared as they flew right over our heads, and Ray Lewis came out of the tunnel and did his dance while fireworks shot into the sky. The stadium went wild. It was thrilling.

I was hooked. I was back in love! The Ravens went on to win the Super Bowl that year—2000.

They won the Super Bowl again in 2012.

I'm not bitter anymore. I'm better, not bitter.

RED WINE SAUCE WITH AHI TUNA

This would be a good sauce to make at a Super Bowl party. You can use it on steak, chicken or ahi tuna steaks. You can grill, or sear. I put some of this scrump-diddly-umptious sauce on top of some seared ahi tuna and it was *magnifico*.

It took me a while to perfect this recipe. I had done ahi tuna with a red wine sauce before, but it wasn't where I wanted it to be. The sauce wasn't right. It was keeping me up at night. Then, one night around dawn, it dawned on me. Tomato paste!

The next time I made the sauce, I added a little tomato paste to the sauce to thicken it up and give it a little zip. Then I added a little dried oregano to give it some zing. Zip! Zing! It turned out great.

A few things before we get started—the tuna steaks I used were about an inch and a half thick. I cooked them for 2 minutes per side over medium-high heat. They turned out perfectly—the pepper/salt/sugar that I had sprinkled on top gave them a nice sear, and they were a beautifully pink on the inside.

Cooking times vary. A thicker piece of fish takes longer.

Also, when you light your Cognac on fire, be careful boys and girls. Yes, the subsequent explosion of flame looks so impressive and very dramatic, but have the fire department on the phone in one hand, and a garden hose in the other.

If you're using this sauce on a steak or chicken, just cook or grill as you normally do, and then add a little sauce on top.

This is a bold sauce. Don't use too much!

INGREDIENTS

2 ahi tuna steaks, about a half pound (8 ounces) each

2 tablespoons butter (1 for the sauce, 1 for the sear)

2 tablespoons extra-virgin olive oil (1 for the sauce, 1 for the sear)

2 tablespoons chopped shallots

1 tablespoon chopped garlic

2 ounces of Cognac (about ¼ cup)

½ cup dry red wine

½ cup stock (I used beef)

½ teaspoon dried oregano

1 tablespoon tomato paste

Fresh-cracked black pepper

Kosher salt

Brown sugar or raw/turbinado sugar (you can use plain sugar in a pinch)

HERE WE GO!

Rinse off your tuna steaks and pat dry with paper towels.

SCAN THE QR CODE TO SEE THE YOUTUBE VIDEO

Let's make the sauce first. In a small pan over medium heat, add 1 tablespoon of butter, and 1 tablespoon of olive oil.

When the butter melts, add the shallots and the garlic.

Cook about 2 minutes until the shallots are clear and the garlic is golden. Stir a few times.

Add the 2 ounces of Cognac.

Stand back, Jack! Get a lighter, one with a long handle. Light the Cognac on fire. Be careful! The flames will shoot up!

When the Cognac burns off, and the fire department has left . . .

Add the red wine and the beef stock.

Let it cook for 3 minutes while stirring.

Add the oregano, and salt and fresh-cracked black pepper to taste. Stir it up!

Add the tomato paste, stir for a minute or so.

Remove from heat.

The sauce is done; now let's cook our tuna.

Put both tuna steaks on a plate.

Add a little fresh-cracked black pepper, a little Kosher salt, and a sprinkle of turbinado or brown sugar on top of each steak.

Get a sauté pan; put it over medium-high heat.

Add 1 tablespoon of butter and 1 tablespoon of olive oil to the pan.

When the butter starts to brown, add the tuna, peppered/salted/sugared side down.

Add a LITTLE SPRINKLE of fresh-cracked black pepper, Kosher salt, and turbinado sugar to the unseasoned top side.

Cook for 2 minutes. You can cover loosely with a piece of aluminum foil to cut down on the splattering.

Lift the tuna out of the pan with tongs. Swirl the butter and olive oil around in the bottom of the pan, so you're not placing the fish in a dry pan.

Turn the tuna over and place in the pan. Cook for 2 minutes on the other side.

Give it a slice, see if it's done to your liking. If it is, dish it up. Keep in mind, the fish will keep cooking, even though you've taken it out of the pan. Err on the side of rare.

Place the tuna on a plate, drizzle just a little red wine sauce over each piece.

I made risotto with peas and Parmigiano to go along with this dish.

Everything was *delizioso*!

MANGIAMO!

PIZZA

with Marc Antoine and Dean Martin

I don't know why Marc and I started calling each other "Bastardo." We had just met.

"How ya doin', bastardo?"

"What's up, bastardo?"

Marc Antoine is a tremendously gifted guitar player, I love his style. He's played with Rod Stewart, Sting, and Celine Dion. Marc was born in Paris; he was living in L.A. when I first met him. A percussionist named Steve Reid had put together a tour; he called it Jazzatopia. Marc on guitar, me on vocals, and Everette Harp (he played with Kenny Loggins) on sax. We traveled all over the U.S.; Marc and I became fast friends during the tour. The year was 1997.

We were in San Antonio playing a place called the White Rabbit, and the night before the show, Marc and I went downtown to the Riverwalk—a collection of bars and cafés alongside the San Antonio River. I was in an open-air Mexican restaurant, and Marc was down by the water. I was sitting at the bar, surrounded by my Spanish-speaking brothers and sisters, when I heard one of my songs come over the sound system. It was one of the first times I'd ever heard my music on the radio. I jumped up and screamed out to Marc, who was about fifty yards away,

"BASTARDO!"

The restaurant went dead silent. A couple of guys pulled out machetes. For a couple moments there, I thought guns might be drawn. Everyone was staring at me, but they finally relaxed when they realized I wasn't screaming at any of them. I just smiled a sheepish smile, waved weakly, and walked out. I don't think Marc and I called each other "bastardo" after that.

The Jazzatopia tour started with rehearsals in an industrial complex outside of L.A. There were three warehouses. In one warehouse they were building white plastic Storm Trooper uniforms for a *Star Wars* movie. There were hundreds of them hanging on racks outside in the sun to dry. It was bizarre.

In another warehouse, Fleetwood Mac was rehearsing for their tour. A year before, I had played a club in D.C. owned by Mick Fleetwood, the drummer. The place was called Fleetwood's; the Slim Man band played there a bunch of times. Mick and I became friendly; he wasn't the kind of friend I could ask to bail me out of jail, but he knew who I was. I stood around and listened to Fleetwood Mac rehearse for a while in their warehouse, then I went over and said hello to Mick. Howdy, neighbor!

Then there was our warehouse, warehouse number three. The Jazzatopia warehouse. At our first rehearsal, Marc got into a fistfight with the drummer, who had to be replaced. Seriously. After that, things calmed down a bit; I think Marc scared the shit out of the rest of the band. Everybody fell in line.

Marc and I were constant amigos during the tour. One night, Marc told me the story about a lovely woman he had just met while he was doing a TV show in Madrid. Marc was playing a song, and a half-dozen professional dancers were doing a little choreographed dance to his music. One of the dancing girls caught his eye; it was love at first sight. Soon after, Marc had to fly back to the States; that's when we did the tour together.

As soon as we were done, Marc went back to Madrid and asked her to marry him. They got married soon after.

Marc invited me to their wedding in Madrid. The wedding was wild, and fun, and crazy. We danced. We ate. We drank. We played. I sang a few songs with the band. The wedding started in the afternoon and went until 4:00 a.m. Or was it 5:00? I think it was 6:00 when I caught a cab back to the hotel.

The day after the wedding, I went to Marbella, a beach town on the Mediterranean. I was at a seaside bar, drinking sangria—the kind they make with white wine, brandy, and Cointreau. It was late afternoon; a song came over the sound system as the sun was setting.

“When the moon hits your eye like a big pizza pie, that’s amore.” Dean Martin was singing. I love Dino; I love that song. But when I thought about that opening line, I turned to the guy standing next to me and said,

“ ‘When the moon hits your eye like a big pizza pie, that’s amore.’ What the hell kinda lyric is that?”

The guy turned to me and said, “I’ve never worked a day in my life because of that song.”

He then told me that one of his relatives had written that song and a bunch of others. His relative had willed him the royalties when he died. The guy who wrote “That’s Amore” was Harry Warren, the son of Italian immigrants. He wrote “Chattanooga Choo Choo,” “Jeepers Creepers,” “You Must Have Been a Beautiful Baby,” and a lot of other smash hits. Harry Warren also won three Academy awards, and was nominated eleven times. No wonder no one in his family had to work. Ever. True story.

I told the story to Marc—he wasn’t surprised. Marc then told me a story; his friend had written a song—not a hit song, just a song—that was included on *The BodyGuard* soundtrack. That’s the movie with Kevin Costner and Whitney Houston where Whitney sings “I Will Always Love You.”

The soundtrack sold millions of copies; the movie was a smash. Marc’s friend’s first royalty check was for about two million dollars. That’s a lot of dough.

Speaking of dough—want me to show you how to make a pizza?

“When the moon hits your eye, like a big pizza pie, that’s amore!”

PIZZA

Pizza is kind of like making love. Even when it's bad, it's pretty good.

First things first—if you're gonna make your own dough, you should do it a day in advance; it tastes best that way. If you're pressed for time, there are lots of shortcuts out there—leave it to me to find the one that takes 24 hours. There was a great deli in Baltimore named Mastellone that sold fresh pizza dough, and it was amazing, better than I could make myself. If you can find a great deli that has fresh dough, use it! If not, make your own, it's a-not-a-so hard!

This recipe will yield enough dough for 2 pizzas.

I make my own tomato sauce; it only takes about 25 minutes. Or you can use bottled tomato sauce. Either way, you'll need about a ½ cup of sauce per pizza.

Unless you have a wood-fired oven, you're gonna need a pizza stone. You'll also need a paddle to get the pizza on and off the stone—because that stone is gonna get really hot. How hot? Five hundred degrees. That's how hot your oven should be. The pizza stone should sit in that hot oven for at least 30 minutes before you put a pizza on it.

Ready?

INGREDIENTS

For the Dough:

3 cups of bread flour, plus a little more for dusting

2 teaspoons turbinado sugar (turbinado sugar has a molasses flavor, but you can use regular sugar if you want)

1½ teaspoons of salt (this is one of those rare instances when I DON'T use Kosher salt, I use table salt)

½ teaspoon rapid rise yeast

1⅓ cups really cold water

1 tablespoon extra-virgin olive oil (plus a tablespoon for the kneading surface)

Corn meal for dusting the pizza paddle

Toppings:

½ cup of tomato sauce per pizza

Basil leaves (about ¼ cup per pizza)

If you want, you can add—sausage, pepperoni, cut-up meatballs, diced chicken cutlets, Feta cheese, Asiago cheese, provolone cheese, spinach, peppers, onions, olives, mushrooms, shallots—feel free to get creative.

Fresh mozzarella cheese, sliced into thin slices, or shredded (about a cup per pizza)

Parmigiano-Reggiano cheese, grated (about ¼ cup per pizza)

HERE WE GO!

SCAN THE QR CODE TO SEE THE YOUTUBE VIDEO

I do the dough by hand in a wooden bowl—it's kinda sexy that way.

Put the flour, sugar, salt and yeast in a wooden bowl. Mix by hand, just a couple stirs.

Make a crater in the middle of the flour. Pour the cold water in the hole, and start folding the flour over the water. Mix by hand for a few minutes.

When everything is combined, and all the flour is soaked up into the dough, take the dough out of the bowl, roll it in a ball and put it back in the bowl. Let it sit for 15 minutes, uncovered.

Then, make a small crater on top of the dough ball, and pour the olive oil in. Fold the dough around the olive oil, so it blends in. Work the olive oil into the dough for a couple of minutes. The dough will be just a little sticky.

Lightly oil a large chopping block—or you can use your counter top. Drizzle some olive oil onto a paper towel, and dampen the chopping block or countertop. Don't throw away that towel. We'll use it again momentarily.

Take the dough out of the bowl, and place it on the chopping block or counter top. Let's knead some dough! Make your hand into a fist, and press your knuckles into the dough, and roll it around, form it into a ball, and do it again. Knead, knead, knead.

After a few minutes, take that lightly oiled paper towel and rub it on the inside of a large glass or ceramic bowl.

Shape the dough back into a ball, place it in the oiled bowl, and cover it tightly with plastic wrap.

Put it in the fridge for 24 hours.

Time to make some pizza. . . .

Take the dough out of the fridge. Cut it into two equal parts. Roll each into a ball. Put both dough balls on a lightly oiled baking pan. Cover loosely with plastic wrap and let it sit.

Put your pizza stone on the middle rack of your oven.

Turn your oven to its highest setting—500 degrees is the highest setting on mine.

Wait 30 minutes for the stone to heat up and for the dough to settle.

Time to grab your dough balls.

Dust a chopping block or counter top with flour. Grab a dough ball, put it on the block, and flatten by hand into an 8-inch circle.

Using a rolling pin, roll the dough into a 12-inch circle.

If you don't have a rolling pin, do it by hand. Start working the edges, using your fingers to spread the dough into a larger circle until it's about 12 inches.

You don't want the dough too thick or too thin.

If things get sticky—your hands or your rolling pin—dust with some flour.

After your dough is formed into a 12-inch circle, dust your pizza paddle with a little corn meal. Corn meal will help the pizza slide on and off the paddle. Corn meal doesn't burn at high temperatures like flour does. Dust your paddle with corn meal, and put your dough on the paddle.

Take a ladle of sauce, about half a cup, and spread it evenly around the dough in a thin layer.

Snip some basil leaves onto the pizza. Add your mozzarella, spread it around evenly, and then sprinkle on the Parmigiano cheese.

If you have any other ingredients you'd like to add —sausage, peppers, olives, etc.—now is the time.

Now to the oven . . .

When your pizza is ready, open the oven, and slide the pizza off the paddle and onto the heated pizza stone.

Cook for about 10 minutes.

Then, check your pizza. When the outer crust is light brown, and the mozzarella on top is browning and gooey, you're done.

If the cheese needs a little help browning, turn on your broiler, and let the cheese brown—THIS ONLY TAKES A MINUTE OR LESS!

Grab your paddle, scoot the pizza off the stone and onto the paddle, and place the pizza on a platter. Eat it up!

Then make another pizza with the second ball of dough. Go back, Jack, do it again! Use some different toppings! When it's done . . .

Slice it up, serve it up, and sing a little song . . .

"When the moon hits your eye like a big pizza pie, that's amore!"

MANGIAMO!

SLIM MANICOTTI stuffed with SHRIMP and SCALLOPS

and The Sounds of Silence

I was singing in a club in Baltimore, Maryland at a place called Nightlife. It was a small club in a strip mall; my band, BootCamp, was doing a show there, and during a song my voice cracked.

I sounded like I was going through puberty. Except I'd already done that back in 1776. I had no idea what was happening with my voice. On the next song, my voice cracked again, the sound was similar to a donkey in heat. I've never been around donkeys in heat, but I can imagine they sound like my voice did that night. Hee-haw. My voice kept cracking; it was embarrassing. I left the club that night dazed and confused.

BootCamp was a really good band. Howard Zizzi on drums, Bob Fallin on guitar, and Tom Alonso on keyboards. If you took the Cars, the Police, and Journey and put them in a blender, that's what we sounded like. If you took the hairdos of the Three Stooges, Flock of Seagulls, and Chinese crested terriers and put them in a blender, that's what we looked like.

BootCamp started off at a club called Mack and Myer's in Essex, Maryland. A few months later, we got a gig in New York in the Hamptons at a place called the Neptune Beach Club. All summer long, we worked six nights a week—10:00 p.m. to 4:00 a.m., with doubles on Saturday and Sunday afternoons. I did most of the singing.

At the end of the summer, when we went back to Baltimore, the gigs kept coming. We were working five and six nights a week, every week; we played up and down the east coast, from small dive bars to big concert halls.

One of our favorite places to play was Painters Mill, outside Baltimore; it was a theater in-the-round that featured all kinds of acts, from Gladys Knight to Rodney Dangerfield to Johnny Cash. The guy that booked Painters Mill was a big BootCamp fan. His name was Larry Hargrove. Whenever Larry needed an opening act, we'd get the call. So, BootCamp ended up doing shows with the B-52s, the Tubes, Squeeze, Split Enz, Johnny Winter.

My mom had the first Johnny Winter album, the one with the black cover and a headshot of him with his white hair, and a gold chain, and a black leather vest. I played the hell out of that album. And when Larry called and asked if we wanted to open for Johnny Winter, I immediately said yes.

When BootCamp took the stage at Painters Mill that night, I looked out at the crowd. It was mostly bikers. Not Lance Armstrong-type bikers, more like Hells Angels bikers. We were dressed in jumpsuits and had on more make-up than most rodeo clowns.

We started our first song, and we got nothin'. Not a clap. Not a cheer. We played a few more songs, same thing. When a bottle of Jack Daniels flew through the air and hit the neck of my bass guitar, I thought it might be best to cut our set a little short. True story. We left the stage after just a few songs. Not long after, I started having problems with my voice.

My mom had great musical instincts; she always told me that I was singing too high in BootCamp. She told me I should be singing in the lower registers, but I was a stubborn young knucklehead, and I didn't listen. And after years of screaming at the top of my lungs, six days a week, almost every week, my voice started to crack. I went to see my doctor, who is also my cousin.

He looked down my throat and told me I had nodules on my vocal cords. He explained that nodules are like little calluses you get from singing and talking too much; he sent me to a specialist. The guy wanted to operate immediately. I don't know why, but I refused. I kept on seeing specialist after specialist, and they all wanted to operate; I kept refusing. Like I said, I was a stubborn young knucklehead.

I didn't give up. Then one afternoon, I went to Sinai Hospital and saw a specialist named Ury Kalehy. He came in and looked down my throat, looked up my nose, pulled out my tongue, and said,

"You chew on the left side of your mouth. You sleep on your right side, you breathe through your left nostril. . . ."

He kept going on and on about all my sleeping, chewing, and breathing habits. He was right about everything. How he knew all this, I'm not sure, but I knew he was The Man. He told me we didn't have to operate, we could do something else. I told him I'd do anything to avoid surgery. He gave me a steroid inhaler; then he told me to shut up for two weeks. Not a word, not a peep, not a whisper or a grunt or a groan. Complete and total silence. He asked me if I could do it. I said yes.

So for two weeks, I shut the hell up. I wrote things down a lot; it was weird at first, and then I started enjoying it.

I didn't answer the phone, I didn't sing a note, I didn't say a word for two weeks. I used a lot of sign language—not real sign language, but a sign language I made up myself. I did a lot of pointing and whistling. After fourteen days, I went back to Dr. Kalehy; he looked down my throat and told me the calluses were gone. He told me I could talk.

I was a little apprehensive, I wasn't sure what I was gonna sound like.

When I spoke, my voice had changed—it was high and clear, not low and gruff. When I talked, I sounded like Michael Jackson. Or Janet Jackson. I didn't sound like me. When I sang, I sounded like I had just inhaled a helium balloon; my voice felt different, it sounded different.

It didn't sound manly anymore. All the grit was gone.

Soon after my vocal rest, BootCamp recorded an EP at Ace Frehley's home studio. Ace was the guitarist in a pretty popular band called KISS. After we released the EP, the music critic for the *Baltimore Sun* said I sounded like "a castrated Michael McDonald."

Ouch.

BootCamp broke up not long after; it was a good run, but time to move on. I went back into the studio to write some new songs, and I decided to pitch my voice low, like I did when I was at Motown. I always loved Nat King Cole and Chet Baker, that low and slow, cool and soft way of singing.

So I wrote and sang a bunch of songs like that, and released the first Slim Man CD, *End of the Rainbow*. The same music critic who said I sounded like a castrated Michael McDonald was writing for *Rolling Stone* when he wrote the following review of the Big Slim Debut:

"A near-perfect example of how jazz and soul can be combined as pop. . . ."

SLIM MANICOTTI STUFFED WITH SHRIMP AND SCALLOPS

Traditional manicotti are not my favorite things to eat. Some of my best friends like manicotti. But all that ricotta cheese just doesn't do it for me.

But I felt the need to create a Slim dish worthy of the Slim Manicotti name. So instead of filling my manly manicotti with ricotta cheese, I use shrimp and scallops in a spicy tomato sauce.

And if that ain't genius enough, I cut the manicotti in half and stack 'em like chimneys. They're easier to fill that way. And they look much cooler as well.

And for my final stroke of brilliance, I bake them and then sprinkle the tops with panko breadcrumbs and broil them for a quick minute, to give them a little crunch. They're scrump-diddly-umptious.

Slim Manicotti. For Slim People.

NOTES:

Make sure your bay scallops are dry. Wet scallops are injected with who-knows-what, and give off a lot of liquid when you cook them. Ask your seafood person, they'll know.

If you can't find bay scallops, you can use sea scallops—the big ones—but they're expensive. Once again, make sure they are dry scallops. Some scallops might have a small muscle on the side, remove it and toss—the muscle, not the scallops!

I don't like farm-raised shrimp. I love people who are raised on farms; they're good, wholesome, down-to-earth folks. But farm-raised shrimp? They don't taste good, and they're mushy. Wild shrimp are the way to go, as wild and as crazy as you can find.

I used Barilla manicotti; there were 14 in the box. I cooked them all, and ended up using 9 of them—the others broke! I cut the cooked, unbroken 9 manicotti shells in half, so I had 18 half-manicotti. I stood them up vertically, like little chimneys, and filled them from the top.

This stellar recipe calls for equal parts shrimp and bay scallops. You can also use equal amounts of shrimp, scallops, and lobster. You can also use just shrimp. Whatever you use, make sure you have 1½ pounds (3 cups chopped).

You can also use this sauce over rice or pasta—spaghetti or linguine would work well.

INGREDIENTS

¾ pound shrimp, de-shelled, de-veined, about 1½ cups (cut into pieces the size of small grapes) SAVE THE SHELLS, AMIGOS!

¾ pound bay scallops, about 1½ cups (they need to be about the same size as the cut-up shrimp)

Kosher salt

1 (28-ounce) can of whole, peeled, Italian tomatoes (San Marzano are best)

4 tablespoons extra-virgin olive oil

1 cup dry white wine

2 tablespoons minced garlic (about 4 cloves, depending on the size)

1 teaspoon oregano (dried is best)

½ teaspoon crushed red pepper (use less if you don't like it spicy!)

2 anchovy filets

¼ cup chopped fresh Italian flat-leaf parsley (curly parsley ain't as good, but will do)

¼ cup of snipped fresh basil (use a scissors, cut it into small pieces, or chop coarsely)

1 pound manicotti

¼ cup plain panko breadcrumbs (I sometimes use Progresso Panko Italian Style)

HERE WE GO!

SCAN THE QR CODE TO SEE THE YOUTUBE VIDEO

Rinse off your shrimp and scallops and pat dry with paper towels—especially the scallops. Keep patting the scallops dry until the paper towels no longer get damp. Scallops throw off a lot of liquid.

Take a large pot, fill it with cold water, and put it on the highest heat you got. This be for the manicotti, Slimigos. As the water comes to a boil, let's make our sauce/manicotti filling.

Put the chopped shrimp and scallops in a bowl. Sprinkle with Kosher salt, about ½ teaspoon, and give them a toss. Set aside.

Grab your colander. The Italians have a wonderful name for a colander. They call it a *scolapasta*. *Scolare* is the Italian word for "to drain."

Put your colander/*scolapasta* over a large bowl. Pour the can of tomatoes into the *scolapasta*. Slice into each tomato a couple times with a spatula so the juice drains out into the large bowl.

Pour the tomatoes out of the *scolapasta* and into a small bowl. Set aside the juices that have drained into the large bowl.

Put 1 tablespoon of olive oil in a large sauté pan over medium-high heat for 2 minutes. Swirl a couple times.

Add the shrimp shells. That's right! Add the SHELLS to the pan and cook and stir for 3 minutes.

Add the wine and let it cook off for 3 minutes. Stir often.

Take the tomato juice that drained in the large bowl. Remember those juices? Add the juices to the sauté pan with the wine and shrimp shells, and cook and stir for 5 minutes.

Put your colander/*scolapasta* over a medium bowl. Pour the shrimp shells/tomato juice/white wine sauce out of the sauté pan into the colander. Let the sauce drain into the bowl.

Throw out the shrimp shells. Save the sauce.

Take your sauté pan—the same one we cooked the shrimp shells in—and give it a quick wipe with a paper towel.

Put the sauté pan over medium heat. Add 2 tablespoons of olive oil, the garlic, the oregano, and the crushed red pepper, and cook and stir for 2 or 3 minutes. Don't burn the garlic! Burnt garlic tastes bitter and nasty.

When you make the following move, make sure nobody sees you. Most people don't like anchovies, but when you mash them like this, they add a really nice flavor.

Add the anchovies, and mash them suckers with the back of a wooden spoon until they disintegrate. Cook for 1 minute.

Add the tomatoes to the pan, and mash with the back of a wooden spoon. Add the tomato juice/white wine sauce to the tomatoes. Add a little salt.

Cook and stir for 5 or 6 minutes.

Add the shrimp and the scallops to the pan. Cook for 5 minutes, give it a stir every minute or so.

Add the parsley and the basil. Give it a stir, SlimNation. Taste for salt and pepper and adjust to your refined sensibilities.

Remove from heat. The Slim Sauce is *pronto*!

And now for the manicotti . . .

Pre-heat your oven to 400 degrees.

You should hopefully have a large pot of water on the stove. It should close to boiling by now. When the water comes to a full boil, add 2 tablespoons of Kosher salt. Add the manicotti.

Only stir once or twice—you don't want to bust up your manicotti. I cooked the Barilla manicotti for 7 minutes—just like the instructions on the box—and they turned out really well. They were not all the way cooked, which was good, because we're gonna bake 'em in the oven for a bit. *Capisce*?

After you drain the manicotti, cut them in half. Don't cut them on an angle, cut them straight, because we want the manicotti to stand up—they WON'T be lying flat, like all the rest of the manicotti in the world.

No! Slim Manicotti is unique! We're going vertical. Upright.

Five of my 14 manicotti broke while cooking. I had 9 manicotti left, which worked out most excellently. I cut each one in half. Just so you don't have to grab your calculator, I had 18 half-manicotti.

Get a small baking dish—8 by 11 inches is good, smaller is even better. Take a half a manicotti. Stand it up vertically in the baking dish, flat-side down, spear-side up, like a small chimney. Prop the manicotti open. Take a teaspoon, and spoon some shrimp and scallop mixture into the manicotti. Fill it up. Each one should take a couple spoons of shrimp and scallop sauce.

Do this with all the half-manicotti.

After you have filled all 18 half-manicotti, if you have any leftover sauce, pour it over the tops, distributing equally amongst our slim manicotti. Be fair and judicious.

Put the manicotti in the oven, and cook for 7 minutes. KEEP IN MIND! Ovens vary wildly in temperature. Times are approximate. The goal here is to bake the manicotti so the seafood gets warm and the manicotti finishes cooking. It won't take long.

Keep an eye on that slim manicotti! Check them every few minutes, make sure they don't burn.

After 7 minutes, remove from the oven.

Set your oven on broil.

Sprinkle just a little breadcrumbs (I use panko) on top of the upright manicotti. Put them under the broiler.

Broil for a minute until the breadcrumbs are golden. Don't burn your breadcrumbs! Keep your eyes on these guys.

When the breadcrumbs start to get just a bit golden, take your slim manicotti out of the oven. Let them sit for a few minutes.

Put two on a plate. Place one vertically, like a chimney. Lay the other flat. Spoon a little sauce from the bottom of the baking dish over the manicotti, and . . .

MANGIAMO!

GRILLED VEGETABLE PASTA

and

How My Dad Almost Killed Me

Most Italians I know have a garden. I don't know why; it just seems to be the case. My grandmother, Angela, had a small garden; my uncle Oscar, had a garden—or rather, he had someone build him a garden and maintain it. Oscar wasn't a dig-in-the-dirt kinda guy; I don't think he ever mowed a lawn in his adult life—he had people who did that kinda thing. But my dad? Oscar's only brother? He loved getting down in the dirt.

I remember one spring, my dad wanted to build a vegetable garden. He lived in an apartment above a big barn on a farm in Long Island, New York. He was a professor of philosophy and literature at the State University of New York in Old Westbury, which was about fifteen miles from the barn. I used to drive up from Baltimore, Maryland, and visit him in his little place on the top floor.

My dad had painted all the walls different bright colors; purple, yellow, orange. For his dining-room table, he had found a huge old wood spool that the phone company had used for wrapping telephone wire. He laid it on its side, and that's what we ate on. His kitchen table was an antique, foot-operated sewing machine.

There was a dog kennel in the barn downstairs, which was a lot of fun when the volunteer fire department sirens would go off in the middle of the night, and the dozen or so dogs would start caterwauling. Along with the dogs, there were also horses residing in the barn below. Well, it wasn't like Smarty Jones or Seattle Slew were living down there. This was a working barn, with working horses, and when you have horses, you usually have horse flies. So in the upstairs apartment my dad put fly strips on the ceiling.

In case you've never lived above a barn with horses and horse flies; fly strips are basically rolls of sticky paper that unravel and hang from the ceiling. When flies fly by, they get stuck to the paper. Since the ceiling at my dad's apartment was slanted and low; if you weren't careful when you walked by, the fly strips would stick to your hair. This wasn't a problem for my dad, who had no hair. But for us long-haired teens, it was a big problem.

I had a hairdo that resembled all three guys in the Jimi Hendrix Experience put together. Whenever I walked by these fly strips, my hair would get stuck, and I'd have to call for my dad to cut me loose. So there were all these fly strips hanging from the ceiling, with dead flies and clumps of curly hair stuck to them.

The other thing you have when you have horses downstairs? Horse shit. With all that free fertilizer in the barn, my dad decided to create a garden. He wanted to border the garden with railroad ties; so one day he borrowed a pickup truck, and we drove to a deserted area of the Long Island Railroad.

My dad couldn't just go to the Home Depot and buy wood borders. He had to go find old railroad ties. He couldn't just go to a furniture store and buy a dining-room table, he had to go find an old wood spool. He couldn't buy a kitchen table at IKEA, he had to use an old sewing machine. He couldn't just find a normal place to live, he had to find a place on top of a barn with a kennel and horses and ceilings that were so slanted that you had to walk around crouched over like Quasimodo.

My dad had it in his head to find railroad ties to border his garden. We found a stack by the side of some abandoned railroad tracks; the railroad ties smelled like creosote, and weighed what seemed like a ton. We put the back gate of the pickup truck down. We were able, the two of us, to get one railroad tie onto the bed of the pickup truck, but the only problem was, the railroad tie was hanging off the back of the pickup. Whenever my dad went over a bump, the end of the railroad tie closest to the cab of the truck would rise in the air, and the other end that was hanging off the back of the truck would hit the ground. It was like a see-saw. A dangerous see-saw. My dad pulled the truck over.

Then he had a brilliant idea; he wanted me to get out of the truck and stand on the end of the railroad tie that was close to the cab, using what little weight I had to keep the railroad tie from flying up in the air. He told me to hang on to the roof of the truck for stability. Brilliant.

My dad yelled a lot. He laughed a lot, too, but he had a temper. I found it hard to say "no" to my dad; so I got out of the truck and stood on the end of the railroad tie, facing forward, holding on to the roof of the cab for dear life. The first bump we hit, I shot into the air like a rocket. It seems kinda funny now. It wasn't real funny to me back then. I was terrified.

That's when I thought it might be best to prop up one end of the railroad tie on top of the cab of the pickup, and close the back gate to hold the other end inside the bed, so it wasn't hanging off the back. And that's the way we rolled. We ended up getting a bunch of railroad ties, and made a huge square outside of the barn. We shoveled horseshit for hours from the barn into the garden.

That garden was incredible. We had Brussel sprouts the size of cabbages. Everything grew to amazing proportions and tasted incredibly fresh and delightful.

GRILLED VEGETABLE PASTA

When I think of vegetables, I always think of that garden—and how I almost died to get it built.

I like to grill. I like pasta. I like vegetables. So, I thought, why not combine all three? That's when I came up with this recipe. I put the "j" back in genius with this dish. You'll want to serve it at room temperature, but add the mozzarella balls when the pasta is hot, so the balls get gooey, so to speak. *Fusilli* pasta works best.

I cut the onion and the orange bell peppers into large pieces, because they're easier to grill and flip that way. When they're done, I chop 'em up into smaller, bite-size pieces. Also, the cherry tomatoes only need about five minutes on the grill, just to heat 'em up.

Serves 4, or 1 teenage kid who's been shoveling horseshit in the sun for hours.

INGREDIENTS

A bulb of garlic, the root end cut off

Extra-virgin olive oil

1 zucchini, scrubbed, ends snipped off, sliced in circular slices

1 yellow summer squash, prepared the same way

2 small eggplants, prepared the same way

2 orange bell peppers, stems and seeds removed, cut in large slices

1 Vidalia onion (or any sweet onion except purple/Spanish), sliced into large circular slices

2 dozen cherry tomatoes

A dozen small balls of mozzarella

½ cup pignoli (pine nuts), toasted to a golden brown in a dry pan over medium heat—you can also use sliced almonds, toasted the same way

Basil leaves, a large handful (a cup)—save a few whole leaves for garnish

1 tablespoon of balsamic vinegar

1 pound of *fusilli* pasta

Freshly grated Parmigiano-Reggiano cheese

Kosher salt and fresh-cracked black pepper

Non-stick cooking spray (optional)

HERE WE GO!

SCAN THE QR CODE TO SEE THE YOUTUBE VIDEO

Make sure your grill surface is clean. A little non-stick cooking spray on the grill surface will help keep your vegetables from sticking. Be careful! Don't spray it into the fire.

If you're using a charcoal grill, light the coals, and let them burn for 20 to 30 minutes, or until the coals are ash-gray. You don't want the fire to be too hot, or you just end up burning the vegetables. If you're using a gas grill, put the heat on medium.

Take the bulb of garlic. Slice the root end off. Put the whole garlic bulb on top of a large piece of aluminum foil. Drizzle it with olive oil, about a teaspoon. Wrap it up, and put it on the outside part of the grill—the place with the least heat—and let it slow-roast for the whole time you're grilling.

For the pasta, get a large pot, fill it with water, and let it come to a boil.

Now for the vegetables. Put them all on a large platter. Drizzle with olive oil, about a tablespoon, make sure they're all lightly coated. Sprinkle with a little salt and fresh-cracked black pepper. Then flip 'em over and do the same on the other side—drizzle with a little olive oil, and sprinkle with a little salt and pepper.

Put all the vegetables on the grill, except the tomatoes. Let everything grill for about 5 to 7 minutes, depending on the heat of your grill, then turn 'em over.

Put the tomatoes on the outside of the grill. Grill all your vegetables for another 5 to 7 minutes.

Remove the vegetables from the grill, and place them on a large platter. Cut the onion and the orange bell peppers into bite size pieces.

For the pasta, when the water is a-boiling, add a few tablespoons of Kosher salt, and then add a pound of *fusilli*. Follow the directions on the box. When the pasta is supposed to be done, give it a taste. Bite through a piece of pasta, look at the center. If it is chalky, it is not done. When the *fusilli* is *al dente* (firm to the bite) drain, put it in a large bowl, drizzle with a tablespoon olive oil, and toss.

Take your garlic bulb out of the aluminum foil, make sure it's cool enough to touch, and grab the bulb by the top. Squeeze the cloves out through the bottom, right onto the pasta. Mix 'em up.

Add your grilled vegetables, give them a stir.

Add your mozzarella balls and toss gently.

Add the toasted pignoli—save some for sprinkling on to each plate.

Take the basil leaves (save a few for each plate for garnish), and snip 'em with scissors into small pieces right onto the pasta. Toss gently.

Add a little more olive oil if you like and toss again, gently.

Add the balsamic vinegar (about a tablespoon or so to taste) and toss once more.

Dish it up! Make it look nice! Add a couple basil leaves to each dish, sprinkle a few toasted pignoli on top, and add a little freshly grated Parmigiano-Reggiano cheese on top, if you like.

MANGIAMO!

LAMB CHOPS with ROSEMARY

and

Elvis and Mixed Nuts

Elvis hated us.

Not the real Elvis. An Elvis impersonator.

I had a band in the late 1970s called Mixed Nuts. The original name was Nick's Nuts, but a gangster guy who booked the band hated the name. He told us to change it, so we changed it to Nix Nuts. He hated that name, too, so we changed it to Mixed Nuts. Gangster guy liked it; it fit.

We played cover songs, mostly Top 40 dance stuff—Earth, Wind and Fire, Marvin Gaye, Ohio Players, along with some jazz—Grover Washington, George Benson, Weather Report. We played clubs in and around our hometown of Baltimore, Maryland. We had some really good musicians in the band. We sounded good; we looked good, which is much more important than sounding good. We didn't take it all too seriously—we were a little nuts.

Our keyboard player, Danny, was the nuttiest of the Nuts. He was the instigator. He was a short, roly-poly guy, looked a lot like Danny DeVito.

One of our first gigs was opening for an Elvis impersonator. When we did the show, we used their equipment—drums, amps, and keyboards. I'm guessing Fake Elvis' keyboard player wasn't very good because he had placed pieces of masking tape on each key of his keyboard. He had written the notes of each key on each piece of tape—so the "C" key had "C" written on the tape, the "D" key had "D" written on it, and so forth, up and down the whole keyboard.

We played for about a half hour. Danny played the guy's keyboard. At the end of our show, Danny changed all the pieces of tape on the keyboard—so the "C" key was no longer "C," and the "D" key was no longer "D."

We left the stage. People didn't throw things at us, but the applause wasn't deafening, either. People were there to see The King, who was waiting in the wings as we walked off. His band went onstage and the keyboard player started their intro, the theme from *2001 A Space Odyssey*.

All the notes were wrong, thanks to Danny. The keyboard player looked down at his keys, and then over at Elvis, who was waiting on the side of the stage. Elvis gave him a dirty look. The keyboard player started the intro again. Nothing but wrong notes.

I don't think the keyboard player hit one good note all night. Needless to say, it wasn't the best night for Elvis and his band. After the show, Elvis came looking for us.

But Mixed Nuts had left the building.

When Mixed Nuts played the Baltimore nightclub circuit, we started at 9:00 p.m. and played until 2:00 a.m. We did five 40-minute sets, 200 minutes of music. We usually played the same club for a week. Then, we'd head to a different club, and play for a week; we did that all year long.

A lot of the clubs we played were owned by Greeks—The Redwood Inn, Rhapsody, Hollywood Palace. The owners were all named John; we gave them nicknames, so we could tell them apart . . . Uncle John. Little John. Big John.

We used to play the Hilton Hotel in a neighborhood called Pikesville. It was one of the few clubs in Baltimore not owned by a Greek named John.

One night, The Nuts were at the Hilton doing our Big Finale, which was a song called "Birdland" by Weather Report. It's a lively little number, a song that we had a request to do. The guy that requested it hit the dance floor as soon as we started the song. He was all by himself, out there on the dance floor, doing a frantic little dance . . .

And then he died of a massive heart attack. Right there in front of us—on the dance floor. True story. We were scheduled to play the Hilton the following week. But we didn't. They didn't want us playing there anymore after the guy died.

It's not like we killed him. But it did give birth to the phrase "We knocked 'em dead last night."

LAMB CHOPS WITH ROSEMARY

When I was in Mixed Nuts, I didn't cook very much, but when I did, I usually made some Italian vegetarian dishes; tomato sauce, pesto, things like that. I didn't eat a lot of red meat.

My dad cooked a birthday dinner for me one year; he made this incredibly elaborate meal, and the main course was a leg of lamb with mustard sauce. My dad had invited Danny—he loved Danny, thought he was ridiculously funny.

After this extravagant dinner, after all the courses had been served, Danny looked at my dad and said,

"Good slop, Phil," which my dad thought was hilarious.

INGREDIENTS

1 pound lamb chops (I had 6, each about ¾ inch thick)

1 tablespoon chopped fresh rosemary

1 clove garlic, minced (a generous teaspoon)

1 teaspoon extra-virgin olive oil, plus 1 tablespoon for searing

1 tablespoon butter

HERE WE GO!

Rinse off your lamb chops and pat them dry with paper towels.

Put the chopped rosemary and the minced garlic on a chopping board.

Even though they're already chopped, chop 'em up together for a minute. These guys need to get to know each other.

Put the chopped rosemary and garlic in a small bowl.

Add a teaspoon of olive oil, mix it up. Set aside.

Place the lamb chops on a large plate.

Rub a little of the rosemary/garlic/olive oil mixture on top of each lamb chop—only on one side! Spread it around evenly, a thin layer.

Add a little Kosher salt and fresh-cracked black pepper.

Get a large sauté pan (I used a 10-inch pan).

Turn the heat to medium-high.

Add the 1 tablespoon of butter, and the remaining 1 tablespoon of olive oil. When the butter starts to brown, add the lamb chops—spiced side down!

Cook for a couple minutes, as in 2 or 3. Thinner pieces take less time, thicker ones, longer.

Using tongs, turn 'em over. Swirl the olive oil and butter around in the bottom of the pan so you're not placing the lamb chops in a dry pan.

Cook for another 2 or 3 minutes on the other side.

Check them for doneness—at 2 or 3 minutes a side they should be medium rare. If you like them well done, cook for a couple minutes more on each side. If you like them rare, cook them less.

That's it!

Dish it up, make it look nice, add a sprig of rosemary, maybe a dollop of risotto, some asparagus Parmigiano, and . . .

MANGIAMO!

FLAMING LIMONCELLO SAUCE
with X Ray Hip

Baked salmon

Sautéed sole

Kevin (L) and Joe (R)

When the first Slim CD, *End of the Rainbow*, was released, it initially did nothing, no sales, no airplay, no gigs. For weeks and weeks, there was a whole lot of nothin' going on; then it started getting some radio play.

I was playing piano at a dive bar in Baltimore, Maryland, called The Horse You Came In On. The bar phone would ring occasionally, and the bartender would answer and then call out to me, "That was your mom! You're number thirty-seven!" The next week, "You're number twenty-nine!"

Suddenly, it went Top Ten, sold tons, and was widely acclaimed—not only in the U.S. but Europe, Japan, and Australia. It happened right quickly. That first Slim CD, *End of the Rainbow*? It done did good, all the way around.

The second Slim CD?

Not so good. It was widely ignored by just about everybody, except some Slim Family members who bought copies out of sympathy. *Closer to Paradise*—that's the name of the second Slim CD, by the way—seemed to take me Further from Paradise. It started off slowly, and then petered out, so to speak. It never caught on.

I recorded the first two Slim CDs in a studio owned by my friend, Cowboy Pickles. It's a small spare bedroom with great gear—topnotch microphones, amps, speakers. Some amazing sounds came out of that little room. It was very comfortable, but for the third Slim Man CD, I decided to swing big. It was time to get out of the comfort zone.

It was time to go for it.

I decided to record Slim CD #3 in a real studio in Manhattan, a place called Sound on Sound. Eric Clapton recorded there. If it's good enough for Eric, it's good enough for Mr. Man. Sound on Sound was like a luxury hotel with a studio on the side. There were more assistants than musicians; assistants who took orders for food, assistant engineers who kept track of everything, assistants who tuned guitars, set up drums, moved pianos, brought you coffee. They did everything but carry you from room to room on their shoulders.

I hired a producer, Carl Griffin. Carl had signed me to Motown years before and he also produced my Motown CD. Griff had recently produced B.B. King's *Live at the Apollo* CD, which earned B.B. and Griff a Grammy. So I got Grammy-Award-winning Griff to produce the third Slim CD. Grammy award-winning producers don't come cheap. I could've bought a car. Well, a really small used car, but still . . .

I decided to dig deep and have some guest stars on the CD, so I hired Rick Braun to play trumpet (Sade), Marc Antoine to play guitar (Sting), Everette Harp on sax (Kenny Loggins), and Chieli Minucci to play guitar (Jennifer Lopez). Each one cost a pretty penny. I brought in my friend Questar, a brilliant sound engineer, to do sound. I hired a professional photographer to shoot the CD cover.

In other words, I hired the best people I could find, I recorded in one of the best studios in Manhattan, and basically went deep into the Slim Pockets to do Slim Man #3. I called the CD *Secret Rendezvous*; it was released in 1997, in the spring.

Right after it was released, I got notice from our distributor that they were declaring bankruptcy. They owed us more than fifty grand; they had sold lots of Slim CDs, but they hadn't paid us in a while, and now we weren't gonna get paid at all. I was counting on that money to pay for the very expensive *Secret Rendezvous* CD I had just recorded. I tried to find another distributor, but nobody would touch us because of the bankruptcy, so *Secret Rendezvous* and the first two Slim Man CDs just sat there in limbo. My hands were tied. My CDs were tied up. It all came crashing down. I had to take a step back.

That's when Carl Griffin called and asked me if I was still writing instrumental music. When Carl and I were working together at Motown, he would ask me every once in a while to write an instrumental piece—a sax song, a piano song, a flute song. So I wrote a few instrumentals while I was a songwriter at Motown. Griff pitched them to Grover Washington, Jr. and a few others, but nothing happened. But I was still writing instrumentals, so I sent some of them to Carl, while the Slim Man CDs were tied up in the bankruptcy. He loved the songs and suggested I do a whole CD of instrumental music.

I asked my friend, Joe Ercole, to help produce the CD, and play some keyboards. He's an amazing pianist and producer—he graduated at the top of his class at Berklee School of Music. Joe was writing and producing jingles for TV and radio; he had developed a very successful jingle company.

Joe had hired me to sing jingles before; I did the John Sebastian sound-alike for Ford Motor Company's "Welcome Back" TV ad campaign, I did jingles for Mobil, the Maryland Lottery, PBS, and a ton of others. Joe's productions were stellar, and I thought he'd be a great fit for the project.

Joe and I started working together. We each wrote six songs, most of them were funky, up-tempo, jazzy stuff that had a little hump to it. We recorded the CD in his studio, an immaculate place in the basement of his home outside Baltimore. Joe played keyboards, I played bass, Kevin Levi played sax.

When we did our promo photo, I put on a fake moustache—I kinda liked the way it looked. Plus, I needed a little separation from the Slim Man bankruptcy thing. Maybe folks wouldn't recognize me . . .

When we finished the CD, I sent it to Carl. He loved it. When he asked me what the name of the band was, I told him I didn't have one. But I came up with a name soon after. At the time there was a sax player named Boney James who was doing well. There was also a band named Down to the Bone that was hitting it big. So I thought that anything with "Bone" in the name would be a good luck charm.

So I named the band Bona Fide.

Carl signed Bona Fide to his label; the first CD was named *Royal Function*, and the label's radio promoter picked the first single, a song called "High Street." It did next to nothing. I was surprised when the record company decided to go with a second single, since the first one had failed so miserably, but they did. Carl picked the second single, a lively little number called "X Ray Hip." I named the song after a guy who played basketball at the University of Maryland, and later played for the Harlem Globetrotters. His name was Exree Hipp.

Carl had a good history of picking hits when he was at Motown; he had found an old Stevie Wonder demo, "Until You Come Back To Me" and placed it with Aretha. He found another old unpublished Stevie song, "Tell Me Something Good" and placed it with Chaka Khan and Rufus.

"X Ray Hip" was released and suddenly . . . nothing happened. Again. For weeks, nothing. But eventually, it started climbing the charts, and it kept climbing and climbing. It went all the way to Number One. My first Number One song. It spent one glorious week at Number One on the jazz charts. Nice. The CD started selling like crazy, big gigs were coming in and Bona Fide was taking off.

We won the Best New Artist award at the Smooth Jazz Awards that year.

Show Biz is like a rollercoaster ride. When you first start, you feel all excited and nervous, in a good way. Then, you get turned upside-down and inside-out. You get flipped over, and you flip out.

One second you're flying blind through dark tunnels, the next you're sky-high, going a million miles an hour. You're exhilarated and scared to death at the same time.

Then, the ride's over, you feel sick to your stomach, and you wonder why you ever did it in the first place. Then you get back on the ride and do it all again.

That's Show Biz, kids. Gotta love it.

FLAMING LIMONCELLO SAUCE

When your career is going down in flames, nothing like a little flaming limoncello sauce to help things along.

When I was a kid, I loved to read biographies. My mom gave me a whole set called Childhoods of Famous Americans. They had titles like *Tom Edison, Boy Inventor* and *Abe Lincoln, Frontier Boy*. I loved to read, and for a while there, I loved fire. Fireworks, bonfires—I felt an attraction to flames when I was a kid. My mom told me they should write a biography about me . . . *Slim Man, Boy Pyromaniac*.

It was just a phase. I didn't burn any houses down, but I did set fire to my cousin's bedroom floor once . . . accidentally.

When I'm cooking, I like the occasional explosion—as long as it's intentional! A little Cognac or vodka set on fire. . . . It's a cool crowd-pleaser—as long as nobody catches on fire.

When I first thought about this sauce, I couldn't wait to try it. I like limoncello. It's a bit sweet, a little sour, and it's got alcohol in it. Set it on fire, and it shoots flames in the air. What's not to love?

Seriously? Be careful, my Slim People. I need every one of ya!

Notes:

I did not add salt and pepper to this sauce. Give it a taste after it's done, if you feel like it needs a little something, add some salt and fresh-cracked black pepper.

I put this sauce over fish. I've used it over baked salmon. It's *delizioso* that way. But my favorite? Sole or flounder—both are from the same fish family; they are light and flaky and *delicato*.

I dust each filet with a little flour that's been salted and peppered.

I sauté them in a tablespoon of butter and a tablespoon of olive oil over medium-high heat for a quick minute or 2 per side, or until they are crispy and golden. Golden!

Then I pour a LITTLE sauce over top of each filet and eat *pronto*!

INGREDIENTS

2 tablespoons of butter

2 tablespoons extra-virgin olive oil

2 tablespoons minced shallot

2 tablespoons limoncello

1 tablespoon minced garlic

⅓ cup dry white wine

½ lemon (about a tablespoon of fresh-squeezed lemon juice, remove any seeds)

1 tablespoon fresh Italian flat-leaf parsley, chopped

HERE WE GO!

SCAN THE QR CODE TO SEE THE YOUTUBE VIDEO

Heat the butter and olive oil in a small pan over medium-high heat.

When the butter starts to bubble, add the shallots and cook for 2 minutes.

Add the limoncello.

Grab a long-handled lighter, put on some asbestos gloves and light up the limoncello! Watch the explosion. BE CAREFUL!

When the flames die down, add the garlic, cook for 2 minutes, stir or swirl often.

Add the white wine and cook for 2 minutes, stir or swirl often.

Add the lemon juice and the parsley and cook for a minute.

Done!

Drizzle a LITTLE bit over a piece of baked salmon or sautéed sole and . . .

MANGIAMO!

MINESTRONE
and
The Wild Ride Home

My uncle Oscar and I were real close. He was my dad's only brother; they grew up poor on the streets of New York City, sons of struggling Italian immigrants. Their Mom, Angela, moved the family to Baltimore, Maryland, when she started organizing the ILGWU—the International Ladies' Garment Workers Union. Oscar (I called him "Unc") went to medical school, became a surgeon, and—with a little encouragement from Angela—started a little health care company for the unions that evolved into a really big health care company. Unc made a ton of dough, started with nothing.

I was just a kid when my folks got divorced. My dad moved back to New York, I stayed with my mom in Baltimore. Unc was like a second father to me; he was the guy I turned to in times of trouble, and in the good times, too. He always lived close by; Unc was my doctor, my confidant, and my go-to guy.

When I was a stupid teenager, I was at a party that got busted for under-age drinking. I had just walked in, and the cops came in right behind me—I was the first kid they cuffed. Unc was the guy who bailed me out, he and my mom came and got me. All charges were dropped.

When Unc went out of town, he used to lend me his big, new Cadillac Brougham with the blue velour bucket seats and the wide-whitewall tires. I'd drive around Baltimore, listening to his Tony Bennett tape on the 8-track.

A couple years ago, when I broke up with XF2 (ex-fiancé number two), Unc was the guy I called. He told me to come over, and stay for a while. I ended up staying for a couple years. Oscar was a great cook; he had attended Marcella Hazan's cooking school in Italy. Marcella's cookbooks on Italian cooking are my favorites; she's legendary. He also took other cooking classes in Italy. Unc really enjoyed cooking and enjoyed teaching me; although, if you listened in on a conversation, it might not seem that way. One time, he was showing me how to skin a fish, and I wasn't doing it fast enough.

"Timmer! Come on! Move a little fucking faster, will ya? I want to eat tonight!"

There was a reason I was going so slowly. Oscar had extremely sharp knives; being a surgeon, I guess he was used to razor-sharp instruments. Unc used to send his kitchen cutlery out to be sharpened on a regular basis. You could have performed an emergency appendectomy with one of his paring knives.

He taught me more about cooking and food in those few years than I had learned in my whole life.

I was in my early twenties, living at my mom's house when Unc called me up one night and asked me if I'd ever drank tequila. I told him no; he told me to come over. I told him I'd be right there—you can't refuse a request from The Godfather.

I had an old Datsun station wagon with rusted out floorboards—you could see the ground below on both the driver's and the passenger's side. It was a stick shift, and it backfired when you shifted—sounded just like gunshots.

I got in the car and drove the ten minutes to Unc's house. When I walked in, he was standing in his kitchen with a bottle of tequila and two glasses. He poured us each a shot and then gave me a slice of lime. He put some salt on the skin between my thumb and index finger, and told me what to do—lick the salt, drink the shot, and suck the lime. I did. It tasted like turpentine. Smelled like it, too. It tasted like something you might drink after ingesting poison, so you could induce vomiting. It burned going down, my eyes were tearing up, my throat was on fire, and I had an instant headache.

Let's have another. We stood in the kitchen and drank some more. His wife was upstairs—smart woman. Good-looking, too. Oscar was a sharp dresser, but that night, he was in his bathrobe and he had no drawers on. How did I know?

Unc was not a modest man; he once got naked and went swimming in the river at his 75th birthday party. There were dozens of people there; he just took off all his clothes and dove in.

Me? I have recurring nightmares about being caught naked in public. But Unc? He didn't mind who saw him naked. It wasn't a sexual thing, Unc just didn't see any problem with letting it all hang out; which he was doing that night.

So there we were in Unc's kitchen, drinking shots of tequila, Unc with his bathrobe untied, and I'm starting to feel a little untied myself. Have you ever tried on someone's eyeglasses, and they've got a really strong prescription? And things look really out of focus, and you get a bit of a headache after a few seconds and then feel nauseated?

That's how I felt. We'd had a couple of shots. I must have looked like a seasick sailor because Unc was giving me worried glances. That's when he said, "You don't look so good. I'll give you a ride home."

Oscar loved my mom, so he welcomed the opportunity to give me a ride home. Why we took my car, I don't know. Unc always had real nice cars; why he wanted to drive my old Datsun piece-of-shit that backfired and had rusted out floorboards was a mystery. Unc got behind the wheel in just his bathrobe with no drawers on and started the engine. It backfired; sounded like a shotgun blast. I looked over, and he had a look of glee in his eyes. He took off.

He had a blast driving that car. Every time he shifted, the car would backfire. BANG! He'd let out a holler and a laugh and drive on. You could look down through the holes in the floorboards and see the street zipping by. It made me dizzy. I felt sick to my stomach. But Unc was having a grand ol' time.

He pulled up to my mom's house, parked on the street out front, and I got out and started staggering up the sidewalk to the front door. Neither Unc nor I realized his wife had heard us leave his house and was following right behind us. When Unc got out of my car and started following me to the front door, she pulled up. She jumped out of her car, grabbed him by the back of his bathrobe, put him in her car, and drove off. I was oblivious. I got to the front door of my mom's house, and turned around to let Unc in, and—

He was nowhere to be found. I looked all around, in the bushes, behind the trees, in the car. I couldn't find him. I was baffled. Where the hell did he go? I looked up and down the street. It was late. It was dark. I walked in the front door and walked into the kitchen.

I woke up the next morning, and my mouth felt like several small animals had spent the night in there.

MINESTRONE

After a night of tequila, ain't nothing like a bowl of minestrone followed by a long schnooze. I made this soup last night, and it was the best I ever made, if I may say so myself.

Italians don't use a lot of corn, but I put some in this recipe. Why? Because it tastes really good, and I like the texture and color it adds, too.

Pancetta is Italian bacon. When you cook pancetta, treat it like bacon. Let the pancetta brown on one side, then give it a stir, and try and get the un-browned pieces to brown on the other side. If you don't have pancetta, you can use bacon. If you're a vegetarian, you can leave it out.

I made this dish recently, and the pancetta was cooking too quickly. I threw in a ¼ cup of white wine to stop it from burning, and the minestrone ended up tasting better than ever. So I added white wine to the recipe.

I use fresh oregano. I normally like dried oregano better, but for some reason, fresh tastes best in this recipe.

You can use diced Italian tomatoes, or whole. If you're using whole Italian tomatoes, they'll need to be smooshed. Open the can, pour them in a bowl, dig in with your mitts, and squeeze the tomatoes so they break up. Remove the yellow center core, and any skin or stems.

The chickpeas and the corn are already cooked. All you need to do is heat them up, so add them last.

You can eat this soup as is or you can put some rice or pasta in it.

I used to put the pasta right in the soup and let it cook in there. The only problem was . . . the pasta would end up absorbing all the broth. So if I want pasta in my minestrone, I cook the pasta separately and add it to each individual bowl before serving.

This recipe yields about 20 cups of soup, which is 5 quarts. I think.

INGREDIENTS

6 ounces pancetta cut into small pieces (a generous cup)

¼ cup extra-virgin olive oil plus 2 tablespoons

Crushed red pepper (I start off with ¼ teaspoon)

¼ cup of dry white wine

1 cup each—chopped onion, carrots, celery

5 cloves minced garlic (about 2 tablespoons)

2 cups each—green zucchini, yellow squash, Savoy cabbage—all cut in small pieces (you can use regular cabbage if you can't find Savoy)

1 (28-ounce) can Italian plum tomatoes, smooshed up (about 3 ½ cups)

8 cups chicken broth (you can also use vegetable broth)

2 tablespoons fresh Italian flat-leaf parsley, coarsely chopped

1 tablespoon fresh oregano, leaves stripped from the stems, chopped (or 1 teaspoon dried oregano)

1 (16-ounce) can garbanzo beans (chick peas)

1 cup yellow corn (fresh, canned, or frozen)

¾ cup grated Pecorino Romano cheese, plus some for sprinkling/topping

Salt (I use Kosher)

½ pound small pasta (*ditalini*, elbow macaroni, mini *farfalle*)

HERE WE GO!

Put a large heavy pot (a Dutch oven would work well) over medium heat for 2 minutes. Add the pancetta, cook for 4 minutes, stir just a couple times. If the pan gets dry, add a drizzle of olive oil.

Give it a stir, let it brown for 4 more minutes, stir a few times.

Add the olive oil and the crushed red pepper. Let it heat up for a minute. Stir.

Add the white wine, and let it cook off for 2 minutes.

Turn the heat to medium-low. Add the onions, carrots, celery, and garlic and cook for 10 minutes. Stir, baby, stir.

Add the green zucchini and the yellow squash. Add a drizzle (1 tablespoon) of olive oil. Cook for 5 minutes.

Add the Savoy cabbage, and add another drizzle (1 tablespoon) of olive oil. Cook for 5 minutes.

Add the tomatoes, the broth, and the water. Turn the heat to high. Let it come to a boil, and then reduce the heat to medium-low.

Cook for 10 minutes or so until the zucchini and squash are semi-soft.

Add the parsley and oregano.

Add the garbanzo beans (chick peas) and the corn.

Add the grated Romano cheese.

Let the soup cook for 10 minutes or so.

Taste for salt and pepper and adjust.

Remove from heat.

FOR THE PASTA:

Get a medium-sized pot, fill it with water, and put it on the highest heat.

When the water comes to a boil, add a couple tablespoons of salt (I use Kosher).

Add your pasta. Cook according to the instructions on the box. It might take longer.

When the pasta is done (*al dente*, firm to the bite), drain, and put in a bowl.

Drizzle with a tablespoon of olive oil and stir. You might not use all the pasta.

Dish it up! Get a soup bowl, fill it about ¾ of the way with soup.

Add some pasta to the soup. Give it a stir.

Top with grated/shaved Romano cheese, serve with some crusty bread, and . . .

MANGIAMO!

SALMON ELLA
with
Ella Fitzgerald

Batu and I were hanging out at the Slim Shack. I had a piece of salmon; we were listening to Ella Fitzgerald, and I became inspired, so I created this recipe. I call it . . .

Salmon Ella.

I love salmon. I love Ella. Put 'em both together, and you got Salmon Ella.

One of my top five favorite CDs ever in the history of the world is a CD Ella Fitzgerald did with Louis Armstrong called *Ella and Louis*. It really is one of my favorites. Louis Armstrong changed my life. When I was five years old, my dad took me to a movie called *The Five Pennies*, and I saw Louis sing and play trumpet. I turned to my dad and said,

"That's what I want to do." I wanted to play and sing like Louis Armstrong.

I begged my dad for a trumpet.

A couple weeks later, for Christmas, my dad got me a plastic toy trumpet. I broke it. I told him I wanted a real trumpet, not a toy. A few weeks later, for my birthday my dad rented me a real trumpet; I could hardly hold it up. I had to dig my elbows into my sides when I played. I loved it. I fell in love with music, and we got married soon after. We've been together ever since. It's been a magnificent relationship.

I played trumpet for years; I did Louis Armstrong imitations. I still love Louis Armstrong, and the CD he did with Ella Fitzgerald is great. They did a couple; the first one, released in 1957, is the best of the bunch. It features the Oscar Peterson Trio; Norman Granz produced it (the production is stellar), and not only is it one of the best CDs ever, it has one of the best cover photos ever.

My mom was an incredibly smart woman and a huge hero of mine. She had a tough go of it, yet forged an incredible life without a whole lot of help. When she and my dad divorced, she found herself with three young kids, no job skills, a high school education, and not much else; she didn't even know how to drive.

Still, she picked herself up, dusted herself off, and did what needed to be done. She learned how to drive. She taught herself the skills she needed. She studied the dictionary, the English language, learned how to type, and how to write. She taught herself foreign languages. She started counseling troubled teens at John Hopkins Hospital, and ended up running the psychology department at Johns Hopkins University. Guys with more degrees than a thermometer were asking my mom to help them with papers, articles, and theses.

She didn't have a lot of money, but she managed to travel and had a chance to see the world—that was important to her. Music was also really important to her; she had a nice stereo, and a great collection of music, but she was frugal. She had to be.

When Ella Fitzgerald came to the Lyric Opera House in Baltimore, Maryland, my mom could only afford one ticket, which she bought for me. She thought it was important that I see Ella, so I caught the bus, went downtown to the concert, and saw Ella Fitzgerald sing with the Billy Taylor Trio.

I sat in the balcony, and soaked it all up. It was a thrill. Ella Fitzgerald was a wonderful singer. What a voice; such a pure tone, great diction, and always in tune. Joyful. Girlish. And swinging like nobody's business. Ella scatted better than anybody, her scats were as good as any Miles Davis solo. It was an incredible concert.

Ella didn't have an easy life; she was born in Virginia, her dad left when she was an infant. Her mom died when Ella was fifteen. Her stepdad abused her, so her aunt took her away from Virginia to New York City. Ella took to the streets of Harlem, was a numbers runner and a lookout for a bordello; she was in and out of reform schools and orphanages.

Then she entered a talent contest at the Apollo Theater and won; the grand prize was $25. She became a regular at the Apollo, and things took off from there. She started singing with Chick Webb, a drummer who led a big band. She started recording, and a song she co-wrote—"A Tisket, a Tasket"—became a hit. Ella started singing at the Jazz at the Philharmonic series in New York, concerts put on by Norman Granz, who became her manager and produced those incredible recordings with Louis Armstrong.

Ella went on to win thirteen Grammys, sell millions of records, and tour the world. She was shy and quiet—but strong and determined. She had it tough, but forged an incredible life. Kind of like my mom. Except my mom was never a lookout for a bordello. Not that I know of, anyway.

SALMON ELLA

In cooking, just like in music, sometimes you have to improvise.

I was going to use honey in this sauce, but I ran out. I used maple syrup instead. My dad lived in upstate New York, and he had this homemade maple syrup that was so stinkin' good. So when I ran out of honey, I used a little of my dad's maple syrup instead, and it was really good.

I use low-sodium soy sauce, the other stuff is way too salty.

This is a bold sauce, use sparingly. In this recipe I use it over baked salmon; you can also sear or grill your fish, and then pour a little reduced sauce on top when it's done.

I like my salmon the way I like my women—wild and Alaskan. (There's a joke in there somewhere, it just hasn't come to me yet.)

Salmon are anadromous. That means they are born in fresh water, migrate to salt water, and then return to fresh water to reproduce.

Just thought I'd toss that out there.

INGREDIENTS

1 pound piece of wild salmon filet, skin removed

For the sauce:

½ cup low sodium soy sauce

1 tablespoon chopped scallions/green onions, bottom root and top leaves cut off and discarded

1 tablespoon grated fresh ginger

1 tablespoon minced garlic

2 tablespoons maple syrup

1 teaspoon hot sauce (use less if you don't like it spicy)

HERE WE GO!

SCAN THE QR CODE TO SEE THE YOUTUBE VIDEO

Rinse off your salmon and pat dry with paper towels.

Preheat your oven to 400 degrees.

Mix all the sauce ingredients together. Set aside.

Put the salmon in a baking dish.

Pour half of the sauce over the salmon. Set the other half aside.

When the oven comes to temperature, put the salmon, uncovered, in the oven on the middle rack.

Cook for 10 minutes.

While the fish cooks, put the remaining sauce in a small saucepan over low heat and reduce.

After 10 minutes, the fish should be done. Thinner pieces take less time, thicker pieces take more. Ovens are crazy, too. Some run hot, some run cold.

Test the fish with a fork. When it flakes on top and is firm and pink in the middle, it's done. Some folks like it rare, some like it cooked well. I like it medium-rare.

Dish it up! Put the fish on a nice platter. Drizzle with a LITTLE of the reduced sauce, dress it up with a scallion. My broccoli and peppers would go well with this dish. Or some roasted vegetables . . .

MANGIAMO!

PASTA CARBONARA
and
I Really Love You!

It was by far the biggest paying gig ever offered to the Slim Men; not only that, but the promoter was going to put us up in a nice hotel and buy us all dinner and drinks at the club after the show. The club was called Odessa, it was a fine-dining, elegant nightclub/restaurant in Laguna Beach, California. Swanky.

Because it was so swanky and brand spanking new, and because they were paying us a lot of do-re-mi, we decided to pull out all the stops. We invited some guest soloists—guitarist Richard Smith and trumpet player Tony Guerrero. We made sure our shoes were shined, and our suits were pressed, and our wigs were in place. Showtime!

John E Coale was on drums. The keyboard player that night was David Bach—it was one of his first shows with us. Mombo Hernandez played percussion. It was crowded, a good turnout of Slim People. Odessa had a 1960s supper-club vibe; well-dressed guests sat at well-dressed tables and enjoyed dinner as they watched the show. We were scheduled to do two one-hour sets.

The first set sounded okay—we were just starting to catch our stride when we had to take a break to do a drawing. In between sets, they had scheduled a drawing for dinner with the band after the show. They brought a big fishbowl filled with tickets up to the stage, and I picked a number from the bowl and called it out to the crowd. There was a short silence, and then a guy stood up. He didn't yell or scream; he just stood up and sauntered to the stage.

He was tall and thin, with blond hair. He was dressed casually, and had a loopy grin. When he showed me his ticket I saw he had the winning number. So this guy and his guest were gonna join us for the post-concert dinner celebration—the after-party slurp and chew.

The Slim Dudes went back on stage and did our second set. There were a couple of rough spots; at one point, Richard Smith came up to me after playing guitar on a couple of songs and said, "Nice trying to play with you."

The Slim Men eventually pulled it together, and the crowd seemed to enjoy themselves. After the show, we walked over to the restaurant area of the club. They had a huge table set for us—each setting had more forks and knives than anyone would ever need. I sat next to the couple who had won the dinner drawing.

Normy was kinda quiet and kinda quirky, his wife, Sam, was sweet with a quick smile.

Normy and I started talking, and he told me that he made clay models for Porsche. Clay models are what they use to create the shells for the bodies of actual cars, and Normy worked with the designers making new Porsche sports cars. I'd been to the Porsche factory in Stuttgart, Germany; I did a private party there. Normy had been to the factory, too. We talked about sports cars, clay models, Porsche, Stuttgart, and how Normy did what he did. It was an intriguing conversation.

We ordered lots of food; we got appetizers, and soups, and salads. We drank more than a few bottles of wine. We had main courses. We had desserts. We had after-dinner drinks. It must have been around midnight when the waitress—who had been working so hard all night—gave me the bill. I was kinda embarrassed, but I told her that the promoter was picking up the tab. She told me the promoter was nowhere to be found.

I got up, and started looking around the club; in front, out back, the men's room, the ladies' room, under tables, in the kitchen—I looked everywhere. I called him. I called the hotel. I sent out smoke signals, helicopters, and drones. Promoter-dude had vanished.

So I took out the old credit card, and prayed that the cops wouldn't leap out of the woodwork and arrest me on the spot when it got declined. The wine alone must have cost at least a thousand bucks. Twelve courses for twelve people in a place like that? I was just hoping I wouldn't have to wash dishes for the rest of my life. My card went through, but I didn't want to chance it with a tip, so we gathered some cash, and gave it to the waitress.

We left the club that night a bit weary, kinda dreary, somewhat embarrassed, and a lot lighter in the wallet. We went to our hotel rooms and crashed. The next day, I was checking us all out, and discovered the promoter had not paid for the rooms. Ouch. He never sent me the money he owed us, and it was a lot. I never heard from him again, but I ended up paying the band anyway. It was a huge loss, but . . .

Normy and Sam have become really good friends of mine. We hang out on a regular basis.

They came to Catalina Island a few years ago to see the Slim Man Band at the Jazz Fest. We went out afterwards, and Normy had quite a few festive beverages. In his defense, Catalina doesn't allow cars, people walk everywhere, so everyone tends to drink a bit more than usual. We were playing pool at a local bar when Normy started shouting at the band,

"I LOVE YOU GUYS! I MEAN IT! I REALLY LOVE YOU!"

He kept saying it; over and over, louder and louder. Quiet Norm was so loud and boisterous, that we ended up leaving the pool hall—after some encouragement from the staff and patrons. We walked on to the narrow streets of Catalina and Normy kept on yelling,

"REALLY! I'M NOT JUST SAYING THIS!! I REALLY LOVE YOU GUYS! REALLY!"

Sweet Sam finally dragged him back to his hotel room, Normy screaming "I REALLY LOVE YOU!" all the way.

The next morning, the Slim Man Band had breakfast with Normy and Sam. Normy was unusually quiet, turning whiter shades of pale with each bite. We quietly told him we really loved him, too. Really.

PASTA CARBONARA

I really love this pasta carbonara. Really. Except it's not the healthiest dish in the world. That's why I only eat it a couple times a year. Any more than that, and you'll have to walk around with a defibrillator in your backpack. It's a heart-stoppin', artery-poppin' dish, but it's one of my favorites. This is my own version. I added white wine, which gives it a little kick.

I use Parmigiano-Reggiano cheese. Most recipes call for Pecorino Romano, which I find a little too salty for this dish, so I use Parmigiano, which is a little sweeter.

You'll need a generous cup of diced pancetta. You can trim off any excess fat.

I almost always cook a full pound of pasta, but I only use about two-thirds or so. These days, I like a little more sauce and a little less pasta. I save the plain, leftover pasta for frittatas, or a small pasta salad.

The name *carbonara* comes from the Italian word for coal, *carbona*. Legend has it that coal miners would put a couple of eggs, a piece of pancetta (Italian bacon) and a hunk of cheese in their pockets, and make this dish on their lunch break, using just one pot.

Putting eggs in your pocket doesn't sound like a good idea to me, especially if you're mining, but what the hell do I know?

INGREDIENTS

3 eggs

1 cup freshly grated Parmigiano-Reggiano cheese

2 tablespoons fresh Italian flat-leaf parsley, chopped

Fresh-cracked black pepper

1¼ cups (about ½ pound) of diced pancetta, excess fat removed

Crushed red pepper (I start off with ¼ teaspoon)

4 cloves of garlic, peeled, and smashed/flattened with the broad side of a knife

¼ cup white wine

1 pound of spaghetti (I cook the full pound, but only use about ⅔)

Kosher salt

Extra-virgin olive (a tablespoon, if needed)

HERE WE GO!

We'll do this all in real time.

SCAN THE QR CODE TO SEE THE YOUTUBE VIDEO

Get a large pot. Fill it with cold water. Put it on the highest heat. This is for the pasta. As it heats up . . .

Get a large bowl, one big enough to hold all the pasta and other goodies.

Break the eggs into the bowl. Add the cheese. Add the chopped parsley. Add some fresh-cracked black pepper.

Beat all this goodness with a fork. Now let's cook our pancetta.

Pancetta is Italian bacon, so treat it like bacon. Don't be flippin' it all around. You want it to brown on each side. It's tough to brown pancetta that's been diced, but you can try!

Get a small sauté pan. Put it over medium heat. Put the diced pancetta in. Let it cook until it's brown, about 4 minutes. If the pan gets dry, add a drizzle of olive oil.

Flip it over, give it a stir, and cook until it's brown on the other side, about 4 minutes.

When the pancetta is done, turn off the heat, and use a slotted spoon to get it out of the pan. Put the pancetta in a small bowl and set aside.

You should have some pancetta drippings left in the bottom of the pan. You'll need about a tablespoon to cook the garlic. If you don't have enough, drizzle a little olive oil in the pan.

Put the pan on medium-low heat.

Add the crushed red pepper and the smashed garlic, cook for a minute or 2 until the garlic is golden.

Turn the garlic over and cook for another minute or 2 until the other side is golden.

Turn the heat to high. Add the wine; let it cook off for a minute or 2 while stirring. Turn off the heat.

Now back to the pasta . . .

When the pasta water comes to a boil, add a couple tablespoons of Kosher salt. Add the pasta.

Follow the cooking instructions on the pasta box. When the pasta is supposed to be done, take a piece and bite into it. Look at the center of the pasta. If it looks chalky, it is not done. If it tastes chewy, it ain't done. When the pasta is *al dente*, firm, but not chalky or chewy, drain it well.

IMMEDIATELY put the pasta into the bowl with the eggs and cheese and parsley. You want the heat from the pasta to cook the eggs. Add the garlic and white wine from the small sauté pan. Toss gently. Add the cooked pancetta and toss gently.

Dish it up! Garnish with a piece of parsley, and . . .

MANGIAMO!

SLIM'S HALIBUT FISH STICKS

with
The Babysitter

My sister had all her kids by C-section. They're all pretty normal, except whenever they leave the house, they go out the window.

When the doctors perform a C-section (cesarean section) they make an incision, and bring the baby out via the abdomen rather than, well, you know. They stitch you back up, and instruct you to stay still for a week or so until your incision has healed. When my sister had her first baby, she asked me to babysit for a week while she recovered. I did. I actually enjoyed it, and I told my sister that whenever she had another kid, I'd do it again.

I had no idea at the time that she'd go on to have four more kids—the doctors should have put a piece of Velcro on her stomach. My sister had kids every two years, like clockwork. At one point I was babysitting a newborn, a two-year-old, a four-year-old, a six-year-old and an eight-year-old. My sister used cloth diapers. Not on herself, on the kids. So whenever the kids peed or pooped, you had to take off the diapers, shake 'em out, and put on a fresh one—with safety pins. And then put on a diaper cover. Pampers are easy. Real diapers ain't.

Babysitting five kids is like living in a tornado—it's a whirlwind of activity. Get 'em up, get 'em dressed, make breakfast, get lunches packed, cut chewing gum out of their hair and then get them off to school. After school, you pick them up, drive 'em around to all their after-school activities, go home, make dinner, clean up, make sure they do their homework, and then put 'em to bed. The next day, you get up and do it all over again for the ingrates.

One especially hectic morning, all the kids were running around screaming. I was trying to make sure all five were dressed; I was making school lunches and trying to get everybody ready for school.

I'm not good at breakfast. I can cook you a dinner that will make you cry tears of joy, or at least not make you sick, but breakfast for me is some fresh fruit, maybe an English muffin. I rarely eat cereal, especially the kind kids like to eat—Peanut Butter Cap'n Crunch, Count Chocula. But when you need to feed the little monsters in the morning and you're in a hurry, cereal is quick and easy, you just fill a bowl and grab some milk.

Which is what I did that crazy morning—except when I grabbed the milk carton, it was empty. Well, there was a drop. Kids love to do that; they'll drink out of the carton, and leave the last drop so they won't have to throw it away.

So there they are, five kids seated at the table, bowls filled with cereal, clock ticking, and no milk. The kids had a rare moment of silence. They all looked at me, wondering what I was going to do next. I looked at the clock; we were running way late. I grabbed a liter bottle of Coca-Cola and poured it over the cereal in each bowl. They first looked at me like I was crazy, and then suddenly they all just thought it was the coolest thing in the world. They ate it up. They left the house that morning on the highest of sugar highs.

Breakfast was a crapshoot, but I almost always cooked a nice dinner for the kids in the evening. But one night, I realized we had nothing in the fridge. It was too late to go to the store and come home and cook dinner, so I ordered Chinese food. Only one problem—they didn't deliver out in the sticks where my sister lived, meaning I'd have to jump in the car and go pick it up.

My favorite car ever? My Jeep Wrangler convertible. I loved that car. It was a manly man's car; stripped down of all luxury. No radio, no AC, a canvas top, and canvas doors with plastic windows. It was a rough ride. I loved to put the dogs in the back, smoke cigars and take a drive; when the weather was nice, and you had the top down and the doors off, it was heavenly. I had taken out the back seat, so it was basically a two-seater.

Which posed a problem that night. I couldn't leave the kids home alone while I went to pick up Chinese food, and I didn't have enough seats or seat belts to strap them all in. What to do?

I grabbed whatever helmets they had—football, baseball, bike—and put them on the kids. I put the two youngest in the front seat and strapped them in tight together. The other three I put in the back, and covered them with a big blanket. It looked like I was trying to smuggle illegals. I told them to shut up, and I gently drove to the Chinese place, picked up dinner, and drove back. It was only a few miles. I took it easy on the brakes—I didn't want those kids rolling around the back of the Jeep. I'm just glad I didn't get stopped by the cops. We got home safe and sound; I took off their helmets, and we went inside and ate.

I did an all-ages show one Christmas in Towson, Maryland. The nieces and nephew were just kids; they came down and sat in the front row. It was the first time they'd seen me on stage; to this day I remember how good that made me feel to see them there.

I introduced the kids to the crowd, and then asked them to come up on stage and sing with "Uncle Slimmy." They were mortified. It was the first time I ever called myself Uncle Slimmy; the name stuck. The kids didn't come up on stage that night—but they've been coming to Slim Shows ever since.

I thought they'd have more sense than that.

SLIM'S HALIBUT FISH STICKS

My mom was a great cook. But when she was in a rush to get dinner on the table for us kids, sometimes she'd pull a package of Mrs. Paul's Fish Sticks out of the freezer and heat 'em up. When I was trying to come up with a recipe for a piece of halibut, I decided to cut it into pieces the size of Mrs. Paul's, and make my own fish sticks. I'm a genius, ain't I?

How did fish get to be so expensive? The halibut I used was $28 a pound. That's ridiculous. What's even more ridiculous is using that expensive halibut to make fish sticks, but they are so ridiculously good.

I love panko breadcrumbs. I mean, I don't eat them out of the bag, but they're great for frying. They're light, crunchy, delicious, and have a great texture.

I was getting ready to make this dish a couple days ago. I had some leftover toasted pine nuts from some pesto, so I chopped them up and put them in the panko breadcrumbs. Then I added a little bit of dried dill, and some salt and pepper, and mixed it all up. Man, they were good.

If you don't want to go through all that, you can use plain panko breadcrumbs. I sometimes use a 50/50 mix of Progresso Italian Style panko breadcrumbs and plain panko breadcrumbs.

As far as the fish goes, you can use any thick, firm-fleshed whitefish—halibut or sea bass. Cod would be an inexpensive alternative. The best way to cut these filets is into rectangles, about four inches long and about an inch wide.

Another thing—don't bread the fish in advance. Dip and fry, that's what I say. If you leave breaded filets sitting around, they get gooey and don't fry right. And you know what Nat King Cole said,

"Straighten up and fry right!"

Slim's Quick Dill and Panko Breadcrumbs for Fish

1½ cups of plain panko breadcrumbs

1 tablespoon dried dill

2 tablespoons toasted pine nuts, chopped (toast in a dry pan over high heat while shaking)

½ teaspoon of salt

Fresh-cracked black pepper to taste.

Mix all the ingredients together. That's it!

INGREDIENTS

1 pound skinless halibut filets, cut into rectangular pieces

2 eggs

Salt and fresh-cracked black pepper

½ cup canola oil (or olive oil)

2 cups panko breadcrumbs on a plate (you might not use them all)

HERE WE GO!

Rinse the fish and pat dry with paper towels. Put the fish on a platter.

SCAN THE QR CODE TO SEE THE YOUTUBE VIDEO

Take the eggs, and put them in a shallow bowl. Add salt and pepper. Beat it!

Heat the canola oil in a large pan over medium-high heat. You can use canola oil for this, because it doesn't smoke at high temperatures. But I've used olive oil many times with great results.

Grab a piece of fish. Dip it in the beaten egg, let the excess drip off.

Then roll it in the panko breadcrumbs. Press each side in, make sure the panko sticks to each side of the fish. Put it on a plate.

Do this with all the pieces of fish.

When all the fish is breaded, take a pinch of the breadcrumbs, and drop 'em in the oil. If they sizzle, the oil is hot and ready.

Place as many pieces of fish as you can in the pan. When you see the bottom edges of the fish turn golden brown—2 or 3 minutes—use some tongs and turn them over. Don't fork it—you don't want to lose any of the juiciness, and you don't want the fish to flake apart on ya.

Brown on the other side for about 2 or 3 minutes.

When both sides are golden brown, place on a plate covered with a layer or two of paper towels.

You gotta eat this dish right away. Plate it up right quickly, garnish with parsley, and serve with lemon slices. My Caprese salad is the perfect side for these fish sticks.

MANGIAMO!

AGLIO e OLIO SAUCE (Garlic and Olive Oil)

with Hugh Grant and Drew Barrymore

A couple years ago, they shot a Hugh Grant/Drew Barrymore movie in Manhattan. It was called *Music and Lyrics*.

I heard about the movie from an online casting agency. I was already in Manhattan with Batu doing some cooking shows for the Italian American Network at my cousin's apartment, so I figured—what the hell? I signed on, and ended up being an extra. The movie is what is known as a Rom-Com, a romantic comedy, except nobody was laughing while we were filming. Everyone from Hugh to the crew looked miserable and tense.

Hugh Grant's character had been a pop star back in the '80s—a Wham!-type band—and he was trying to stage a comeback by writing a hit song for a famous young girl singer.

Drew Barrymore was the woman who watered Hugh's houseplants. One day she started blurting out lyrics to the song Hugh was writing on the piano, but Hugh didn't want any help, especially from the plant-watering girl. He was pissed off. They start off hating each other, and then—surprise—they end up writing songs together and falling in love.

Washed-up Hugh is still doing a few Oldies gigs here and there to make ends meet—state fairs, amusement parks—and he gets booked to play a high-end high school reunion. They filmed it in a swanky hotel ballroom in Manhattan, and that's where my scene was shot. They shot the reunion scene in one ballroom, and they had all us extras corralled into another ballroom across the hall.

I saw Hugh Grant quite a bit; they shot the scene dozens of times. They kept playing this song—it sounded just like "Careless Whisper" by George Michael—over and over again, and they kept shooting the same scene for twelve hours. No exaggeration. No wonder everybody looked so miserable and tense; Hugh looked like he was in pain, like he was passing a kidney stone or something. On one hand, I felt for Hugh; doing the same scene twenty-five times in a row is enough to drive you crazy. On the other hand, you're getting paid a couple million bucks to make love to Drew Barrymore.

I wore a white suit and a white shirt. I looked like the ice cream man. Or a Latin American dictator. For twelve hours, I stood around in that stinkin' suit, listening to the same song, over, and over, and over again. Towards the end of the day, I found a big empty room and sat by myself at one of the tables; I was beat, dead-tired from doing nothing. Drew Barrymore walked in with her female assistant, and they sat at my table. There were dozens of other empty tables in the room, but they sat at mine.

We sat there for a few minutes. I looked over every once in a while to wave or say hi, but neither of the women would even look at me; they'd look away. It was weird. The film folks told us not to approach Hugh or Drew, but this was different—they had approached me. I felt like saying,

"Do you come here often?"

"Haven't I seen you before?"

"I'm not wearing any pants."

But I didn't. After about a half hour they both got up and walked away. They didn't say goodbye; they just got up and walked out.

I rented the movie after it came out; the scene we spent twelve hours shooting took up about five minutes of the movie. I guess my big film debut got left on the cutting room floor, because I never saw myself, not once. I did make $84.00 for twelve hours work, which comes to roughly $7.00 an hour. Isn't that illegal?

I thought the movie was pretty good. But I swore I'd never do it again. But a couple years later . . .

I got a call from a casting agent named Joyce. I was living in Nashville, Tennessee. Music City, USA. Joyce asked me if I would like to be an extra on a new TV show that ABC was shooting in Nashville, a show called . . . *Nashville*. She told me they had seen my photos online and liked them. I declined.

Joyce kept calling me. She called and told me the director liked my look. She told me there might be a bigger part available. She called and told me the shoot wasn't far from the Slim Shack. She called me so often, I felt like I was married. I didn't have much going on in Nashville; I was pitching some songs to publishers, making some demos, shopping stuff around. I had a few poles in the water, but nothing was biting, so, I thought, why not? I told Joyce I would do it. She told me where to go and what to wear—I needed to dress like I was going to the Grammys.

A couple days later, early in the morning, I was driving from the Slim Shack to Titans stadium, where the Tennessee Titans play football. There was a holding area for the extras, and there were about a hundred people inside. I signed in, and then we all got on old school buses that drove us to the General Jackson, an old steamboat docked on the Cumberland River in downtown Nashville next to the stadium.

We boarded the steamboat, and went into the concert area—a ballroom on the first level that was decked out with a big raised stage. Tall cocktail tables were scattered around, and there was a second-floor balcony overlooking the whole scene. The assistant director stood up, got everybody's attention, and then described the scene we were about to shoot. An older female country singer, Rayna James, and her young rival, Juliette, are nominated for the same country music award—Female Vocalist of the Year. Juliette—played by Hayden Panettiere—shows up on the steamboat drunk and does her new song on stage, all liquored up. That was the scene.

Hayden/Juliette came out and sang her song. I'll admit this—it was a really good song. I liked it.

I didn't like it so much after hearing it for five hours straight. They shot the scene over and over again. Every time they changed a camera angle, they'd have to re-position the lights, re-position the cameras, and re-position the actors. Then it was time to break for lunch; we all went to the third floor of the boat. There were a couple tables laid out with . . .

Two big tubs of Costco peanut butter and jelly, loaves of bread, Tootsie Pops, and Goldfish crackers. It was a nice lunch—if you were in kindergarten. After about an hour, we went back down to the concert area and shot the same scene over and over again. After about five more hours, at around 10:00 p.m., we broke for dinner—a buffet that wasn't so bad. After dinner, we sat around an empty banquet hall and waited. And waited. And waited. An assistant director walked in, and started looking us over. He looked at me and crooked his finger, so I went over to where he was standing. He whispered,

"We need a guy to play a slick record executive type, an older guy. Are you interested?"

When he said "older guy," I felt like boxing his ears in. But I just said "yes."

He walked me upstairs to where they were shooting the scene. It was being shot on the top deck, which was open-air with a lovely view of downtown Nashville. It was freezing. I stood in a small group of people, around a small table all decked out with flowers and ribbons, and the prop guy handed me a glass of champagne.

I took a sip; it was ginger ale. The director came over and explained the scene; one of the stars of the show, Scarlett, was coming over to talk to this small group of four folks, and I was supposed to have a fake conversation with this girl standing in front of me.

Fake conversation? The director wanted me to move my lips, but not make any sound—they were gonna overdub the voices later. So I had a fake conversation with my fake glass of champagne with this really good-looking girl. We finally wrapped up around 2:30 a.m. I had been on the set for seventeen hours. I drove home, let Batu out, made some *aglio e olio*, and went to sleep.

My scenes actually made it into the show. When I appeared on TV, a friend took a photo of their TV set and sent it to me. There were no reports of people firing handguns at their TV sets when I appeared. I only had a couple minutes of screen time, but I got a lot of messages, phone calls and texts, mostly from my family.

"Hey, Mr. Big Shot, Mr. TV Star! Too good for us now, huh, Donkey Face?"

AGLIO E OLIO

What do Romans fix to eat as a late night snack? *Aglio e olio*, pasta with garlic and olive oil.

This is a great dish to fix after a long hot day of doing nothing on the set.

When I make this dish, I add a little chopped red bell pepper, or yellow bell pepper. Or both. Why? I like the color it gives to this dish. After the sauce is mixed in with the pasta, I add a little chopped fresh Italian parsley. Serves 3. Maybe 2 if you're in my family.

INGREDIENTS

3 tablespoons extra-virgin olive oil

6 cloves garlic sliced thin (about 2 tablespoons)

Crushed red pepper (I start with ¼ teaspoon)

1 red bell pepper (cored, de-seeded, and chopped) about ¾ cup

½ pound pasta (I use *spaghetti*, *penne rigate* works well, too)

2 tablespoons fresh clean Italian flat-leaf parsley—coarsely chopped

Kosher salt

HERE WE GO!

Fill a large pot with cold water and put it on the highest heat you got. This is for your pasta.

As the water heats up, start your sauce.

Put the olive oil in a small saucepan on medium-low heat.

SCAN THE QR CODE TO SEE THE YOUTUBE VIDEO

Add the garlic, the crushed red pepper, and the bell peppers.

Add a little Kosher salt. Stir.

Let the sauce simmer as we make our pasta.

When the pasta water comes to a raging boil, toss in 2 tablespoons of Kosher salt.

Add the pasta.

Stir every few minutes.

Follow the directions on the box of pasta. When it's supposed to be done, take a bite of a piece of pasta. If it's chewy, or chalky in the center, it is not done. When the pasta is *al dente*, (firm to the bite), drain and transfer to a bowl.

Add the sauce, the chopped parsley, and toss again.

Dish it up. The Romans don't put cheese on this dish.

But if your Sweetie McPetey wants freshly grated Parmigiano-Reggiano cheese, save yourself some trouble, just shut up and grate.

MANGIAMO!

ASPARAGUS PARMIGIANO

and

I Want My MTV

Our manager told us about this new television network that was about to launch, a twenty-four-hour network that was going to play nothing but music videos. They were gonna call it . . .

MTV. Music Television.

He played us a few videos that were scheduled for rotation, and asked us if we could do a couple like that. We, the boys in the band, looked at each other and told him, "Yes, we can."

But we didn't have a lot of time; the launch of MTV was about to happen. Our manager was Carl Griffin (Griff), the same guy who signed me to Motown. Our band was BootCamp; we had just released a 7-inch, vinyl single with two songs, "Hold On to the Night" and "I'm a Victim." It was doing really well.

We had no idea how to make a music video; we didn't even know what a music video was until Griff showed us the MTV demo reel. But we knew a guy who worked as a cameraman for the local TV station. He worked in the news van, doing live remotes. We called him, and he told us he could "borrow" the cameras and stuff from the TV station, but it had to be after hours. My guess is that he was gonna borrow this stuff without asking, because he asked us to keep it on the down-low, the hush-hush.

The first video we shot was for the song "Hold on to the Night." I wanted to shoot the video at night (clever!) on The Block, which is a two-block section of Baltimore Street in downtown Baltimore that has strip clubs, adult bookstores, and peep shows. And a hot dog place called Pollack Johnny's. But how were we gonna get Baltimore Street closed down in the middle of the night, when all the action was going on?

I called the Baltimore Police Department and told them we were shooting a movie with Ben Vereen—it was the first name that came to mind. To my surprise, the BPD agreed to shut down the street. Ben Vereen is an actor and singer, he was in Roots—the TV series, not the band—and he was pretty popular in Baltimore, had done a bunch of concerts there. So the Baltimore Police Department put out the order to close Baltimore Street for a few hours for a movie shoot for Ben Vereen.

We showed up with our TV cameraman, and a couple of guitars, and . . . we had no idea what to do. We had no script. We had no Ben Vereen. We had a boom box and an empty street. It started to drizzle, so we pressed "record" and started rolling, in the rain.

Action! We did take after take. The drizzle worked in our favor—it made the street look shiny and slick. The camera guy was really creative, he did takes where he was lying on the wet ground with the camera looking up. He swooped and swerved and shot some crazy footage. Hit Man Howie Z was banging his drumsticks on the side of a trashcan when some garbage got stuck on one of his sticks, and crap started flying everywhere. The cameraman was getting it all, but if he had panned out, you would have seen a sergeant with the BPD standing right next to Howie, yelling at him . . .

"You better clean up all that shit when you're done, son!"

We did some more takes, and . . .

Maybe the cops finally figured out that this wasn't a Ben Vereen movie, or maybe the strippers were complaining about us driving away the customers, but the police put a halt to the filming. They took down the barricades, and traffic started flowing slowly down Baltimore Street again. We left without having any idea if what we shot was good, bad or ugly.

One down. One to go. A friend of mine had just finished working on an Al Pacino movie that was shot in Baltimore, *And Justice for All*. The filmmakers had used an old courthouse and the old Baltimore City jail for the movie, and the sets were just sitting there vacant, waiting to be torn down.

All the props and the furniture had been left behind, completely intact. It would be perfect for the "I'm a Victim" video. Once again, we had to do it all on the hush-hush; we didn't really have permission to use the vacant *And Justice for All* set. We just showed up on the sly and started shooting. Our camera guy had "borrowed" the gear from the TV station once again, and we all sneaked into the courthouse and the jail, and commenced with the craziness.

We just started filming and improvising. The camera guy was shooting everything, trying to get as much footage as possible in the little time we had. We had one camera, that's it; we didn't have any microphones, or audio, we just sang along with a battery-powered boom box. We didn't have any lighting, we didn't have any assistants, or stylists, or producers, or directors telling us what to do, where to go, or what to wear.

At one point, we were filming in an old jail cell, and the door accidentally slammed shut with a CLANG! I was locked inside and they couldn't get the door back open. It freaked me out a bit. I have recurring nightmares about being in prison. They eventually got it open. It was good to be out of jail.

I was just hoping the real cops wouldn't bust in, arrest us for trespassing and send us to a real jail. We wrapped up—no sense in pressing our luck. Once again, we left the shoot with no idea if what we shot was any good.

The cameraman edited both videos on his own. He snuck into the editing suite at the local TV station, and "borrowed" a few hours at a time. He eventually cut all the footage together, and showed us the two videos.

They had a certain charm, for sure. The cameraman did an excellent job, with the shooting and the editing. Our acting wasn't gonna keep Robert DeNiro up at night worrying about us stealing his next job, but the videos had a unique down-home allure. Griff sent them to MTV. We, the BootCamp Boys, didn't think much about it after that. We had no idea how big MTV would become.

When the network launched, MTV included the two BootCamp videos. They were two of the first 100 videos MTV ever played. They put us in regular rotation. MTV caught fire, and we started getting calls—labels, agents, producers.

MTV took off. So did BootCamp.

ASPARAGUS PARMIGIANO

When you've just finished a video shoot outside a strip club, ain't nothing like a little asparagus to make your pee smell funny.

I like to use thin asparagus—the size of a pencil; they're more tender and tastier than the big boys. So try to find asparagus that's not the size of a tree trunk. As a general rule, the larger the vegetable, the tougher it is. If the asparagus are really thick, you'll have to peel the skin off the outer stalks. Use the slim ones!

This dish should serve 4 people, depending on the people. Members of my family eat like horses. That's why I feed them in the barn.

INGREDIENTS

1 pound thin asparagus

2 tablespoons extra-virgin olive oil

Kosher salt

Fresh-cracked black pepper

¼ cup freshly grated Parmigiano-Reggiano cheese, plus a little more for sprinkling

HERE WE GO!

SCAN THE QR CODE TO SEE THE YOUTUBE VIDEO

Rinse off your asparagus and pat dry with paper towels.

Preheat your oven to 400 degrees.

You need to break off the bottom ends of the asparagus. Grab an asparagus spear. Grab one end with your thumb and forefinger, and the other end with the thumb and forefinger of your other hand, and bend until it snaps. Discard the bottom end.

Do this to all the asparagus. Rinse well, pat dry with paper towels.

Put them in a glass or ceramic baking dish.

Drizzle with olive oil, about 2 tablespoons.

Mix them up; make sure each spear is coated.

Add some Kosher salt and some fresh-cracked black pepper.

Mix them up again.

Put the dish in the oven.

Bake for 15 minutes. Check the asparagus, make sure they're done. If they ain't, put 'em back in for 5 minutes. They should be firm, but not crunchy.

Take the dish out of the oven, sprinkle the asparagus with the grated cheese.

Set the oven to broil. Put the dish back in the oven for A MINUTE OR TWO! Keep an eye on these guys!

When you see the Parmigiano start to brown, take the baking dish out of the oven, try an asparagus spear, make sure it's done, and dish it up!

This dish goes well with Slim chicken Marsala, or chicken Milanese, or lemon chicken.

MANGIAMO!

SHRIMP with SPINACH and SUN-DRIED TOMATOES

with Momma Max

My first band was named Momma Max. We were a punk-rock band, although they hadn't come up with that phrase yet. We did a lot of original material, and some covers—mostly songs by our favorite band, The Stooges.

Not Larry, Moe, and Curly. Iggy Pop and the Stooges. "Now I Wanna Be Your Dog," "Down on the Street"—those were just a couple of the Stooges songs that we covered.

Momma Max played a lot at a club called the Bluesette, which was on Charles Street in Baltimore, Maryland. It was a club that didn't admit anyone over the age of twenty-one; the kids that hung out in the club were the kids who didn't fit anywhere else.

Hippies, rock stars, black radicals, black hippies, runaways, dropouts, gays, musicians, artists—it was a crazy mix of young people who found a place to hang in a town where there was nowhere else for kids like that to go. And Momma Max was one of the bands that played the Bluesette. We also played high school dances, festivals, and concerts; but the Bluesette was our hang.

I lived on a dead-end street named Rosebank. There was a kid up the street who played guitar—Rob Grant. A friend of his played drums, and the three of us started jamming in my mom's basement.

My childhood was great; up until the age of fifteen, things could not have been better. I loved school, had great grades, was president of the class, teacher's pet, loved my neighborhood, had lots of friends, rode bikes, had fun, loved my family, played baseball and football, and played lots of music.

Then all hell broke loose.

My folks divorced; the three kids stayed in Baltimore with my mom, and my dad moved back to New York. High school was a veritable hell; I didn't fit in anywhere and was getting in fights almost every day. So I started a band; it was the outlet for my teenage rage. We wrote a lot of angry, aggressive songs.

My dad had a dog named Momma Max, and I thought it would be a great name for the band. Momma Max started playing and word got out. Word of mouth was the way most kids heard about music; Iggy Pop wasn't on the cover of *People* magazine, Led Zeppelin wasn't on the *Tonight Show*. Kids found out about music from other kids, and when word got out about Momma Max, it spread like wildfire, and we started selling out shows.

There was a club outside of Baltimore called the Latin Casino. They occasionally brought in big-name acts, and when they needed a band to open up for Iggy Pop and the Stooges, they called Momma Max. It was a perfect fit; we were ecstatic. We played our hearts out that night, and then we watched the Stooges from the side of the stage. Iggy Pop was in full effect—he came out shirtless, and sang and danced and broke glasses on the floor and crawled around the stage on his bare stomach.

It was an incredibly exciting show. The Stooges did a live recording that night—I found a copy on the Internet. Momma Max was not included, but we did get a couple more gigs out of that show. When we got an offer to open up for the Raspberries at the Latin Casino, we were a little apprehensive, but we took the gig. The Raspberries were a power-pop band, with matching suits and hairdos you could bounce rocks off of. Momma Max was a rough and tumble punk-rock trio. Momma Max and the Raspberries? Not a great fit, but we took the gig—we needed the money.

I brought a date, something I rarely did. She wasn't a girlfriend, but she was beautiful and sexy, and I wouldn't have minded having her as my girlfriend. I thought maybe my chances would improve if she saw me on the big stage.

Momma Max opened the show; people didn't throw rocks at us, but the response was underwhelming. Then the Raspberries came out and did their show. I wasn't too impressed, but they must have made quite an impression on the girl I brought, because at the end of the night, I saw her walking out the back door with the lead singer, Eric Carmen.

Welcome to the glamorous life of Show Biz, kid.

SHRIMP WITH SPINACH AND SUN-DRIED TOMATOES

There's nothing like a dish of pasta after a night of punk-rocking and mosh-pitting.

A couple of things to mention here—I don't use farm-raised shrimp. They taste funny and have the consistency of wet cardboard. Use wild shrimp, as wild as you can get 'em!

You can de-shell and de-vein your own shrimp. It's easy—remove the shell, make a split down the spine, remove the dark vein, and rinse. You can also buy shrimp that have already been de-shelled and de-veined.

I use sun-dried tomatoes in oil. The dry ones soak up too much sauce.

A note about pasta . . . I recently cooked a pound of DeCecco spaghetti (number 12) over the highest heat I had. The directions on the box said to cook it for 10 to 12 minutes. I tasted it after 12 minutes, and it was not done. It ended up taking 16 minutes.

Start tasting your pasta when the directions say it's supposed to be done. If it is chalky in the center, and chewy, it's not done. Keep tasting it every 2 minutes until it's *al dente*, firm to the bite.

I almost always cook a full pound of pasta. I only end up using about ¾ pound for the sauce. These days, I am using a little more sauce and a little less pasta. I put the leftover pasta in the fridge, and use it in frittatas, or put a little butter and cheese on it and serve it to the young'uns—it's my Slim Mac and Cheese.

Let's start cooking. . . .

INGREDIENTS

1 pound large shrimp, de-shelled and de-veined

3 tablespoons extra-virgin olive oil

5 cloves garlic, sliced thin (about 2 tablespoons)

Crushed red pepper (I start off with ¼ teaspoon)

¼ cup dry white wine

Kosher salt

½ cup sun-dried tomatoes cut into small strips (drained of excess oil)

½ lemon (2 generous tablespoons of fresh-squeezed lemon juice—remove the seeds)

3 cups baby spinach

1 pound of pasta; spaghetti or linguine

HERE WE GO!

SCAN THE QR CODE TO SEE THE YOUTUBE VIDEO

Rinse off the shrimp and pat them dry with paper towels.

Let's get the pasta water started. Get a large pot, fill it with cold water, and put it on high heat. As the water starts to heat up, let's make our sauce.

Put a large sauté pan over medium-low heat. Add the olive oil. Let it heat for 2 minutes, then add the sliced garlic and some crushed red pepper. Let the garlic cook for 2 or 3 minutes, until pale gold.

Add the white wine, turn the heat to high. Let it cook off for 2 minutes. Turn the heat back down to medium-low. Add the shrimp. Sprinkle a little Kosher salt on top, and let the shrimp cook for 3 minutes then turn them over.

Add the sun-dried tomatoes; spread them around in between the shrimp.

Take the half of a lemon, and squeeze the juice through your fingers over the shrimp, making sure no seeds get into your sauce. You don't want Aunt Esmerelda busting her dentures on a lemon seed.

Add the spinach. As the spinach cooks down, use a wooden spoon to mix it in between the shrimp. Let it cook for 2 minutes or so until wilted, and remove from the heat. Taste for salt and adjust.

When the pasta water comes to a boil, add 2 tablespoons of Kosher salt, and the pound of pasta. Follow the directions on the box. Taste the pasta. It should be firm, not chalky or too chewy. If it's not done, cook and check every 2 minutes until it is. When it's *al dente*—firm to the bite—drain it in a colander.

Put the pasta in a large bowl, and drizzle it with a tablespoon of olive oil, and give it a gentle toss.

Add half the sauce to the pasta. Gently mix the sauce into the pasta.

Dish it up! Add a little bit of extra sauce on top of each plate.

One of my exes loved to put grated Parmigiano cheese on this dish. I was going to say something to her about how in Italy they don't put cheese on seafood, but I just grated the cheese and kept my mouth shut.

Like my dad used to say, "Nobody gets in trouble by keeping their mouth shut."

MANGIAMO!

POTATO and LEEK SOUP

with
Supermodels in Paris

Hit Man (L) and Jaime (R)

I was walking down the streets of Paris with Hit Man Howie Z when I heard a woman's voice calling my name. This was weird because it was my first time in Paris; I didn't know anybody there. Who the hell could it be?

I turned around and was staring at two of the most beautiful women I'd ever seen. One I knew.

Her name was Barbie, and she used to be a cocktail waitress at a club that Howie and I used to play in Baltimore, Maryland, a place called Girard's. The other gal I didn't know. Barbie introduced us to her friend. When I asked Barbie what she was doing in Paris, she told me she was doing some modeling for *Vogue* magazine. She told me her friend had just been on the cover of *Italian Vogue*. I invited them to dinner that night; it would probably cost every penny I had, but how many times are you gonna have an opportunity like this? Paris? Supermodels?

When Barbie asked me what Howie and I were doing in Paris, I told to her that we were in London, trying to get something going with our band, BootCamp. Howie and I had come over to Paris to meet my cousin, who was having her art exhibited at a gallery. That's what I told them, which was all true, but not the whole truth. The whole truth?

We had rented a cheap flat in London for a week or so. It was me, Howie (drums), Bob (guitar) and a friend of ours named Mac. We were struggling musicians, except for Mac. He didn't look like he was struggling—he was wearing custom silk suits and buying expensive antiques—the rest of us were on a real tight budget.

One evening, we went to a pub and had some drinks. We were having a good ol' time in London Town when I noticed Mac in the corner, talking to some Rastafarian. He gave Mac a little package, and then RastaMan screamed, "RUN!" All hell broke loose.

A couple of British policemen started running towards the pub, blowing their whistles and we took off running. We exploded out of that pub; we ran through yards, gardens, we sprinted down alleys, leaping over cars. It's amazing how fast you move when cops are chasing you. Not that it happens to me very often.

We made it back to the flat—how, I don't know. Turns out Mac had bought some hashish from the Jamaican. It seemed to me like a good time to get out of London, so Howie and I took off for Paris. We decided to get on a Hovercraft to cross the English Channel. A Hovercraft is a huge boat. Massive. It sits on what looks like an immense flat tire; you board the boat, and they inflate the tire, and you start rising and rising, way up in the air.

Then they turn on these gigantic fans on the back of the boat, and it blows you across the water, like you're on a huge inner tube. The English Channel was choppy that day, it was a real rough ride, and Howie was really hungover from the night before.

He laid down on a row of seats behind me. Every few minutes, he'd poke his head up, and each time he did, he was a different shade of green. He looked like he was gonna die. We finally made it across the Channel, and caught a train to Paris.

My cousin picked us up. She's quite an artist, her paintings are intriguing and original and worthy of an exhibition at any gallery. She gave us a ride to the apartment where she was staying with a friend. Her friend's name was Jaime, and he was quite a character; he was an artist, and did surreal paintings, similar in style to Salvador Dali. He had a goatee and long brown hair, and wore scarves and black crushed velvet smoking jackets with colored silk pocket squares. His paintings, his clothes; they were cool, I dug his style.

His apartment was cozy and comfy; Jaime put us up for a couple days.

A few days later, Howie and I were walking down the street when we met the Vogue supermodels. A few hours later, we were in a swanky restaurant in Paris called Chez Georges, and it was intoxicating.

The chef came over to the table and started talking to us. He spoke into a microphone that was hooked up to a small speaker that hung around his neck. I didn't understand a word he said; the speaker was distorted, but it sounded like he was speaking Russian.

We ordered dinner, and it was lovely. One of the many wonderful things about Europe is the way they take their time when they eat out. At the end of the dinner, Russian chef guy came back with a bottle of vodka—no label, just an old, clear bottle with all sorts of stuff in the bottom, black peppercorns, red pepper, green pepperoncini. It looked like birdseed soaking in grain alcohol.

He placed a big metal shot glass in front of Howie, poured it full, and shouted something in Russian. He motioned for Howie to drink, and the table got real quiet. Howie didn't budge. Russian chef barked at Howie again. We looked at Howie. He looked at us, and then looked at the shot glass. He drank.

After he swallowed, his eyes started to tear up, his face turned red and he started sweating. I thought his head was gonna explode. Then the mad Russian turned to me and poured a shot in the same metal glass. I looked around the table. He barked something in Russian and I picked up the glass and drank it all down. It was like swallowing a red-hot piece of charcoal. My throat was on fire, my eyes watered, and I felt like I was gonna projectile vomit. But I didn't.

After dinner, we invited the girls back to Jaime's apartment. That's when the circus began. We walked in the front door, and Jaime had a certain look in his eye.

Howie and I were hoping that maybe he would be going off to bed. No such luck. I think Jaime had other things in mind. We poured some drinks, and then Jaime turned on the charm, full blast. He moved in real close to the girls and started with the French flattery. They didn't understand a word Jaime was saying, but his intentions were loud and clear. He was making moves that Pepé Le Pew would have been proud of.

I think Jaime must have scared them, because those supermodels hurried out of that place like it was on fire. If they had leapt from the balcony, I wouldn't have been surprised.

Howie and I never saw them again. Just as well, I guess. Supermodels must be expensive girlfriends. Should I pay the mortgage? Or buy her a new handbag? Get health insurance? Or get her a new pair of shoes?

POTATO AND LEEK SOUP

If you're looking for a French dish to cook after two supermodels have just walked out of your life, have I got a dish for you. The French call this *vichyssoise*.

This soup is so quick, so easy, so inexpensive to make, I can't believe I don't make it more often.

You can serve it hot. You can serve it chilled. You can serve it at room temperature. You can serve it chunky, or you can put it in a blender and serve it smooth. It's delicious, which is the most important thing.

The last time I made this soup, I thought it needed a little crunch on top. So I cut a leek into matchstick-size pieces, dusted them with flour that I had salted and peppered, and fried them for about a minute.

When I served the soup, I stuck the slivers into the soup so it looked like a little teepee in the center of the bowl. My dad would have smacked me on the back of the head and given me grief over that, but they tasted great, and it looked cool.

You'll need 4 leeks for the soup.

Cut off about an inch of the white root at the bottom, and cut off most of the green upper part of the stalks. You'll have about 6 or 7 inches or so of stalk left. RINSE WELL, especially in between the leaves.

Peel off the outer leaf of each leek. You'll use these for the garnish. You'll also see just how dirty leeks can be. You gotta clean 'em up!

Chop the stalks into chunky pieces, which should give you 4 cups for the soup.

Slice the leaves you pulled off into matchstick size slivers—you'll fry these for the garnish.

INGREDIENTS

For the soup:

4 tablespoons butter

4 cups chopped potatoes

4 cups chopped leeks

4 cups chicken broth (or vegetable)

Salt and pepper

For the fried leeks:

4 tablespoons of olive oil

¼ cup of flour

4 whole leek leaves, cut into matchstick-size slivers

Salt and fresh-cracked black pepper

HERE WE GO!

Let's do the soup first.

Put the butter in the bottom of a large pan over medium-low heat. Add the 4 cups of chopped potatoes, and the 4 cups of chopped leeks.

SCAN THE QR CODE TO SEE THE YOUTUBE VIDEO

Cook for 10 minutes, stir often.

Add the broth—I used chicken—and put the heat on high. When the soup comes to a boil, reduce the heat to medium-low, add salt and fresh-cracked black pepper, and cook for 30 minutes. Stir often.

While the soup cooks, let's sauté our leek slivers.

Get a sauté pan, put the olive oil in the bottom, and turn the heat to medium-high.

Put the flour on a plate and add salt and pepper.

Put the leek slivers in the flour, roll 'em around, shake off the excess, and place in the sauté pan.

Cook for about 30 seconds to 1 minute, until golden brown, then turn them over and cook for another 30 seconds to 1 minute on the other side until golden brown.

Remove them from the pan and place them on paper towels.

Now back to the soup.

When the soup has cooked for 30 minutes, it should be done. Stick a fork in a piece of potato to make sure. Taste for salt and pepper and adjust.

At this point, you've got a decision to make—smooth or chunky. In cold weather, I like it chunky and hot. In hot weather, I like it smooth and cool, like a supermodel.

If you want it chunky, take a slotted spoon, or a masher, and mash the potatoes and leeks, right there in the pot.

If you want it smooth, put the soup in a blender and give it a couple of pulses. If you want it chilled, stick it in the fridge for a little while.

Put some soup in a bowl. Garnish with the fried leeks—make a little teepee in the center. Serve the soup with some hot and crusty bread and . . .

MANGIAMO!

SWORDFISH with CAPERS and WHITE WINE

and Cal Ripken, Jr.

I grew up in Baltimore, Maryland, about three miles from Memorial Stadium. The Baltimore Colts played football there; it's also where the Baltimore Orioles played baseball. My brother and I were huge fans of both teams; but going to a football game required the presence of an adult; fans at football games can get rambunctious.

But baseball games? They were a lot safer and gentler for a ten-year-old kid.

In the summertime, my brother and I would go to Orioles games by ourselves, just the two of us. We were way too young to drive, so we'd get to the stadium anyway we could; walk, ride a bike, or take the bus. We'd get there early, so we could catch batting practice. We'd stand out in the left-field bleachers with our gloves, two raggedy young kids, hoping to snag a batting practice home run, or a foul ball. Anything.

My brother and I collected Orioles baseball cards. We belonged to the Junior Orioles. When we played baseball in the backyard, we'd take the names of our favorite O's players. My brother wanted to be called "Brooks" after Brooks Robinson (third base). I wanted to be Paul Blair, a black centerfielder. He was my favorite player. Paul Blair once threw me a baseball during batting practice after I screamed, "Hey, Paul, throw me a ball!" about 300 times in a row. I'm surprised he didn't try to bean me.

Section 9 was our spot for baseball in Memorial Stadium—the outfield bleachers, the cheap seats. There were rows of pale yellow aluminum benches with no backs and no padding; when the weather was hot, it was like sitting on a stove, when it was cold, it was like sitting on a block of ice. It didn't matter to us. We loved the O's. Still do.

My brother and I played little league baseball for years; we played on a team called the Tigers. At the beginning of the season, we'd go over to the coach's house. He had a big trunk of mismatched jerseys and pants, and we'd all go over to the trunk and try to find something that fit, while Coach stood in the corner, smoking cigarettes.

My brother was really good; he got all the trophies. I wasn't any good, but I loved playing. I always liked batting cages. A batting cage is a fenced-in cage; one end is open, and about sixty feet away is a pitching machine that throws baseballs at you. You stand at home plate and try to hit them with your bat; I used to carry a Louisville Slugger—a wood bat—around in my car.

One summer, my band BootCamp was playing at a club in Ocean City, Maryland. There was a batting cage right behind the club. I had to try it; there was no way I was gonna miss an opportunity like that. The afternoon before our Big Show, the drummer, Hit Man Howie Z, and our friend Roger—who would later name his only son Brooks—went down to the batting cage. We three were the only ones there.

I was wearing a thin, baggy, nylon bathing suit and a T-shirt. It was the beach; it was summer. I grabbed my bat, put my money in the machine, and stepped into the cage. This was hardball; I was staring at an eighty mile-per-hour fastball machine. I stood next to home plate, bat poised, waiting for the first pitch. It catapulted out of the machine and screamed towards me.

I swung, and hit the ball with all my might. The ball shot straight down, hit home plate, and shot straight up like a rocket and hit me squarely in the you-know-whats.

I hit the ground like a sack of cement. I curled up in the fetal position, racked in pain, breathless. I couldn't have screamed if I wanted to. But fastballs were screaming over my head, smacking into the backboard, and bouncing all around. Hit Man and Rog were trying to grab me in between pitches, trying to avoid getting hit by eighty mile-per hour fastballs. My legs wouldn't uncurl. They eventually dragged me—still curled up tight in the fetal position—by my feet, out of harm's way.

For the rest of the day, I was on the couch in the dressing room, still curled up in the fetal position. I couldn't eat. I couldn't walk. I could barely talk. The BootCamp show that night was not as lively as usual; I sang while standing in one spot, all night long. If I ever get back into a batting cage, I'll be wearing a cast iron codpiece.

Cal Ripken, Jr. played shortstop for the Orioles in 2,632 consecutive games—without an injury—which is pretty incredible because about twenty times a day, a pitcher is throwing a hardball as fast as he possibly can within inches of your body. Day after day, hitters smack baseballs directly at you; balls as hard as rocks travel at blinding speeds as you try and field them. And for years and years, Cal never got injured, never took a day off. It's an amazing streak, one that will probably never be broken.

Cal was raised in a small town north of Baltimore called Aberdeen. My first girlfriend was from Aberdeen; I used to play music in clubs in Aberdeen. Cal Jr. played baseball at Aberdeen High, and I had heard about him way before he got to the major leagues. When the Orioles drafted Cal, everybody was so excited about the hot new prospect. I went to see him play at Memorial Stadium more than twenty times in his rookie season. He won Rookie of the Year that year, 1982. The Orioles won the World Series the next year. Not a bad first two years for young Cal. I was a big fan.

About ten years later, I was driving to downtown Baltimore to see my dentist, who's also a good friend. I thought I'd bring along a copy of the *End of the Rainbow* CD, which I'd just released. His office was in a luxury high-rise, he was on one of the top floors. The views were amazing, but it never seemed to matter much when you were tilted back in the chair, kicking your feet in the air while he was pinning you down doing a double root canal.

I parked in an underground lot, and got in a limited access elevator—it only went to the top two floors. Guess who got in right behind me? Cal Ripken, Jr. I introduced myself, told him I was a big fan. He shook my hand, and I gave him the *End of the Rainbow* CD that I was saving for my dentist. I told Cal it was my first CD; he gave it a look, and thanked me.

Not long after, the Orioles asked me to sing the national anthem. I was honored. "The Star-Spangled Banner" almost always brings tears to my eyes; it was written in Baltimore at Fort McHenry. And singing the anthem is a real privilege, plain and simple. Singing the anthem for my hometown team in their hometown park? Heavenly. I immediately accepted.

I practiced "The Star-Spangled Banner" day and night for weeks. My neighbors probably thought I was either really crazy, or really patriotic, or both. I tried singing the anthem every way I could. I sang it high. I sang it low. I sang it fast. I sang it slow. I sang it half-fast, which is the way I normally sing.

The day finally arrived. I got to ballpark that September evening, and a young woman from the Orioles office led me on to the field. The sky was cloudy, it looked like it might rain. Hit Man was with me, so was Roger. So was Griff, the guy who signed me to Motown—he's a huge baseball fan. My mom, in her wheelchair, was in the stands nearby; she was a big Orioles fan and used to listen to the games on the radio in the kitchen at Rosebank.

The players were standing by as I walked up to the microphone at home plate. The crowd stood on their feet, hats off, hands on hearts, and then the announcer introduced me, and I started singing. I did "The Star Spangled Banner" Slim Man style—low and slow. The woman who had led me on the field kept waving her arms in a circle, motioning for me to speed it up. She looked like a third base coach waving a runner home.

But, like Frank Sinatra, I did it my way.

I thought it sounded good. The anthem is not an easy song to sing. At least I remembered all the words. When I finished, I walked by Cal Ripken Jr., who was warming up outside the dugout.

He smiled, shook my hand and said, "Nice job, Slim."

"Thanks, Cal."

I went to watch the game with my mom.

SWORDFISH WITH CAPERS AND WHITE WINE

A couple things . . . before you buy or cook your fish, take a sniff. It should smell like the sea. Fresh. Your nose knows. When in doubt, throw it out.

Swordfish sometimes has small, dark areas. I cut these out. They tend to taste really fishy. You can use any firm-fleshed whitefish—halibut, sea bass, or grouper.

Cooking times are always approximate. The thicker the fish, the longer it takes.

Serves 3.

INGREDIENTS

3 pieces of swordfish, about ½ pound each, about 1 inch thick, skin removed

1 tablespoon extra-virgin olive oil

1 tablespoon butter

Flour (a ½ cup is more than enough)

2 tablespoons minced shallots

2 tablespoons capers, plus a tablespoon of their juice

2 tablespoons chopped fresh Italian flat-leaf parsley

¼ cup dry white wine

Salt and fresh-cracked black pepper to taste

HERE WE GO!

Rinse off the fish, and pat dry with paper towels. Sometimes frozen fish retains water, so pat dry until the paper towel is not damp.

Heat your oven to the lowest possible temperature, which is usually 170 degrees. The oven at Slim's Shady Trailer Park has a "keep warm" setting that works nicely.

Heat the olive oil and the butter over medium-high heat in a sauté pan, big enough for all 3 pieces of swordfish. Let the olive oil and butter heat until the butter starts to bubble, about 2 minutes.

While it's heating, put some flour on a plate. Add a little salt and pepper to the flour, mix it up.

Press each piece of fish into the flour, lightly coating each side. Lightly!

Put each piece of swordfish in the pan.

Cook for 2 or 3 minutes, depending on the thickness (thicker pieces take longer). Grab your tongs, pick up the fish. Swirl the olive oil and butter in the bottom of the pan before you put the fish back in. You don't want to put it in a dry pan.

Turn the fish over, put it in the pan. Cook for 2 or 3 minutes.

Remove the fish to a plate. Put it in the warm oven.

Add the chopped shallots to the pan (the one you cooked the swordfish in) and cook for 30 seconds or more until golden brown.

Add the capers and their juice, cook for 30 seconds or more. Then add the parsley and white wine, and cook for 2 minutes.

Turn off the heat under the pan.

Remove the fish from the oven.

Dish it up! Put a piece of swordfish on a plate.

Pour a little sauce over top of each piece of swordfish.

Add a circular slice of lemon (remove the seeds), and a sprig of fresh Italian parsley**.** My incredible Italian kale recipe goes well alongside this fish dish, or maybe my amazing spinach and almonds recipe. Or perhaps Uncle Slimmy's rock 'em, sock 'em broccoli and peppers? Yes indeedy!

MANGIAMO!

PASTA e FAGIOLI
and
Pretend You're Dead

Christmas Eve was always a whole lot more fun than Christmas Day for me.

My uncle Oscar threw these crazy Christmas Eve parties. They were the highlight of my year. I loved partying with Unc, loved being around the family.

This is how it usually went down . . . I'd arrive around 7:00 p.m. at Oscar's house on Cat Tail Creek. The trees that line the gravel driveway would be twinkling with Christmas lights. I'd park the car and walk up the front steps. The door would be unlocked, but I'd ring the doorbell anyway. The "Theme from The Godfather" would chime inside.

I'd walk in the door and yell "Zio!"—Italian for "uncle." He'd yell "Timmer!"—which is what he called me. We'd open the wine; he'd start cooking, I'd try to help, and Oscar would constantly yell at me, "What the fuck are you doing? That's all wrong! I give you one thing to do, and you fuck it up! Let me show you how it's done. Shit, Timmer!"

It may not sound like fun, but it was.

The rest of the family would be there, along with wives, girlfriends, boyfriends, and husbands. Oscar was King of the Castle and I was jester and troubadour. Those parties were so much fun.

One Christmas Eve, I had a show at the Rams Head Tavern in Annapolis, Maryland. Annapolis is a bayside Colonial town, right on the Chesapeake Bay. Annapolis is my mom's hometown; Oscar's house was not far away. The Rams Head Tavern is one of the coolest small clubs in the country—it holds about 300 people, and has been voted best concert venue in the world under 500 seats many times. It's one of my favorite places to play.

Oscar had booked a bunch of tables, front and center, for the Slim Christmas Show. The whole family was gonna come. I was at Oscar's house, getting ready to leave for the show that night when all of a sudden—

Everyone started getting sick. Violently ill. Almost everyone in the house was suddenly under severe and violent gastro-intestinal distress. One minute, someone would be feeling perfectly fine, and then suddenly, the attack would occur. It was disgusting. People were trotting around in a panic, and folks were banging on bathroom doors—from the inside and out. It was not very festive; I was just glad it wasn't from something I cooked.

As much as I wanted to stay, I had to leave for the Big Slim Christmas Show. When I left, one of the Slim Family—true story—was laying on a rug outside the bathroom door, doubled over and moaning.

Merry Christmas. Love you!

I drove to the Rams Head. I felt fine, but apparently, a lot of folks in the area had the stomach virus too, because there were some empty tables at the Rams Head that night, even though it was sold-out. None of the Slim Family showed up—they all had the stomach bug. I had brought a date to the Rams Head; we had been going out for a few weeks. The Slim Man show went well. So did the date.

After the Rams Head show, the two of us went back to Oscar's house. It was as quiet as could be, everybody had gone to bed. There was no one in the huge living room, but the fire was still glowing in the fireplace. I stoked the fire, so to speak, and Slim Gal and I sat on the couch in front of the glowing embers, the Christmas tree twinkling in the corner of the room. After a few minutes, I grabbed a couple pillows and a blanket from the couch, and we lay down on the rug in front of the fire. I put the blanket over us; it was very snuggly. Things started heating up, and some outer layers of clothing were shed to ward off the heat prostration.

The house was dead silent, everyone was sleeping, and it was so romantic, quiet, and lovely in the middle of the night.

"Twas the night before Christmas, and all through the house, not a creature was stirring not even a mouse."

That's when the creatures started stirring. My dad came out of his bedroom and sat on the couch, just a few feet away from us. He turned on the TV, which was next to the fireplace. My dad is deaf, *duro d'orecchio*, the TV came on and the sound was so loud you could hear it across the bay. The volume was deafening and startling; my dad, of course, had no idea.

My cousin's extremely large Rottweiler started barking furiously, and came bounding down the stairs, heading right for me and Girly-Girl. I rolled on top of Slim Babe, pulled the blanket over our heads, and whispered in her ear, "Pretend you're dead!"

I really did say that. The dog came over and sniffed. Someone came down the stairs and let the dog out. Some other Slim Family members started wandering out of their bedrooms, wondering what all the commotion was about. They had to have seen me on the floor, I guess everybody thought it was just me under that thin cotton throw.

Slim Gal and I were trying hard not to laugh. Of course, no one would have heard anything over the blaring TV, anyway.

"Phil! Phil!! PHIL!!!"

Somebody finally got the remote from my dad, and turned the TV off. Some folks started milling around the kitchen, getting water and Kaopectate and Pepto-Bismol, and then everybody went back to sleep. My dad went back to bed. There was a short symphony of gaseous emissions coming from the various bedrooms, and then things got real quiet again.

We started getting cuddly again, as the fire glowed. Things began to get a bit amorous—

Until Oscar's wife came running out of her bathroom, waving a plunger over her head, screaming that the toilet had backed up and was flowing all over the bathroom floor. Everybody leaped out of bed, and started charging around. Folks were bounding down the stairs; people were grabbing rolls of paper towels, buckets, and mops and dashing in and out of the bathroom. It was pandemonium.

The Slim Babe and I were still lying on the rug in front of the dying fire, hiding under the small blanket, hoping nobody would notice us. They finally got the toilet plunged, got the mess cleaned up, and went back to bed.

We waited for a few minutes, to see if any other craziness might occur. There was no more vomiting. No more trots. No more TVs blaring. No more toilets overflowing. It was finally quiet. Finally!

" 'Twas the night before Christmas and all through the house . . . "

But the vibe was busted. The fire had gone out—literally and figuratively. I walked her to the door and gave her a big Slim Kiss.

Soooo . . . how do you like The Family?

PASTA E FAGIOLI

The Slim Babe who was with me that Christmas Eve by the fire? She made a great *pasta e fagioli*, and she had some of the best cooking instincts I've ever witnessed. Oscar let her have free reign over his kitchen, which is something he didn't even give me.

I love this soup. It is *perfetto* around the Holidays when the family is gathered around the table, exchanging blows.

Fagioli is the Italian word for "beans." So *pasta e fagioli* means "pasta and beans." Some folks just call it *pasta fagioli*. Some Americans call it *pasta fazool*.

One of my favorite Dean Martin songs is "That's Amore." There's a line in it that goes like this . . .

"When the stars make you drool just like *pasta fazool*, that's amore!"

It's a really good song, and this is a really good soup. The main ingredient is beans, so a big bowl of this might not be a real good idea right before a long car ride with the family.

I've made this dish two ways, one with beans, and one with beans and ham. They're both pretty harkin' good, if I may say so myself. A couple things . . .

I cooked this yesterday. I went to the store and bought what I needed, and went back to Slim's Shady Trailer Park. When I opened the cans of beans and poured them in a bowl, they didn't look right. They looked kinda gray, so I took a bite of one and it tasted like soggy cardboard.

I've never actually tasted soggy cardboard. I'm not encouraging anyone to go out and taste it either. All I'm saying is, the beans didn't taste good, so I took them back and bought another brand. They looked great and were *delizioso*.

Here's my point. If you're making *pasta e fagioli*, and beans are your main ingredient, make sure they taste good before you toss 'em in there. This goes for all recipes.

Slim People! You gotta give things a taste before you get started. Maybe not with raw chicken, but most of the time, give your main ingredient a sniff and a chew. When in doubt, toss it out.

This recipe calls for pancetta. Pancetta is bacon. You want to cook pancetta just like you'd cook bacon—brown it on one side, then brown it on the other. When you're using pieces of pancetta, it can be tricky. Try and get it browned on all sides.

You can use a whole piece of pancetta and dice it. I recently used a package of Boar's Head sliced pancetta, and cut it in slivers, it tasted really good. You can use bacon, if you need to substitute. If you're a vegetarian, just leave it out.

Another thing . . . the rinds of Parmigiano-Reggiano cheese really make this soup delish. Parmigiano-Reggiano is ridiculously expensive, but ridiculously good. I cut the rinds off a piece of cheese that I had in the fridge. One rind was about the size of a playing card, the other was a little smaller. I put them both in the soup. Make sure you take them out when the soup is done, because you don't want to serve a big old gnarly cheese rind to your uncle Oscar.

If you don't have cheese rinds, you can give a generous sprinkling of freshly grated Parmigiano-Reggiano cheese on top of each bowl when you serve it. When I use cheese rinds in the soup, I usually don't add any extra cheese.

But if your Snarlin' Little Darlin' wants some cheese, just shut up and grate.

And finally! I've never cooked a turkey, but I once bought a ham for the Holidays. There was a lot left over, so I trimmed almost all the ham off the ham bone, and removed as much fat off the meat as I could. I had about 2 cups of chopped ham and a ham bone. I put it in my *pasta e fagioli* and it was heavenly. If you want to add ham to your *pasta e fagioli*, go ahead. Pork and beans go together, like cheese and crackers!

Serves 6.

INGREDIENTS

4 ounces of pancetta, diced

3 tablespoons extra-virgin olive oil

1 cup each—chopped carrots, chopped celery, chopped Spanish/purple onion

1 tablespoon minced garlic, about 4 cloves

¾ cup dry white wine

1 tablespoon chopped fresh rosemary

1 (28-ounce) can crushed/diced Italian tomatoes (San Marzano are best)

1 large rind of Parmigiano-Reggiano cheese (or 2 small)

2 (15-ounce) cans of cannellini beans

1 quart chicken broth (or vegetable broth)

Salt (I use Kosher, *mazel tov*!)

¼ cup fresh chopped Italian flat-leaf parsley

½ pound *tubetti* (or any other small pasta like *ditalini*, small elbow macaroni)

OPTIONAL: 2 cups or more of chopped ham, and a ham bone

HERE WE GO!

SCAN THE QR CODE TO SEE THE YOUTUBE VIDEO

Get a large Dutch oven or a large heavy soup pot.

Put the heat on medium, and add the pancetta. Let it cook for 3 or 4 minutes, then give it a stir and let it cook for another 3 or 4 minutes. We want the pancetta to brown, so you don't need to stir it but once or twice. If the pan is too dry, you can add a drizzle of olive oil.

When the pancetta has browned, turn the heat to medium-low and add the 3 tablespoons of olive oil.

Add the carrots, celery, onion and garlic. Give 'em a stir. Let 'em cook for 8 minutes. Stir occasionally.

Turn the heat to medium-high, and add the wine. Stir, stir, stir for 2 minutes.

Add the rosemary and let it cook for 2 minutes. Stir, stir, stir.

Turn the heat to high, and add the tomatoes, cheese rinds and the beans. Stir gently a few times. You don't want your beans going all mushy.

OPTIONAL: you can add 2 cups or so of chopped ham, and a ham bone.

When it all comes to a boil, put the heat on low and simmer for 10 minutes. Stir gently just a couple of times.

Add the chicken broth and a teaspoon of salt. Stir gently a few times.

Put the heat on high, and when it comes to a boil, lower the heat to low and let it simmer for 10 minutes. Stir gently just a few times.

Remove from heat, and add the parsley.

Now would be a good time to remove the cheese rinds and the ham bone (if you used one).

Some folks like to cook their pasta right in the soup. I prefer to cook it separately, and add a little to each bowl, and stir it in. Some Lady People I know are avoiding pasta these days. Sophia Loren loved pasta, and she's been sexy her whole life. Just thought I'd toss that out there.

Cook the pasta according to the directions on the box. When the pasta is *al dente* (firm to the bite), drain it, put it in a bowl and drizzle with a LITTLE extra-virgin olive oil, about a teaspoon, and mix.

Put some soup in a bowl. Add a little pasta and give it a stir.

If you haven't used cheese rinds, now would be a good time to add a little freshly grated Parmigiano-Reggiano cheese. Or a little Pecorino Romano, and . . .

MANGIAMO!

SALMORIGLIO SAUCE over SEARED SEA BASS

with Batu the Singing Dog

Baked grouper

Seared sea bass

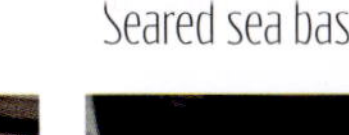

Back in the mid-1990s, a guy named Art Good—jazz DJ and promoter—organized a Christmas tour, and asked me to join. Peter White was on guitar, Freddie Ravel on piano, and Paul Taylor on sax. Most of these guys started off as sidemen with other bands—Al Jarreau, Earth Wind and Fire, Al Stewart. Peter White played guitar on the Al Stewart song "The Year of the Cat," which I liked to call "The Year I Got Fat."

I agreed to do the Christmas tour, but was a reluctant participant. I didn't know a lot of Christmas music, and I didn't know any of the guys in the band. I wasn't looking forward to being away from the Slim Shack for the month of December, so when the tour started, I was just counting off the days, like a convict waiting for his release.

I didn't really get into the swing of things until about halfway through the tour when we did a concert at the Timberline Lodge in Mount Hood, Oregon. It looks like a haunted castle and was featured in the horror movie *The Shining* with Jack Nicholson. Heeeeere's Johnny!

The snowdrifts outside were six feet tall, and the fireplace inside was big enough to cook a moose. The interior of the lodge was stone and wood; the band was set-up on a small stage, and folks were gathered around. The fire was roaring, the eggnog was pouring, the lights were twinkling, and we started playing Christmas songs. Peter White was the bandleader. It was a magical show, if I do say so myself. We closed with "White Christmas"; people started singing along, it began to snow, and I thought Bing Crosby was gonna walk out on stage and start crooning,

The Christmas Spirit. It hit me right between the eyes that night. Bing! I suddenly got it. When I finished the tour, I decided to do a Christmas CD.

I recorded the first Slim Christmas CD, *All I Want for Christmas*, in the home studio at the Slim Shack. It was the first time I'd had my own studio, and I was loving it; being able to record any time, day or night, was luxurious.

The first person I asked to play on the first Slim Christmas CD was Herb Alpert. I loved the albums he did with the Tijuana Brass. I played trumpet along with those records when I was a kid, and thought it would be great to have Herb play on a song or two. I got a nice rejection letter in the mail. I got Randy Brecker from the Brecker Brothers to play instead. He did a great job on "Christmas Time Is Here."

I asked Peter White to play guitar on "White Christmas"—what else? I sent the song to Peter in L.A., and he sent back his guitar tracks. They sounded great, except I kept hearing an alarm going off in the intro of the song . . . beep-beep-beep-beep. I thought maybe I was going crazy—well, crazier—until I played Peter's guitar track all by itself. You could hear his electronic watch beeping, clear as day. There was nothing I could do to get rid of it. So, if you're listening to "White Christmas" and you hear an alarm beeping, don't get alarmed.

A few years later, when I decided to do a second Slim Christmas CD, I knew exactly what I wanted to call it. *Christmas Eve*. Christmas Eve was always the Big Deal with the Slim Family. My uncle Oscar threw the best Christmas Eve parties. I had a title for the CD, now what? I didn't have a home studio anymore—I had moved. I was still living in Baltimore, Maryland, but I was in this wonderful apartment in an old mansion in Roland Park with three bowling alleys off to the side.

But no studio.

I called up my true blue amigo Marc Antoine. He has a really nice studio in his house in Madrid. He invited me over. It was an overnight flight, but I didn't sleep a wink. I have a hard time sleeping on airplanes; I'm afraid I might nod off and start drooling on my neighbor.

Marc picked me up at the airport, and we drove right to a coffee shop in his small village outside Madrid. It was nine in the morning. He ordered two *Liquore d'Hierbas*.

Liquore d'Hierbas is a strong, boozy beverage made from herbs. What kind of herbs? I didn't know, and didn't want to know. The bartender put a couple pieces of ice in a brandy snifter and poured what looked like antifreeze over the cubes. I took a sip. It tasted like cough syrup, smelled like old grass-clippings, and had a punch like Muhammad Ali. It knocked me out; the rest of the day was a haze.

The next morning, I woke up in the guest bedroom at Marc's house. I walked downstairs to the basement studio, and the sound that was coming out of the speakers brought tears to my eyes. Marc had been working all night on guitar parts, and they sounded so good. What a wonderful present; it was like waking up on Christmas morning.

Except it was July and 100 degrees outside. Madrid was in the middle of a heat wave.

Marc played guitar on a whole bunch of songs on the *Christmas Eve* CD. My favorite? "Baby, It's Cold Outside." His guitar playing is inspired on that tune. Stellar. Now all I needed was a woman to do the duet with.

I flew back to Baltimore. I was in the kitchen, cooking and listening to Christmas music, when I heard a gal's voice coming from my speakers. She sounded great, kinda girlish, reminded me of Ella Fitzgerald, with a hint of Rickie Lee Jones. I looked at the CD; it was an old Christmas compilation that had a song of mine—"All I Want for Christmas"—on it. I had never listened to the CD. I looked at the credits to see who the girl singer was. Antonia Bennett. I did some digging on the Internet, and found out who she was. Her dad was a singer, a guy named Tony Bennett.

I reached out to Antonia's manager. He put me in touch with her, and I called Antonia and told her what I wanted; I wanted to do the duet, but I wanted her to sing the man's part, and I wanted to sing the woman's part. She liked my Big Idea.

I booked a studio on 57th Street in New York, a vintage analog studio where Ella Fitzgerald had recorded. The engineer set up two microphones facing each other. Antonio sang looking at me, and I sang looking at her, the way they used to back in the old days.

"Baby, It's Cold Outside."

We only did a few takes. I could have stayed there for another hour or ten. Antonia has a wonderful voice, beautiful blue eyes, and long, red, wavy hair.

The engineer told us he had what he needed, and loved what we did. He suggested Antonia and I go out for a drink, and come back when he was done doing what engineers do. Antonia and I went to Trattoria dell'Arte, an Italian place down the street, across from the old Motown offices and Carnegie Hall. We had a few drinks, had a chat, and went back to the studio. We listened to the song; it sounded better than I ever could have imagined.

Antonia and I walked outside, and said our goodbyes. I hailed her a cab, and then drove back to Baltimore.

I decided to do a video for the title track. I borrowed Oscar's Dean Martin dolls; he had two Dino Dolls, you pressed a button on the base, and they would sing and dance. Batu and I drove from Baltimore to Ocean City, Maryland. Summer was coming to an end. My friend Clubby Clubb had a house on the bay with a big fireplace, and we started a raging fire in that fireplace, and started filming the "Christmas Eve" video right in front. We did dozens of takes, and Batu was in almost every shot.

I had on a white velvet tux jacket; I was drenched in sweat. Batu was panting like crazy. It was hot as hell, outside and in. I was hoping and praying that Oscar's Dino dolls wouldn't catch fire. The video took all day, but we got the footage we needed.

I put the video on YouTube. It got 20,000 hits in the first few days.

Probably because Batu was singing in the video.

Who doesn't love a singing dog?

Salmoriglio Sauce over Seared Sea Bass

One of the Slim exes didn't like anything that was fried or sautéed. She didn't like anything that had butter in it. She loved salmon, though; she ate salmon so often that she started to get an orange glow to her skin, and she became really good at swimming upstream.

It was a challenge trying to cook for her. But I was determined to find a sauce that would go with salmon, and that would meet all her requirements.

I created this sauce last night, and it is so good. The Slim ex would have loved it. Too bad we broke up before I perfected it.

Salmoriglio sauce is a Sicilian sauce usually used on grilled swordfish. It is a simple sauce that I managed to Slim-mify. The sauce calls for white wine, but in an intense moment of inspiration, I thought it would be great to use moscato instead of white wine.

Moscato is a slightly sweet Italian white wine that you can buy sparkling or flat. I used a sparkling moscato that worked so well in this sauce that I'm giving myself a gold star. And moscato is not expensive! Plus, you use a ¼ cup of moscato for this sauce, and you and your funny little honey can drink the rest. Party time!

If you don't have moscato, or would prefer something drier, use a dry white wine or Prosecco—an inexpensive Italian sparkling white wine.

I used Meyer lemons, which are absolutely delicious. They are sweeter and milder than normal lemons. If you can't find Meyer lemons, use a ripe, soft, regular lemon, but I strongly suggest you seek out the Meyer lemons.

The sweetness of the wine and the tartness of the lemon worked so well together.

I used this sauce on baked grouper and on some seared sea bass. I used a ½ pound of each. I cooked both fish at the same time, to do a little taste test. They were both delish.

Bake:

To bake the grouper, I put about a tablespoon of extra-virgin olive oil in a small glass baking dish. I rubbed the olive oil over the grouper, and salted and peppered both sides. I put a thin circular slice of Meyer lemon and a sprig of fresh oregano in the bottom of the dish. I placed the piece of grouper on top of the Meyer lemon and the oregano sprig.

I took a couple tablespoons of moscato and added it to the bottom of the dish, and squeezed a little Meyer lemon juice into the dish—not directly on the fish—to add a little moisture while it was baking.

I baked the grouper for 20 minutes at 400 degrees. It was a thick piece—about 3 inches, so it took a while. When it was done, I took it out of the oven, and spooned a little salmoriglio sauce over the fish. *Delizioso*!

Sear:

To sear the sea bass, I cut it into 3 smaller pieces, each about 3 inches square. Keep in mind, thick pieces take longer to cook than thin pieces. You can place a piece of aluminum foil loosely over the pan if you want to cut down on the splattering.

I salted and peppered the top side, and then I sprinkled a little bit of brown sugar on top.

I put a tablespoon of butter and a tablespoon of extra-virgin olive oil in a sauté pan over medium-high heat.

When the butter started to bubble, I put the salted/peppered/sugared side down first, and cooked the sea bass for 3 minutes. As it was cooking, I sprinkled the tops of each piece with a little salt, pepper and brown sugar.

After 3 minutes, I used a spatula to turn over the sea bass.

I seared the other side for 3 minutes.

When it was done, I spooned a little salmoriglio sauce over top. Wow. She was a-so nice!

Grill:

You can use this sauce over grilled fish as well. Swordfish would work well. Heat your clean, lightly oiled grill to medium-high. Rub your swordfish with a little extra-virgin olive oil. Add some salt and pepper. Place your fish on the grill and cook for a few minutes—don't move it around! We need those grill marks.

Flip it over—carefully—and grill the other side for a few minutes, don't move it around.

Remove the fish from your grill and drizzle with some salmoriglio sauce.

Baked, seared, grilled—this sauce goes well with them all. You can also use this sauce on red snapper, salmon, or any thick, firm-fleshed fish you like.

I roasted some beets to go along with this dish. I just cleaned them, peeled them, cut them in quarters, added a little olive oil, some salt and pepper, and roasted them in the oven for 30 minutes at 400 degrees.

INGREDIENTS

¼ cup of olive oil

¼ cup of Moscato sparkling wine (plus a few tablespoons for the baking dish—if you're baking)

3 tablespoons fresh-squeezed Meyer lemon juice (remove all seeds)

1 teaspoon minced garlic

1 teaspoon dried oregano

2 tablespoons chopped fresh Italian flat-leaf parsley

Kosher salt (to taste)

Fresh-cracked black pepper (to taste)

A couple sprigs of fresh oregano (to place under the fish, if you're baking, plus a few for garnish)

A few circular slices of Meyer lemon (one to place under the fish if you're baking, plus a few for garnish)

HERE WE GO!

Put the first 8 ingredients in a small bowl and whisk.

Put a small saucepan over high heat.

Pour the sauce from the bowl into the pan.

SCAN THE QR CODE TO SEE THE YOUTUBE VIDEO

When the sauce starts to bubble, reduce the heat to low and simmer for 5 minutes. Stir a couple times.

Remove from heat.

That's it!

Spoon a little sauce over baked grouper, seared sea bass or grilled swordfish, and . . .

MANGIAMO!

BOLOGNESE SAUCE
and
Noclothesaphobia

Michael

Fleur, Christian, Petite Louis

A few years ago, I did a New Year's Eve gig in Austria. It was organized by Michael van Droff; Michael and his business partner, Christian Chaléat, run a record company in Germany called Wave Music. They've used a lot of my songs on their compilation CDs, and Michael, Christian, and I have become great friends over the years.

Michael asked me to do a New Year's Eve gig at a mountaintop resort outside of Salzburg. It's called Hotel Vollererhof, and it is one wonderful place. There is a small hut in the woods behind the hotel where they have parties. I was scheduled to do a New Year's Eve concert in the party hut; I flew in a couple of days before and left a couple days after.

Michael drove from Germany with his very pregnant wife, Daniela, and Christian drove in with his French wife, Fleur, and their infant son, Petite Louis. We all stayed in a private villa next to the hotel. The villa was unbelievable—too many bedrooms, each with its own fireplace, bath and balcony, overlooking the Alps. The floors were marble, all the fixtures were brass, and the rooms were huge.

It was luxurious and the views were breath taking. They treated us like movie stars, brought us special desserts—the kind where they use blowtorches and pyrotechnics to create impressive, jaw-dropping, heart-stopping sweets. Incredible.

The hotel was also incredible. They had an indoor-outdoor saltwater pool; you started swimming inside, and you could dive down and swim through a tunnel to the outdoor side. When you surfaced, you were outdoors; the pool was steaming and surrounded by a few feet of snow. You could get out of the pool, jump in the snow, and jump back into the warm salt water, which is what I did—a bunch of times.

The hotel also had a salt cave, a eucalyptus shower room, a steam room, and a sauna. The first time I walked into the sauna, I was the only one there. I had a towel around my waist, and sat down for a few minutes. I decided to lie down on the wooden bench; I was so relaxed, I was almost asleep. Then I heard the door open. When I turned my head, I was looking at the genitalia of a naked man standing right next to me. His boys were dangling right level with my eyeballs.

My first thought was . . .

There should be a warning system in place for things like this. In golf, they yell "FORE!" to warn you that a golf ball is about to bust you on the noggin. In a sauna, they ought to yell "INCOMING!" or something like that to warn you that an old naked guy is about to bust in waving his sausage and peppers in front of your face.

My second thought was . . .

When my dad got to be a certain age, he didn't mind who saw him naked. I took him clothes shopping one afternoon, and he left the dressing room door wide open while I picked out some clothes. When I got back, he was completely naked, anybody could see in, and the store was crowded.

I don't think he was trying to point out that we shouldn't be ashamed of our naked bodies. I think he was trying to torture me. It was like he was saying, "This is what you're gonna look like one day!" It freaked me out a bit.

It's probably why I have a fear of being caught naked in public. I think it's called noclothesaphobia. I'm a little bit shy when it comes to waving the *braciole* out there for the whole wide world to see, so whenever I went into the spa, I kept my towel around my waist.

One day we wanted to go sledding; the hotel had a huge tractor take us all to the top of the mountain, and we went back down the slopes on old wooden sleds. Everybody went—Christian and his wife, Fleur, and their infant son, Petite Louis; Michael's wife, Daniela, pregnant as could be, even went down the slopes. It was an amazing sleigh ride—it felt like we had stepped back in time. Old wooden sleds going down the ancient Alps.

One frigid afternoon, we took a trip into the town of Salzburg and saw the house where Mozart was born; a small townhouse, painted pale yellow. Salzburg was freezing cold that day; we walked down narrow cobblestone streets and drank warm booze-spiked cider that we bought from streetside stands. People were having fun—Christmas had just been celebrated, and it was the party week that happens right before New Year's Eve. On New Year's Eve, we all had a quiet dinner in the hotel, and then walked along a narrow snow-lined path through the woods to the small party hut.

I sang and played piano for the guests—about fifty folks. After I finished my set, Michael came on, and started spinning records. The only people left were The Villa Crew (Daniela, Christian, and Fleur) and the help—waitresses, waiters, and busboys—and we had a blast. The young Germans and Austrians know how to party. We danced until the sun came up.

And then we all went back to the Killa Villa, and I cooked in the incredible kitchen. What did I cook? Well, the Germans and Austrians have a thing for pasta Bolognese, you see it on the menus in all the restaurants. It's everywhere. So the first thing I cooked, on the first day of the New Year? Pasta Bolognese. Happy New Year!

BOLOGNESE SAUCE

My dad sent me a newspaper interview with a restaurant owner in New York. The guy told the story about his Bolognese sauce; it was an old family recipe, and he served it at his restaurant, but didn't have it on the menu.

He didn't put it on the menu because the recipe was all wrong. There was too much red wine; there were too many tomatoes. He was afraid the critics might beat him up over it. So he left it off the menu, but people loved it and ordered it all the time.

I tried to recreate the recipe from the article. I've cooked this recipe dozens of times. I tried using less red wine, and fewer tomatoes, but it wasn't as good. A couple weeks ago, I made two batches—one with the normal amount of wine and tomatoes and one with half the amount.

I had my family and friends taste both batches—blind taste-tests. The sauce with more wine and more tomatoes won. Hands down, even though it's all wrong, according to the experts.

Here is the recipe with lots of wine and tomatoes. You can cut the wine and tomato amounts in half if you like.

You'll need to smoosh your tomatoes first. Open the cans of Italian tomatoes and put them in a large bowl. Roll up your shirtsleeves and start smooshing and squeezing them by hand, one by one. Remove the thin V-shaped bitter yellow core in the center. Remove any skin—they should already have the skin removed, but sometimes there is a little left over.

Finally, I used imported Italian pancetta, and it was really good, not a lot of fat, and had beautiful color. You can use Boar's Head, or a similar brand of American pancetta, if you can't find imported pancetta.

In the video, I use a little more butter than I do now. These days, I need to stay . . . Slim.

VARIATION: When I'm feeling meaty, I sometimes add a ½ pound of ground pork to the pound of ground beef.

INGREDIENTS

½ pound of pancetta, chopped into small cubes, excess fat removed

3 tablespoons butter

3 tablespoons extra-virgin olive oil

1 cup each—chopped onions, celery, carrots

3 cloves garlic, minced, about 2 large tablespoons

½ cup dry white wine

1 pound of ground beef

1 small can (6 ounces) tomato paste

2 cups dry red wine

2 (28-ounce) cans of whole, peeled Italian tomatoes (about 7 cups), San Marzano are best

4 cups stock (I use organic beef stock)

1 pound pasta (I use *rigatoni*)

Kosher salt and fresh-cracked pepper

HERE WE GO!

Put a large heavy pot—a Dutch oven or similar—over medium heat for 2 minutes.

Add the pancetta and let it brown for about 4 or 5 minutes.

SCAN THE QR CODE TO SEE THE YOUTUBE VIDEO

Give it a stir and cook for another 4 or 5 minutes. Think of pancetta as bacon—you wanna try and cook it one side until it's a little crispy, and then flip it over, and cook it on the other side. If the pan gets dry, add a splash of olive oil.

When the pancetta has browned, you can drain off most of the fat, if there is any. If there's not a lot, I leave it in.

Add the butter and olive oil, heat until the butter melts.

Add the onions, celery, carrot and garlic.

Cook for about 5 minutes. Stir, stir, stir.

Add the white wine, and cook for another 5 or 10 minutes until the vegetables are soft. Stir occasionally.

Add the ground beef. If you're also using ground pork, add it now. Break up the ground meat with a spoon. Add a little salt and fresh-cracked black pepper.

Think of the ground beef as a hamburger. Cook it on one side until it's golden brown, about 5 minutes, then stir it up and cook it for another 5 minutes. Break it up again with a wooden spoon.

Stir in the tomato paste.

Cook for 5 minutes, stirring occasionally. It should look like Sloppy Joes—Italian Sloppy Joes.

Add the red wine and let it reduce for about 10 minutes. Stir occasionally.

Add the tomatoes, including all their juices.

Add the stock and turn up the heat to high.

When the tomatoes and stock come to a boil, reduce to a simmer and cook for 2 hours.

Stir occasionally.

When done, skim off the fat, if there is any.

Let's cook our pasta . . .

Put some cold water in a large pot over high heat.

When it boils, add a couple tablespoons of Kosher salt.

Add the pasta and follow the directions on the box. When it's supposed to be done, taste the pasta. Grab a piece and bite through it. If it's chalky in the center, it is not done.

When the pasta is *al dente* (firm to the bite), drain it in a colander and transfer to a warm bowl.

Add a tablespoon or so of olive oil, and stir.

Add some sauce, three or four ladles, and mix it up.

Dish it up! Add a dollop of sauce on top of each plate, and then, if you want, add some grated Parmigiano-Reggiano cheese and . . .

MANGIAMO!

CODFISH CAKES

with

Sherlock Bones, Pet Detective

LOST DOG!!!!!!!!
NEEDS MEDICATION!!!!!!!

BLACK AND WHITE BULL TERRIER

RED COLLAR FRIENDLY REWARD

NAME: BATU

PLEASE CALL WITH ANY INFO----

I had let Batu out into the back yard like I had done a thousand times before. But this time, when I called him, he didn't come. I had just had arthroscopic knee surgery.

I went outside and called Batu's name again and again. Nothing. So I started looking; I grabbed my crutches, and started hopping around the neighborhood like a fool, looking everywhere. I ended up walking for miles. I started to panic as night fell; I had no idea where he was, or what had happened.

Batu is not a street dog, he doesn't know about cars and traffic, or anything like that. He did have a bright red collar with my name and number on it, but nobody called. As night fell, I started making calls to every shelter, every vet, every place I could think of.

Nobody had seen him. Batu is hard to miss, he's a unique-looking dog. He's a bull terrier; there are only about 1,500 in the U.S. I couldn't sleep that night, so I got up and made a poster. That morning, I put them all over town—Baltimore, Maryland. I lived in the city, in a neighborhood called Roland Park. The house had a creek out back, with woods and a trail, and there was a tiny alley in front of the house.

I put up posters everywhere; I started out close to the house, and kept widening the circle. I put up posters on every telephone pole, grocery store, and 7-11 I could find.

No calls.

That second night was hell; I checked my phone a thousand times. I had no idea what had happened to Batu. A neighbor told me she heard he got hit by a car in the alley and had bolted into the woods.

That night my phone rang, and they told me they got the number from Batu's collar. My heart soared.

Until they told me Batu was not attached to the collar. They had found the collar in a shopping mall three miles away, but somehow, the collar had fallen off his neck. They got my number off his dog tag, which was still attached to the collar, which was not attached to Batu. My heart sank.

I got on my bike and rode over to where the collar had been found, and started calling his name, handing out flyers to anyone who would take them, posting them anywhere I could. That night, the third night, I couldn't sleep, so I grabbed a flashlight, got on my bike, and started riding around, calling out his name.

"Batu!"

I'm surprised I didn't get shot. There I was, riding around the city of Baltimore on a bike at 2:00 a.m., waving a flashlight around, screaming, "Batu!" in the dead of night.

Still there was no sign of Batu. I was sick with panic—it was an extremely hot summer, and Batu didn't do well in the heat. Plus, he had a heart condition—an enlarged heart. He was on medication, medication that he needed. I called pet detectives, including Sherlock Bones (true). I called pet psychics. I called every shelter and every vet over and over. I even rented a large animal trap and put it where Batu was last seen. I put up more posters. I placed classified ads.

Two girls called me up, Rebecca and Angela—they had seen one of my posters and offered to help. It was clear that these two attractive young ladies loved dogs and somehow felt a connection to Batu. We started canvassing the city. We drove. We walked. We biked. We hiked.

Still no Batu. It was now four days.

Every vet, every pet detective, every professional dog person I contacted told me that after three days, I might as well give up hope—hardly any dogs are recovered after that long. That didn't stop me from looking—I tried twice as hard. I went to the best neighborhoods, where there were only mansions, and I went to the worst neighborhoods, where there were only crack houses. Seriously. In both places I got funny looks—a crippled white guy on a bike handing out flyers offering a reward for a missing dog. I didn't care.

Rebecca and Angela were in constant contact and helped whenever they could. We were becoming friends, but there was still no Batu. I was terrified. Five days with no food, no water, and without his medicine. I searched high and low, night and day. I couldn't eat, and I couldn't sleep. I lost ten pounds.

When Angela and Rebecca got off work, they'd help me search. Six days turned into seven days as time crawled by. I was depressed and desperate, so I called my friend, Tim, who was a meteorologist at the local TV station and he made a mention on the air.

I got a call that night, someone had seen Batu in their yard in Guilford, one of the nicest neighborhoods in Baltimore, about three miles from the Slim Shack. I drove like James Bond over to the sighting. Rebecca and Angela met me there. We looked behind the house, and there was Batu. I called out his name.

He bolted, took off like a cheetah. We chased after him, but he got away. We looked for hours. Angela and Rebecca went home, but I kept looking until dawn. Then, I went back to the Slim Shack, printed up more posters, and papered all of Guilford. I'm surprised I didn't get arrested. But I didn't give a shit.

After that, I went back to the shack and crashed; I hadn't slept in days. Then my phone rang. A woman introduced herself, Baltimore City Councilwoman Maggie McIntosh, and then she told me she had seen Batu in her neighbor's backyard in Guilford. I jumped in my Jeep and burned rubber. When I got to the house, Maggie McIntosh was there, and she pointed to the neighbor's backyard. There was an iron fence around the yard, and Batu was inside. How he got in is still a mystery. I called his name, but he didn't even know who I was. When I held out one of his treats, he came running. I loaded him into the Jeep.

Batu ate the whole box of biscuits. No wonder. It had been nine days; in the middle of summer, in the middle of the city, with no food, no water, and no medicine. I called Rebecca and Angela, and they met me at the Slim Shack. We had a little party. We drank, we laughed, we cried, and we danced.

Actually, it was Angela who danced. Turns out this really attractive, sexy, dog-loving Italian babe was also a belly dancer. So many prayers answered in one day.

After our little celebration, I took Batu to the hospital. They put him in the DICU, the Doggy Intensive Care Unit for four days. He was emaciated, dehydrated, malnourished, had some internal injuries. He really needed Intensive Care.

So did I when I got the bill.

CODFISH CAKES

In Baltimore, where I spent most of my Slim Boyhood, almost every little neighborhood grocery store had "coddies"—codfish cakes—on the counter by the cash register. The two ingredients were codfish and mashed potatoes. The "coddies" were on wax paper, displayed on a tray, along with Saltine crackers and plain, yellow mustard.

Herman's, the basement grocery store down the street from my grandmother Angela's house, had them. I loved 'em.

When codfish went on sale a few weeks ago at the local grocery store near Slim's Shady Trailer Park in Palm Springs, California, I thought it would be a great time to create my own codfish cake recipe. I call my new creation . . .

Slim Man's Cod Pieces.

INGREDIENTS

6 cups water

3 medium Yukon gold potatoes, cut into 2-inch cubes (about 2 cups)

1 pound codfish filet, skinless, cut into 2-inch cubes (about 2 cups)

2 tablespoons butter

Kosher salt

Fresh-cracked black pepper

4 tablespoons extra-virgin olive oil

1 tablespoon minced garlic

2 tablespoons minced shallot

1 tablespoon chopped fresh rosemary

1 egg

½ cup of panko breadcrumbs

Flour (½ cup should do)

HERE WE GO!

Get a large pot, put in 6 cups of water or so, and put it on the highest heat. Put the taters in the water and let them cook as the water comes to a boil.

SCAN THE QR CODE TO SEE THE YOUTUBE VIDEO

When almost tender—it took mine about 10 minutes after the water came to a boil—add the fish cubes. That's right, put the fish right in the boiling water with the potatoes.

Cook for 5 minutes.

Drain in a colander.

Put the fish and the potatoes in a bowl, add 1 tablespoon of butter, and salt and pepper, and mash coarsely.

IMPORTANT! Keep it chunky! If it's too smooth, the codfish cakes won't fry right.

Let it sit until it's warm to the touch.

As it cools, get a sauté pan and put it over medium heat. I used a 10-inch pan.

Add 1 tablespoon of butter and 1 tablespoon of olive oil.

When the butter starts to bubble, add the garlic and shallot.

Sauté for 3 minutes until the shallots are clear and the garlic is pale gold. Stir a few times.

Add the rosemary and let it cook for 2 minutes. Stir a few times.

Take the shallot/garlic/rosemary mixture that's in the pan and add it to the codfish and potatoes.

Mix it up, but keep it chunky.

Grab your egg, put it in a bowl, and beat it.

Add the beaten egg to the codfish and taters, and mix.

Add the breadcrumbs and mix by hand.

If the mixture is too liquid, add more breadcrumbs.

When the mixture feels right—not too wet, not too dry—make cakes.

I like my cakes about the size of a tangerine. This recipe yielded 8 codfish cakes.

Put the codfish cakes on a plate.

Take the sauté pan that you used for the garlic/shallots/rosemary.

Put it over medium-high heat.

Add 3 tablespoons of olive oil.

As the oil heats up, get a flat plate, and put the flour on it.

Lightly dredge each codfish cake in the flour. Make sure each side is lightly dusted with flour.

When the olive oil is hot, put the cakes in the pan, and sauté for 3 minutes or until the bottoms are golden brown.

Flip 'em over—be gentle—and cook on the other side for 3 minutes or until golden brown.

Place on paper towels when done.

Serve with spicy brown mustard, or plain old yellow mustard like we used to do in Bawlmer!

MANGIAMO!

ASPARAGUS PORTOBELLO and GORGONZOLA SAUCE

with Mombo

(L-R) Giorgio, Kevin, John E, Mombo

The first time I saw Mombo, he pulled up in an old VW bus in a cloud of exhaust smoke and dust. He got out holding two large paper bags and said, "Anybody hungry?"

The night before, the Slim Men had played the State Theater in Modesto, California. I had never been to Modesto before: the radio station there was playing a lot of songs from the first Slim Man CD—*End of the Rainbow*, so I called them up to see if there were any places to play in Modesto. They told me about John Griswold.

John was, and still is, a valiant promoter of the arts. I called up John, and he booked me—sight unseen—at the State Theater, a timeless Art-Deco movie theater that had been renovated. It was beautiful, with red velvet seats, a big wooden stage, and a balcony overlooking everything. The first Slim Man show there was a blast. After the show, a young lady came up to me and said,

"My husband plays percussion. He's really good. You should have him play with you sometime."

I looked at the sparkle in her eye and said,

"Tell him to show up in Sacramento tomorrow. We've got a show there at the California State Fair."

The next afternoon a VW bus pulled up to the side of the outdoor stage as we were waiting to do our sound check. A large Mexican-American man got out, introduced himself, and asked us if we were hungry. We went into the dressing room, which was a small trailer to the side of the stage. Mombo pulled out some burritos the size of footballs. John E Coale, faithful Slim Man drummer, and Rick O'Rick, loyal Slim Man keyboard player, looked at the huge burritos.

We each ate one. Mombo had made the burritos himself. They were delicious. Turns out Mombo owned a small restaurant in a nearby town called Lodi. After we finished the big burritos, we went out to do our sound check. Mombo set up his congas and bongos, and we, the Slim Men, did our sound check. Mombo sounded good. Really good.

The year was 1996. Those first few Slim Man Tours were pretty crazy—we were on a real tight budget. It was basically John E, Rick, and I traveling around the U.S. in an Isuzu Rodeo, packed to the max with all our gear. We'd add a sax player, a trumpet player or a percussionist wherever we went.

It's always an adventure when you go on stage with someone you've never played with before, especially when you're playing for a big crowd in a town you've never been to. And that's what we were facing as we took the stage that night in Sacramento. It was a pretty summer night, the stars were out, and the large stage was facing a sea of people. The announcer introduced us, the lights went up, and we started playing. From the first note, Mombo played his heart out. He fit in like he'd been playing with us from day one. Mombo has played just about every gig the Slim Men have done in California since then.

Mombo and I have become great friends. A man who loves music and cooking? What's not to love? His wife, Kim (I call her Kimbo) and their daughters have a special place in the Slim Heart. To this day, we all keep in touch on a regular basis. This great friendship happened because Kimbo had the guts to ask me if Mombo could play with us. I took a chance on an unknown guy, and it paid off big. John Griswold took a chance on an unknown band named Slim Man, and not only did he open up a new market for us to play, John and I have become true blue amigos. It all worked out magnificently. Better than I ever could have imagined. How lucky can one guy be?

I learned two very important lessons that first night with Mombo in Sacramento. One was to keep an open mind—open to new people, places, and experiences.

The other thing I learned that night was—don't eat a burrito the size of a football before a big show. There was enough gas on that stage to get us halfway across the country.

ASPARAGUS, PORTOBELLO AND GORGONZOLA SAUCE

This sauce would be great in a burrito. An Italian burrito!

When we did our first tour, we played in San Francisco at the very cool Great American Music Hall. It was a real thrill, our first big crowd, our first big show. A couple nights later, we had dinner with Kent and Keith Zimmerman at a really nice Italian restaurant in a fancy hotel in downtown San Francisco, where the doormen dressed like the Swiss Guard.

Keith and Kent are twins, they were editors at a music magazine called *Gavin Report*, a magazine that tagged me as "A male Sade." Kent and Keith wrote a lot of good stuff in *Gavin* about the Slim Man CDs. They also wrote a lot of good books together. I read their book about Sonny Barger, the guy who started the Hell's Angels motorcycle club. It's a good read. They just finished a book about Earth, Wind and Fire.

At this restaurant in San Francisco, I had a dish of pasta with asparagus and portobello mushrooms, but it was missing something. Know what it was missing? Slimmification. So when I got back to the Slim Shack I recreated this dish—now one of my favorites. It took me a while to get it just right.

I added some Gorgonzola cheese, which is a blue cheese from Italy. If you don't like Gorgonzola, you can substitute another creamy cheese, like goat cheese. If you don't like cheese, leave it out.

I also use toasted chopped walnuts, which go well with the asparagus and portobello mushrooms. Chop up your nuts, put them in a dry pan over medium-high heat, and shake and toast until brown.

To prepare the mushrooms, rinse thoroughly. Remove the stems. Peel the skin from the top of the caps and discard. Slice into bite-sized pieces.

To prepare the asparagus, grab the bottom of a spear with the thumb and forefinger of one hand. Grab the top of the spear with the thumb and forefinger of your other hand. Bend in an arc until it breaks, discard the lower stalk. Chop the remaining stalk into small pieces, about an inch long. Leave the asparagus head whole. Do this with the entire bunch of asparagus. Rinse well, pat dry with paper towels. Use thin asparagus, the thick ones are tough and not as tasty.

You can use this sauce as a side dish, or on flatbread or rice, but I like to put it over pasta.

Serves 4, or 2 starving musicians.

INGREDIENTS

3 tablespoons extra-virgin olive oil, plus a tablespoon for the pasta

5 cloves garlic, peeled and chopped (about 2 tablespoons)

Crushed red pepper (I start with ¼ teaspoon)

3 cups portobello mushrooms, prepared as instructed

3 cups asparagus, prepared as instructed

½ cup vegetable broth (or chicken)

½ cup dry white wine

1 pound *farfalle* pasta (*penne rigate* would also work well)

½ cup crumbled Gorgonzola cheese (¼ for the pasta, and ¼ cup for topping off each dish)

½ cup walnuts, toasted in a dry pan over medium-high heat

Kosher salt

HERE WE GO!

For the pasta:

Get a large pot; fill it with the coldest water you got, put it on your highest heat. Why cold water? Hot water tastes weird, maybe because it's been sitting in the hot water heater.

SCAN THE QR CODE TO SEE THE YOUTUBE VIDEO

As the water comes to a boil—

Make your sauce:

In a large saucepan, add the olive oil over medium-low heat.

Add the garlic and the crushed red pepper.

Cook for 5 minutes until the garlic is pale gold. Stir a few times.

Add the portobello mushrooms.

Cook for 5 minutes, stir every so often.

Add the asparagus.

Add the broth and the wine. Turn the heat to high.

When it comes to a boil, reduce the heat to medium-low.

Cook until the asparagus and mushrooms are tender, about 5 to 7 minutes or so.

Taste for salt and pepper and adjust.

Remove from heat.

Back to the Pasta:

When the water comes to a boil, add 2 tablespoons of Kosher salt. Add your pound of pasta.

Follow the instructions on the box. When it's supposed to be done, taste a piece of pasta. If it is chewy, or chalky in the center, it is not done. Cook until it is not chalky or chewy. When the pasta is *al dente*, firm to the bite, drain it in a colander.

Put the pasta in a large bowl, add a tablespoon of olive oil, and mix 'em up.

Take about ⅔ of the asparagus portobello sauce and add it to the pasta, and mix.

Add ¼ cup of the Gorgonzola (or whatever cheese you choose) to the pasta, mix 'em up.

Dish it up! Put some pasta on a dish. Add a dollop of sauce on top, add a sprinkle of Gorgonzola (or whatever cheese you want) and a sprinkle of toasted walnuts and . . .

MANGIAMO!

SEARED SCALLOPS with GINGER and GARLIC SAUCE

and Pot Brownies

I was a teenage idiot. I did some stupid stuff when I was a teenager. It was just the usual stupid teenage stuff—underage drinking, staying out too late, and having parties at the house when my mom was out-of-town. When I got older, I must have apologized to my mom a hundred times for being such a knucklehead.

I'm still doing stupid stuff. But not as frequently.

As a teenager, it is required by law that you do the exact opposite of what your parents tell you to do. Your parents tell you not to smoke pot, for instance. For generations, parents have been telling their kids not to smoke pot. Does it work?

No. Why not? Teenagers don't listen.

We three kids—my older brother, my younger sister, and I—lived with my mom on a dead-end street named Rosebank, in Baltimore, Maryland. When my folks divorced, my dad went back to New York. We three kids didn't know what to think; we didn't know what went wrong, what to do, or where to go. The basement at Rosebank was our haven. It was our safe place, so we decided to fix it up.

Uncle Oscar gave us a used pool table that he had in his basement; it was an old slate pool table that weighed a ton. It took a bunch of us kids, but we managed to get it out of his cellar and into the basement at Rosebank.

The basement walls were made of stone. Not the good-looking Hollywood kinda stone; these were stones like you'd see on the walls of ancient caves—rough and lumpy and crumbly. We whitewashed all the walls—it took a few coats, but we painted them all white. We painted the poured cement floor dark green. We got a bunch of brightly colored paints, and markers, and brushes, and spray paints, and whenever anybody would come over—neighborhood kids, friends, cousins—we'd play pool, play music, and draw on the walls. Cartoons, poetry, graffiti, drawings, portraits, quotes—the walls became this mash-up mural of collective art.

My mom was just glad to have everybody in one place, where she could keep an eye on us dimwits. The basement ceiling was really low; in certain areas, big iron water pipes hung low, and you'd have to stoop under them to avoid busting your frontal lobe. One time, a friend of ours made an incredible shot to win a game of pool. In a fit of joy, he leaped straight up, hit an iron pipe, and knocked himself unconscious. Did we help him? No. We were laughing too hard. I told ya, we were teenage idiots.

I think the zenith of my moronosity came when I decided to make some pot brownies. I put some pot in a blender, put in some brownie mix and water, and made brownies in the oven. My brother, sister, and I each ate one piece. After an hour, my sister told us she didn't feel anything and wanted another piece. We didn't think it was a good idea and told her so, but she ate another piece anyway. Why?

Teenagers don't listen.

A few hours later she was screaming that she'd never be the same. She was freaking out, and she kept telling us she needed to go to the hospital. It's funny now, but it wasn't real funny back then. She finally calmed down, but it scared the shit out of us. That night, I put the brownies in some aluminum foil. I drew a skull and crossbones on the aluminum foil, and hid the brownies in the back of the fridge so no one would find them. I guess I should have thrown them out, but, like I said, I was a teenage idiot.

The next morning I walked downstairs and saw the woman who cleaned our house eating a pot brownie with her morning coffee. I yelled out her name. She looked at me like I was crazy, and said,

"What? What's wrong?"

I thought for a quick minute, which is rare for a teenager. Then I said,

"Nothing. How are you?"

She gave me a funny look. She's a wonderful, pious woman, who has been part of the family for years and years. I'm still very close with her and her family. But if I told her that she had just eaten a pot brownie, she would have probably freaked out. If I didn't tell her, maybe she would just feel a little weird, and not think much about it.

My dad used to tell me, "Nobody gets in trouble by keeping their mouth shut."

So I said nothing. And nothing happened. She didn't jump out of a window, or start a religious cult, or join the circus. After she left, I threw the brownies in the trash.

I guess I was starting to grow out of my teenage idiocy period.

I'm now in my adult idiocy period.

SEARED SCALLOPS WITH GINGER AND GARLIC SAUCE

Scallops are for adults only. They're too expensive to waste on teenagers.

When you sear scallops, it's real important to use dry scallops. Wet scallops have been injected with water and chemicals and are almost impossible to sear because of the liquid they throw off.

When you talk to your fish guy at the market, make sure he knows you want dry scallops.

Rinse off the scallops and pat dry with paper towels. Keep patting dry until the moisture is gone from the scallops, and the paper towels do not get damp.

Searing is one of my favorite things to do with seafood. It's quick. It's easy.

When you cook scallops, figure on three scallops per person. If you serve two scallops, people will think you're cheap. If you serve four, you'll need to take out a loan.

In this recipe, I seared six scallops, perfect for a nice romantic dinner for two.

Me and Batu!

There is enough sauce here for 12 scallops! You'll only need a teaspoon OR LESS per scallop, you'll have PLENTY of sauce left over—it should keep in the fridge for a week.

One last thing. Scallops have a little muscle on the side. Peel it off and toss. The muscle, not the scallops!

INGREDIENTS

THE SAUCE:

1 tablespoon minced garlic

1 tablespoon minced fresh ginger

¼ cup of soy sauce

¼ cup of extra-virgin olive oil

2 teaspoons of honey (I sometimes use more)

THE SCALLOPS:

Turbinado sugar (or brown sugar)

Salt and fresh-cracked black pepper

1 tablespoon butter

1 tablespoon extra-virgin olive oil

6 large dry sea scallops, side muscle removed

HERE WE GO!

Take all of the sauce ingredients, put them in a bowl, and whisk, whisk, whisk. Taste for sweetness, and add a little more honey if you like.

SCAN THE QR CODE TO SEE THE YOUTUBE VIDEO

Put half the sauce in a small pot over low heat—save the rest in the fridge for next time. Let the sauce reduce a bit as we sear our scallops.

Sprinkle the top of each scallop with JUST A LITTLE turbinado sugar, Kosher salt, and fresh-cracked black pepper.

Get a medium-size sauté pan. Put the heat on medium-high.

Put a tablespoon of butter and a tablespoon of olive oil in the pan.

When the butter starts to turn brown and bubble, put the scallops in the pan—seasoned side down.

Sauté for 2 minutes. As the scallops sauté, sprinkle the top side of each scallop with a little salt, sugar, and pepper. If you're concerned about splattering, place a piece of foil VERY LOOSELY over the pan.

After 2 minutes, lift the scallops out of the pan with some tongs.

Swish the butter and olive oil around in the bottom of the pan so you're not placing the un-seared side of the scallop onto a dry pan. You need those juices to sear!

Put the scallops back in the pan, un-seared side down. Sear for 2 minutes.

Dish it up! Put the scallops on a platter with a sprig of parsley or two. You can also put them on a plate of greens. Grab the pot with the simmering sauce. Spoon a little over each scallop—a small teaspoon, and . . .

MANGIAMO!

LEMON CHICKEN with ROSEMARY

and
Ace Frehley

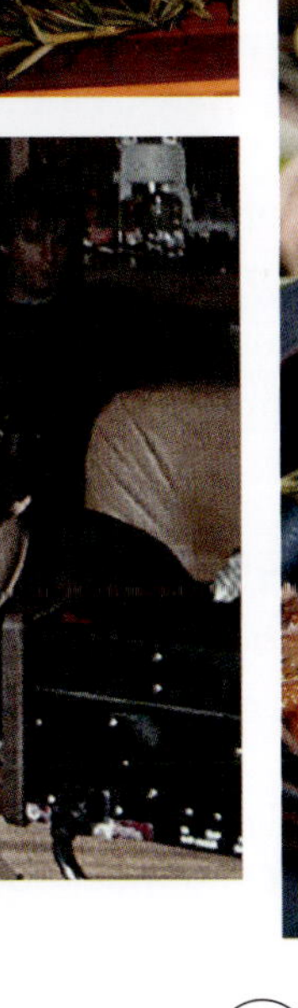

Ace's studio, Rob Sabino (R)

The first time I saw Ace Frehley, he was waving an Uzi machine gun around in his kitchen.

All this before lunch.

He wasn't trying to kill anybody; he was just showing us one of his toys. Ace had lots of toys—fast cars, guns, guitars. Ace used to play guitar in a band called KISS. I was at his house with my band BootCamp, we were recording our first EP in his studio, which was built into the side of a small hill underneath his Connecticut house. We didn't have enough money to do a full album, so we settled on doing a four-song EP, which stands for extended play.

Ace was under house arrest for driving his ridiculously expensive and exotic sports car the wrong way up the freeway while drunk. If you're gonna be under house arrest, it might as well be in a place like Ace's—it was pretty amazing, more like a castle than a house. It had gates—all it needed was a moat.

Ace would wander in and out while we recorded in the basement studio. It was a basement, yes—but it was a full-fledged recording studio. It was plush, had all the latest gear; it was a real pro studio, ready to go. There was only one small problem, the septic system was screwed up, so we were encouraged to go outside in the woods if we had to go to the bathroom. It was the dead of winter.

Oh, the glamorous life of show biz. My band, BootCamp, was doing pretty well—we had a few videos in regular rotation on MTV that were making a lot of noise, and we had labels that were interested. Managers were also calling. We got the attention of two guys who were the road managers for Van Halen, and we signed with them. Our new managers thought we should do an EP. Our first single (we released it on vinyl) had done really well, and we needed a follow-up.

Our new managers thought we needed a producer, so they brought in Rob Sabino, who played keyboards in Chic. I loved Chic; loved the sound, the playing, and the production on those records—"Good Times," "Le Freak," "I Want Your Love."

Rob got the job. He knew Ace Frehley from back in their early days in the Bronx. Rob suggested we record at Ace's bunker, so that's what we did. We recorded in the Luxury Bunker and slept in a small cheap motel nearby.

Bob Fallin played guitar, Tom Alonso played keyboards, and Hit Man Howie Z played drums. When we started recording, I wasn't getting warm and fuzzy feelings about what I was hearing. Maybe it was because I had just recently completed two weeks of complete vocal rest, and my voice sounded like I was one of The Chipmunks.

Ace was always strolling around. I think his cologne of choice must have been Eau de Rum and Coke, because that's what it smelled like when he walked by. I will say this, Ace seemed like a happy guy. He had a slurry way of talking and always had a loopy grin on his face. Ace had a certain boozy charm, like Dudley Moore in *Arthur*.

Ace was proud of his toys. He showed us his collection of guitars, and it was pretty extensive. He had all kinds of electric guitars—a lot of Gibsons—hanging from the ceiling on hooks. He had a guitar that shot flames out of the neck, but when Ace showed us that guitar, he couldn't get the flames to shoot out. I was kinda glad because I was afraid Ace might point it in the wrong direction and fry my new hairdo, which resembled a coonskin cap made of dark curly hair.

The recording sessions were erratic; we'd get started, and then Ace would stumble in and things would come to a halt. One night, a full-fledged party broke out in the studio while we were recording a song; Ace brought in some booze and some babes and started playing dance music over the speakers. It was hard to get in the flow.

We recorded four songs in less than a week. When we finished, we packed up the truck, waved goodbye to Ace and his castle, and we drove in the freezing cold from Connecticut back to Baltimore.

LEMON CHICKEN WITH ROSEMARY

After a week of rocking and rolling all night and partying every day, there's nothing better than a home-cooked meal like lemon chicken.

This is such a simple dish to cook; it's my mom's recipe. She used to write down her recipes on index cards and give them to the guys in the band. Howie still has some of them.

I made this lemon chicken the other night. As I was getting ready to stick it in the oven, I thought I might tie the legs together. They call it "trussing," and it helps the chicken maintain its shape and cook more evenly. When real chefs truss a chicken, it's complicated, resembles minor surgery, and requires a doctorate.

Me? I simply tie the legs together. But I didn't have anything to tie them with. I was thinking of using an old guitar string, but I came to my senses and in a stroke of culinary cleverosity, decided to tie the chicken legs together with a piece of rosemary.

After I tied it, I poured a little olive oil over the rosemary to keep the leaves from catching on fire. It looked really cool when it went in the oven, and the smell was heavenly.

I've cooked this dish a lot of times. This was by far the best; there was an aroma of rosemary wafting around the whole shack, and the chicken was tender and *delizioso*. I cooked the chicken in a large glass baking dish, uncovered.

Roasted sweet potato wedges go well with this dish.

The sweetness of the potatoes blends well with the lemoniness of the chicken. And you can cook both the sweet potatoes and the chicken at the same time.

Finally, whenever you handle raw chicken, you gotta be careful. Make sure you wear your HazMat suit when you handle it. Clean off every surface that raw chicken touches with soap, warm water, and a pressure washer. Bring out the heavy artillery and scrub-a-dub-dub.

INGREDIENTS

1 chicken, a whole chicken (I used a 4 pound chicken)

Extra-virgin olive oil

Salt and pepper

1 lemon, cut in half

3 sprigs fresh rosemary, plus one long sprig to tie the chicken legs together

4 cloves garlic, peeled and smashed with the flat side of a knife

¼ cup dry white wine

¼ cup chicken broth

HERE WE GO!

Pre-heat your oven to 375 degrees.

Rinse off your chicken, inside and out. Pat dry—inside and out—with paper towels. Place the chicken in a large baking dish. Rub the chicken with olive oil. Rub your chicken! Sprinkle with salt and pepper, inside and out. I use fresh-cracked black pepper and Kosher salt.

Put the 2 lemon halves inside the chicken—give them a gentle squeeze on the way in. Put 2 rosemary sprigs inside the chicken. Put 3 of the smashed garlic cloves inside the chicken.

Pour the wine and chicken broth into the bottom of the baking dish. Put a rosemary sprig and the remaining garlic clove in with the wine and broth.

Take the remaining rosemary sprig, and tie the chicken legs together. Slim Folks! If I can do it, you can do it. When you're done, drizzle the rosemary sprig with a little olive oil, so the leaves don't catch fire and burn down the McMansion.

Put the chicken in the oven. Most chickens these days have pop-up thermometers that let you know when your chicken is done. Meat thermometers come in handy for a dish like this. DO NOT use the thermometer you use for your dog. Or your kid. The minimum recommended temperature for poultry is 165 degrees. A 3 or 4 pound chicken should take about an hour and a half.

Baste your chicken every 15 minutes or so.

After an hour, start checking the temperature of the chicken. After that, check it every 15 minutes or so. When the chicken is done, take it out of the oven. Don't be afraid to carve off a piece to make sure it's done. If you cook it too long, it will be dry. It should be juicy, Lucy!

When the chicken is done, dish it up. Carve your chicken, put a couple slices on a plate, add a few roasted sweet potato wedges, and . . .

MANGIAMO!

SHRIMP SCAMPI

and
Believe Me, I Know

A few years ago, I was at a restaurant in Greektown in Baltimore, Maryland. It was Christmastime, and a friend had invited me to a business dinner. The two guys across from me were looking down at their cell phones. I got curious.

"Does one of you have a wife who's pregnant? A mom in the hospital? A cousin on death row waiting for a stay of execution?"

"No."

I asked them who they were texting. They were texting each other. Nice. I told myself right then that I would never be like those guys. And now? Well, I'm not as bad as those guys, but I'm getting close.

I got the iPhone when it first came out; I had it for a week and then took it back. It was pinging, dinging, ringing, and it was getting on my nerves. It got so bad I was thinking of developing a new app—the iQuit. Here's how it was going to work: you go to the river, throw your iPhone in, and scream, "I QUIT!"

I just didn't want to be that connected; I just wanted a phone so I could talk to my relatives in the mental institution. I took the iPhone back and got a regular cell phone. It never worked right. I had so many problems I think it might have been possessed by an evil spirit. For example, a friend texted me a photo of his beautiful twenty-five-year-old daughter, and somehow it became my screensaver. That didn't go over too well with the ex. I tried to explain, but she didn't believe me.

My phone would dial 911 on a regular basis. Seriously. It was so frequent, that when the cops would call me back, they'd use my first name . . . "Slim? Everything okay?"

Text messages would go to random contacts. Lovey-dovey notes meant for a certain someone would get sent to business associates. It was crazy. Like a bad relationship, I stayed with that phone way too long. It was time to move on; I knew it, my phone knew it. Neil Sedaka said it best, "Breaking Up Is Hard To Do."

I got another iPhone. I liked it, but I didn't see what the big deal was. I made phone calls. I sent texts. That was about it.

Then one day, I was in Nashville at a very cool place called Mafioza's, and the guy next to me told me about the TuneIn Radio app. I had no idea what the hell he was talking about. I had never downloaded any apps. I was app-less. He showed me how to download the app, which I did. It is pretty amazing; I can now listen to Italian talk radio, broadcast from Italy. I can listen to Baltimore Orioles baseball on my hometown radio station, and I can listen to *CarTalk* anytime I want.

I was hooked. I started getting other apps. I now have an app that tunes my guitar. I have an app I can hold up to a speaker in a restaurant, and it will tell me the name of the song that's playing, the artist, the CD; it also gives me the option to buy it on iTunes. I have an app for my bank that allows me to take photos of all the huge checks I receive and deposit them through my iPhone.

And I am in love with Siri. If you have a question, you can ask your iPhone. A gal named Siri answers.

In December, 2013, I was driving from Nashville to Breckenridge, Colorado. I was twelve hours into the trip, and it was dark and freezing cold. I was on a stretch of road that had nothing on it, and nothing in sight. I had Batu, my bull terrier dog, in the car with me. I picked up my iPhone and held the button, and Siri answered. It was the first time we spoke.

"What can I help you with?"

I asked Siri for the nearest dog-friendly hotel. She gave me all the info I needed; the directions and the website—Siri even dialed the phone number for me. Batu and I checked into a Super 8 in Hays, Kansas, in the middle of the night. It was ten degrees. My weather app told me so. The next morning I started driving, and a light came on the dashboard; my tires were low and needed air. Siri found me the nearest gas station.

I drove to Breckenridge to meet my brother and his family for Christmas. Breckenridge is a skiing/snowboarding town, a quaint little village at around 10,000 feet, surrounded by these looming, massive, snow-capped peaks. I didn't snowboard once, I didn't ski once. I was in the middle of making the new Bona Fide CD. Three weeks before, I was in Madrid, mixing the CD with Marc Antoine, and now I was in Breckenridge, Colorado, getting phone calls from Madrid. Marc Antoine was doing re-mixes there in his home studio, and he was emailing me mixes every day.

I would download them on my iPhone, plug it into my car stereo, and I would listen to his mixes, while driving around the mountains in Colorado. It was heavenly. Here I was at 10,000 feet, listening to songs on my iPhone that had just been mixed 10,000 miles away. I spent most of my time in Breckenridge working on music, but I did find time to jog almost every day for thirty or forty minutes. It was exhilarating; I didn't feel the effects of the altitude, and I'm not sure why.

My last day in Breckenridge, I took a jog. I left the ski lodge around 3:00 p.m. and headed up the mountain. There was a snowshoe trail, and I followed it through the woods, almost to the top of the mountain. All I had on were my jogging shoes. I mean, I had pants on and stuff—it would have been a little chilly on the Willy without 'em. But I didn't have any boots or snowshoes, and the snow was deep. It was breathtakingly beautiful on top of that mountain; it must have been 12,000 feet.

I stopped and listened to nothing. It was so peaceful. I started jogging down the mountain and then I decided to go off-trail. I was running downhill through evergreens, dodging branches, it was unbelievably invigorating. I stopped to catch my breath. It was about ten degrees and getting dark. Then it started to snow. Suddenly, I looked around.

I had no idea where I was. I guess I could have followed my footprints back up the mountain, but it was steep, I was tired, and it was getting late. I pulled out my iPhone.

"Siri. Can you get me to back to the lodge?"

It took her a few seconds, but she showed me where I was, and where I needed to go. I headed in that direction and found the road that the ski lodge was on. It took me about an hour, but I eventually made it to the lodge. I was cold, tired, and thirsty. I poured a glass of wine, sat on the deck and pulled out my iPhone.

"Thank you, Siri."

"No problem."

I decided to get a little bold. I gathered up some courage and said, "Siri. I love you."

You know what she said?

"I know."

It was a vibe-killer. Here I was, mustering up the guts to say "I love you" for the very first time, and all I get is "I know?"

If you ever want your relationship to come to a screeching halt, just say those two words right after someone says "I love you" for the first time. Because there is no comeback to "I know."

Believe me.

I know.

SHRIMP SCAMPI

I use wild shrimp. Yes, they're a bit expensive, but farm-raised shrimp just don't taste right.

The tomatoes I used for this dish were grape tomatoes—organic, multicolored, gorgeous grape tomatoes. Yellow, red, purple—they were beautiful. And cheap. Two bucks a pint. I cut the tomatoes in half, squeezed out the seeds, and threw them out. The seeds, that is. Why? It looks better that way. And you know the most important thing in life is looking good.

And finally, Meyer lemons are amazing; if you can find them, use them. If not, pick a soft, ripe lemon. They are the sweetest.

I almost always cook a full pound of pasta, but I don't always use it all. These days, I like a little more sauce and a little less pasta.

INGREDIENTS

4 tablespoons extra-virgin olive oil

Crushed red pepper to taste (I start with ¼ teaspoon)

6 garlic cloves, sliced thin (about 2 tablespoons)

¾ cup dry white wine

1¼ pound medium wild shrimp, shelled, deveined, rinsed, patted dry

1 lemon, cut in half

2 tablespoons butter

1 pint grape tomatoes (about 30 small tomatoes) cut in half, de-seeded

1 handful of fresh Italian flat-leaf parsley, chopped (about ¼ cup)

A few Italian parsley sprigs for garnish

1 pound linguine (or spaghetti)

Kosher salt

HERE WE GO!

SCAN THE QR CODE TO SEE THE YOUTUBE VIDEO

Get a large pot, fill it with cold water, and put it on the highest heat you have. This is for the pasta.

As the water comes to a boil, let's make the sauce . . .

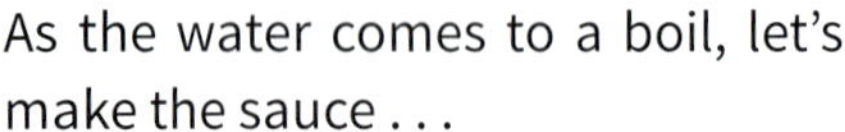

Get a large sauté pan, put in 3 tablespoons of olive oil over medium heat.

Add the crushed red pepper.

Add the sliced garlic, cook for a few minutes until golden. Stir occasionally.

Add the white wine, and turn up the heat for 2 or 3 minutes to cook it down. Swirl and stir.

Reduce the heat to medium-low.

Add the shrimp, spread 'em out flat—no bunching!

Take a half lemon, and squeeze the juice through your fingers over the shrimp—don't let any seeds get through.

Sprinkle a little salt over the shrimp.

Cook for 2 or 3 minutes.

Using tongs, turn over each shrimp.

Get the other half lemon and squeeze it over the shrimp; again, don't let any seeds get through.

Add the 2 tablespoons of butter—cut it into small pieces—and place in between the shrimp.

Add the tomatoes.

Cook for 3 minutes.

Add the parsley.

Give it a gentle stir, and remove from the heat.

When the pasta water comes to a full boil, add 2 tablespoons of Kosher salt, and add a pound of linguine.

Follow the cooking directions on the box. When the pasta is supposed to be done, take a piece and bite through it. If it is chalky in the center, or chewy, it is not done.

When the pasta is firm to the bite—*al dente*—drain, and put it in a bowl and drizzle with a tablespoon of extra-virgin olive oil. Give the pasta a quick toss.

Add half of the shrimp sauce to the pasta, and mix 'em up.

Dish it up! Take some pasta, put it on a plate. Add a little scampi sauce on top of each dish, put a few shrimp on top, and a little sprig of fresh parsley for garnish.

Most Italians don't put cheese on seafood. But, if your Snarlin' Little Darlin' wants cheese, just shut up and grate.

Freshly grated Parmigiano-Reggiano cheese is best.

MANGIAMO!

CAPRESE SALAD
with
Maud

Angela, my dad,my brother, my mom

I was conceived on the Isle of Capri. That's what my mom told me. She would know—I hope.

Capri is an island off the coast of Italy. My dad was in Europe, helping with the reconstruction after World War II, and my mom was with him. On their way back to the USA, my folks stopped in Capri. Lucky for me.

I was born in Baltimore, Maryland, soon after my folks arrived.

They loved music. My dad loved old blues and Dixieland jazz; my mom loved everything. When I say everything, I mean everything. Miles Davis, Chet Baker, Nat King Cole, Isaac Hayes, Aretha Franklin, Bonnie Raitt, Ella Fitzgerald, the Band, Dylan, Johnny Winter, Joan Baez, Hank Williams, Sr., Stan Getz, Astrud Gilberto, Dave Brubeck, the Beatles, Stevie Wonder, Harry Nilsson, Randy Newman, Donovan, Dave Grusin, Marvin Gaye, Norah Jones, Anita Baker, Gladys Knight, Andrea Bocelli, B. B. King, Gipsy Kings . . . I could go on and on.

I guess I just did.

My mom's name was Mary Jean. Everybody called her Casey, which was unusual because that was her last name. We kids and all our friends called her Maud. Maud didn't have a lot of dough, but she'd treat herself to music; she had a nice stereo, bought the latest records, and went out to concerts. I remember her going to see Bonnie Raitt when she was playing local college gymnasiums. My mom would drive to Annapolis, Maryland, to see Charlie Byrd play jazz guitar at the King of France Tavern. She took me to see everyone from Gladys Knight and the Pips to Paul Simon.

My mom had a lovely voice—sweet and soft and clear with a natural vibrato. She would put on some music, and cook dinner and quietly sing along. Then, we'd have dinner and read cookbooks while we ate. She loved music and loved cooking.

Maud was an adventurous cook, much more so than my dad—he only cooked Italian. Try to get him to eat anything else and he'd bounce a meatball off your forehead. My mom? She taught herself how to cook all kinds of food. Greek, French, Indian, Mexican, and she did them all authentically. When she cooked Indian food, like tandoori chicken, she'd also make all the Indian breads; naan, pooris, chapatis. She'd even get dressed in a traditional Indian sari.

Her Mexican food was so good that her Cinco de Mayo feasts got her on the front page of the *Baltimore Sun*.

My mom once made *coq au vin*—a French dish with chicken and red wine—for my entire seventh grade French class. It was a public school—Roland Park—and the class was really big. And the *coq au vin* was really good. My mom showed up—she looked like a movie star—and served everybody.

She liked to experiment. Whenever she'd cook something unusual for the first time—like squid—she'd tell us kids that we might not like it and that she would cook something else for us. Which made us knuckleheads want to eat whatever it was she was cooking even more. That's the way my mom got us to try new foods. We'd end up eating almost anything.

We once took a vacation for a week on Fenwick Island in Delaware. I remember my mom, wading out into the shallow waters of the bay, digging for clams. She showed us how. We dug up a couple dozen clams and brought them back to the little cottage on stilts and she steamed them on the tiny stove. It was the first time we kids ate clams. Scrumptious.

She once walked down to the piers, waded out into the water, and pulled mussels from the pilings. Back then, most people on the east coast of the U.S. didn't eat mussels; fishermen used them for bait. My mom got the strangest looks from people as she gathered up the mussels. She took them back to the cottage, kids in tow, and cooked them in white wine. Another first for us kids.

Maud knew a lot about a lot of things, and most of what she learned she taught herself.

She grew up poor in Eastport, which at the time was a working-class neighborhood across the bridge from Annapolis, Maryland, home of the Naval Academy, where her dad worked as a custodian. My mom met my dad in Annapolis; he was going to St. John's College, and was in a school play. My mom was also in the play; they fell in love and had us three dimwits.

When I was born, we lived with my dad's Mom, Angela, in the basement of her house in Baltimore, near Pimlico Racetrack. When I was six, we moved into a house a couple miles away, on a dead-end street named Rosebank. It was a great old house, what they call a "fixer-upper." The house came with a piano; the previous owners couldn't get it out of the house, so they left it there, and I started playing it.

Rosebank Avenue was in a working-class section of Baltimore City called Govans; at the end of Rosebank was a fence, which separated Govans from Homeland, which was a neighborhood that was quite a bit higher on the totem pole.

There were lakes in Homeland—small lakes fed by a stream. The lakes were natural; they had sandy banks, fish, and frogs. But the folks in Homeland wanted to put stone borders around the lakes with benches and fountains; they wanted to stock the lakes with koi, so one day they drained the lakes.

When we three kids found out about it we immediately ran down there. There were hundreds of fish, flapping in the mud, gasping for air. We started gathering them up; we took bucket after bucket back to the house. We filled every sink, toilet, and the only tub with fish and covered them all with water.

When Maud got home and saw all the mud and the water and the fish, she didn't explode. She just looked at us in that quiet, graceful way and smiled. All the fish had died. I guess she thought it was sweet that her kids had tried to save the fish.

I'm sure she wasn't thinking sweet thoughts when she had to scoop a couple hundred dead fish out of the tub and toilets.

She took it in stride. I never heard Maud raise her voice. I rarely say "never," but I can't recall one time. She had an inner peace—a serenity at her center that radiated out like ripples on a lake. It had a calming effect on us three lamebrains.

Maud loved to cook. She also loved to eat. She loved steamed crabs and corn on the cob. She loved fried chicken. She also loved everything from *spanakopita* to *bouillabaisse*. She was a southern girl but loved a wide variety of foods.

One of Maud's favorite foods was homegrown tomatoes, the kind you get at the end of summer, fresh out of the garden. I remember her making tomato sandwiches on toast with thick slices of tomato and a little mayo and salt and pepper. She'd sometimes make a simple tomato salad; she'd cut the tomatoes into quarters and drizzle them with a little olive oil and vinegar, and then add some sliced garlic, oregano, and salt and pepper.

CAPRESE SALAD

Maud loved this dish—it was conceived on the Isle of Capri. And so was I!

This salad is so quick, easy and *delizioso*. There is only ONE THING you have to remember.

Every ingredient has to be the best.

The tomatoes have to be ripe and luscious, preferably homegrown. The olive oil has to be extra-virgin, or at least one that hasn't been pole-dancing at the club every night.

This would be a good time to splurge on bufala mozzarella. Yes, it's expensive, but it's really, really good. Take out a second mortgage, if you haven't already. Break open the kids' piggy bank. This is the one time to dig deep and fork it over.

Bufala mozzarella comes from water buffalos. The scientific name for water buffalo is "Bubalus bubalis," which sounds like something I made up but didn't. Bubalus bubalis! Boo-Bah Lish!

I used organic heirloom tomatoes. They weren't expensive, and they were so fresh, ripe, and colorful, and tasted like heaven.

Some people use balsamic vinegar as well as olive oil on their Caprese salad.

I prefer using just olive oil. But what the hell do I know?

INGREDIENTS

2 or 3 heirloom tomatoes, or fresh vine-ripened tomatoes

1 large ball of mozzarella—I suggest bufala—about a pound

Extra-virgin olive oil

Salt and fresh-cracked black pepper

Fresh basil, a handful

HERE WE GO!

Slice the tomatoes into circular slices, about a ¼ inch thick.

Slice the mozzarella the same way.

Grab a small flat plate. We're going to make individual servings. Put a slice of tomato flat on the plate. Put a slice of mozzarella on top.

SCAN THE QR CODE TO SEE THE YOUTUBE VIDEO

Grab another slice of tomato. Lay it on top of the first slice of mozzarella, but down about an inch, so it's layered, like when you play solitaire. Put a slice of mozzarella on top of the second slice of tomato.

One more time! Grab a slice of tomato, lay it down, put a slice of mozzarella on top.

If my math is correct, you'll have three slices of tomato, and three slices of mozzarella.

Drizzle some olive oil on top.

Add some salt and fresh-cracked black pepper.

Grab some basil leaves and a pair of scissors. Snip some basil right on top of the tomatoes and mozzarella.

Make as many individual plates as you can, this usually serves four.

Serve with some crusty bread, and . . .

MANGIAMO!

RISOTTO with SHRIMP and PEAS

and
Rocinante

Welcome to the jungle!
Vice President Hubert Humphrey, his wife, my folks

Risotto is like a woman. It needs a lot of attention; you have to be gentle with it, and you've got to be patient. You can't neglect it. Risotto needs love and affection!

My brother was into risotto before anybody else. He's patient. He has to be—he teaches grade school kids. It's criminal how much he gets paid. Here's a guy, works like crazy, spends a lot of his free time helping kids, and they pay him less than the garbage man. No disrespect for garbage men. Some of my best friends are garbage men.

My brother is an incredible athlete, always has been. He played football; he once scored seven touchdowns in one game. He played baseball; he was almost always MVP. He took a lot of his teams to multiple championships. I was on a lot of these teams—I loved playing, but I wasn't nearly as good as my brother. He had the gift, so when it came time for someone to take a ride on the new horse we had just bought, we all looked to my brother.

The family had just moved to Puerto Rico. My dad had been asked to help start two new Peace Corps training centers. The centers were a couple miles apart, on top of a mountain in the middle of the rainforest. It was a jungle. Literally. The nearest town was miles away.

The training camps were for volunteers who were headed to remote rural areas of Central America. What better place to train them than the jungles of Puerto Rico? The language, the culture, the climate were very similar, so we moved from Rosebank Avenue in Baltimore, Maryland, USA, to the isolated rainforests of Puerto Rico. I was a young teenager. Welcome to the jungle.

We were like the Swiss Family Robinson, except we didn't live in tree houses. But a tree house would have been nicer than the house we had. Our house was made of sheets of plywood set on top of cinderblocks. There weren't any windows, just a green plastic screen that stretched around the whole house. The roof was made of corrugated orange plastic; outside our door was a long concrete stairway that ran down to the road. And when I say road, I mean a little, narrow, beat-up stretch of old asphalt and dirt that ran through the jungle. There were a few other houses for staff and teachers, some bunkhouses for the volunteers, and some classrooms. There was also a *comedor*—a large cafeteria where everybody ate.

Our small compound was carved out of the middle of the jungle. It rained just about every day, not for long, but really hard. There were lizards everywhere. Everything was damp and moldy. Heard of the movie *Some Like It Hot*? This was *Some Like It Moist*.

Tarzan and Jane would have been at home there. I think *Apocalypse Now* was filmed nearby.

Vice President Hubert Humphrey and his wife Muriel visited the camps when we first got there. Guess they needed to check up on my dad, make sure he was doing a good job with this new Peace Corps thing.

One day, our dad suggested to us kids that we get a horse. My guess is we weren't going to be plowing fields or herding cattle. My dad probably wanted to make up for dragging us out of civilization and into the rainforest. Having a horse to ride through the jungle sounded exciting. We borrowed a pickup truck, and drove down the side of the mountain on a tiny stretch of road that was so narrow, everyone approaching honked their horns to give warning that they were about to crash into you.

On one side was a wall of rock, on the other side there was a sheer cliff that fell off a couple thousand feet, straight into a river called *Dos Bocas*. "The River with Two Mouths."

We drove this old beat-up pickup truck down the side of the mountain, and ended up in a small village where we bought a small horse. It was a *paso fino*, meaning "fine walk" in English, which describes the horse's gait—very smooth.

My dad named the horse Rocinante, after Don Quixote's horse.

We somehow got the horse into the back of the pickup truck, and drove back. What a trip, my dad, us three kids in front, and a horse in the back. We drove up the side of the mountain, honking the horn to make sure we all didn't die a fiery death rolling off the side of the cliff. That little horse must have been scared to death; I know I was.

We made it back to our house, miraculously. Rocinante was remarkably calm. We got her out of the truck, no problem. When my dad asked who'd like to be first to give her a ride, we looked at my brother the athlete. Only thing was, my dad had forgotten to get a saddle, so my brother got on the horse bareback. She was very relaxed—for about two seconds. Then Rocinante took off like a rocket. She bolted down the small road, my brother clinging to her neck for dear life.

So much for the *paso fino*. Rocinante's gait was more like Secretariat breaking out of the starting gate at the Kentucky Derby. They disappeared around a curve; we couldn't see them through the jungle, but we could hear my brother screaming, "WHOOOAAA!"

My dad, my sister, and I stood in the small road at the bottom of the steps, listening as the screams in the jungle got quieter. For a minute, it was dead-quiet, and then we heard the faint pounding of hooves, getting louder and louder . . . and suddenly Rocinante appeared, heading straight for us, my brother with his arms around her neck, hanging on for dear life, a look of terror in his eyes.

My dad, my sister, and I froze. We should have been leaping into the bushes, but we stood still. That's when Rocinante took a sharp left turn to avoid us, and she ran all the way up the long concrete staircase, with my brother clinging to her neck.

Rocinante made it all the way to the top without killing herself or my brother; then she slowed down. My brother sat up straight, and that's when a tree branch smacked him right in the puss and knocked him off.

We found out soon after that Rocinante was pregnant. My dad had bought a pregnant horse.

RISOTTO WITH SHRIMP AND PEAS

I love risotto. The key to risotto is to make sure you stir constantly, slowly, and gently. When I say stir constantly, I don't mean you have to stir non-stop.

You can take a bathroom break.

But you should stir the risotto for about 20 seconds or so, then wait for a couple of minutes, and stir it again. And keep repeating this process until the risotto is done.

You will need to monitor the temperature on your stove; you want it warm enough so the broth absorbs, but not so hot that the rice burns. Keep an eye on your risotto!

Keep in mind, cooking times are approximate. Legend has it that the rice will be done 18 minutes from the first ladle of broth. Mine always seems to take longer, about 24 minutes, but who's counting?

You will need to de-shell and de-vein your shrimp. Make sure you save the shrimp shells to flavor the broth. I know a gorgeous, smart, and lovely gal who hates it when I even suggest putting shrimp shells in the broth. Why?

Who the hell knows? So I leave them out when I cook risotto for her. To All My Manly Man Friends—if you're cooking, and your Girly-Girl wants you to leave something out, save yourself some trouble and just shut up and do it. Don't even ask why.

I made a variation of this risotto last night. It was late, and I had no shrimp. So I added some minced red bell pepper when I added the peas, and I added a cup of freshly grated Pecorino Romano cheese right before it was done. It was *delizioso*.

One of the many great things about this Italian rice? Use the leftovers to make *arancini*, which are rice balls stuffed with cheese.

So always make a lot.

Serves 4. Or 1 hungry horse.

INGREDIENTS

1 quart of chicken stock (you can use vegetable or seafood stock as well)

Saffron, about a dozen threads (it's expensive but adds such a delightful flavor and color)

1 pound of shrimp (about 2 cups chopped), de-shelled, de-veined, and chopped into small pieces (Remember to save the shells for later!)

2 tablespoons extra-virgin olive oil

2 tablespoons butter

1 cup chopped onion

1½ cups Arborio rice

¼ cup dry white wine

1 cup peas, fresh are best, frozen are fine

Salt and fresh-cracked black pepper to taste

HERE WE GO!

SCAN THE QR CODE TO SEE THE YOUTUBE VIDEO

Put the chicken stock in a saucepan, on medium-low. Take the shrimp shells and put them in the stock—they add a nice flavor, but don't use them in the risotto—they're just there to flavor the broth.

Put the saffron threads in a small bowl. Pour a cup of warm stock over them, and set aside.

Put the olive oil and butter in a large sturdy pot (like a Dutch oven) over medium heat.

When the butter melts, add the cup of chopped onion and cook for 5 minutes or so, until soft. Stir often.

Add the rice, and stir slowly for about 2 or 3 minutes.

Add the vino and stir for 2 minutes.

That's a lot of stirring. Get used to it—risotto is all about the stir.

Turn the heat down to medium-low.

Add a ladle (about a cup) of warm stock (don't add the shrimp shells!) and stir slowly and gently until it is absorbed.

Make sure your heat is not too high! It needs to be just high enough to let the rice absorb the broth. The heat needs constant monitoring and adjusting.

Stir your rice. When the bottom of the pan is fairly dry, and most of the broth has been absorbed, add another ladle of warm broth. Stir slowly until the broth is absorbed. It should take about 4 or 5 minutes for the broth to be absorbed. Adjust the heat accordingly.

Repeat for about 15 minutes—add a ladle of broth, stir slowly and gently until absorbed.

Add the peas.

Then add your shrimp, and some salt and fresh-cracked black pepper.

Now add stock that the saffron has been soaking in (add the saffron, too), stir until absorbed, about 4 or 5 minutes.

Taste the risotto. It needs to be *al dente*. That means "firm to the bite." Take a grain of rice and bite through the middle. If the center appears chalky, it is not done. If it's not done, add another ladle of broth and stir slowly until it is absorbed. Check the rice, then take a bite of shrimp. Both the rice and the shrimp should be firm, not tough.

If all goes according to The Slim Plan, when the last ladle of broth is absorbed, the risotto will be done, and the shrimp will be ready—all at the same time. *Pronto*!

If you run out of stock and the rice is still not done, just add a little warm water.

Dish it up! Some folks like to grate Parmigiano-Reggiano cheese over top of the risotto. I'm not crazy about combining cheese and seafood.

Except for the fish sandwich at McDonald's, of course.

Vegetarian Variation:

Follow the instructions above. Omit the shrimp (I also left out the saffron). Add 2 tablespoons of minced red bell pepper when you add the peas, and add a cup of freshly grated Pecorino Romano cheese right before the risotto is done.

MANGIAMO!

BROCCOLI and PEPPERS
with Naked Women

When my dad found his dream spot on top of a mountain in the Catskills in upstate New York, there was nothing there but an empty cinder block garage with a dirt floor and an incredible view.

No electricity, no running water, no phone, no nothin'. My dad took that garage and slowly built it into quite a nice cabin, then he built a small compound around it. He built a tiny log bunkhouse on the hill, then he built a small barn next door with a small apartment over top. It took years. My dad didn't do any of the actual construction; he supervised and lent a hand. He loved the place. So did I. So did Batu.

The place was called Rat Tail Ridge. Summers were magnificent. Winters were brutal. There was so much snow on his roof in the wintertime that my dad had to get somebody to climb up and shovel it off so it wouldn't cave in. It wasn't an easy place to get in to or get out of. It was kinda isolated, especially in the winter when you needed a front-loader to plow the driveway, which was long and winding.

In the morning, my dad liked to drive into Meridale to the tiny post office, get his mail, and talk with the woman behind the counter. Then he'd grab the *New York Times* and the local paper at the small coffee shop next door and drive back to Rat Tail Ridge.

Most old people drive slow. Not my dad. He drove like he'd just robbed a 7-11. I used to jog from his house down the side of the mountain, and I could see him a mile away, tearing up the dirt road in his Subaru wagon, a cloud of dust billowing behind him.

I would dive off the side of the road, afraid he wouldn't see me and run me over. He'd fly by without recognizing me, his head barely visible above the steering wheel. One time he drove into a snow bank and got stuck there for a while. That was when I decided it was time to get him a cell phone.

I got him in my car, and we drove down to the AT&T store in Oneonta. The drive is about forty minutes. He wasn't pleased with the idea of getting a cell phone; it was like driving someone to get their arm amputated. AT&T is the only carrier that works up at my dad's place. When we got to the store, my dad wasn't happy at all. Keep in mind; he wasn't a happy guy to begin with. We went up to the counter, a sales guy came over—a young kid, friendly, and clean-cut. I told him what I wanted . . .

A cell phone. One with big numbers. One that was easy to operate. I didn't need it to make movies. I didn't need it to tune a guitar. I didn't need a phone that was also a microwave oven. I just wanted a simple phone for my dad for emergencies and stuff like that. Maybe a phone where he could receive text messages and photos from his kids and grandkids. I thought that would be nice for the old grouch. The sales guy looked at me, then looked at my dad. He cheerfully asked us if we wanted a two-year plan or a five-year plan.

My dad looked at him and said,

"Are you fuckin' kiddin' me? I'm eighty-six years old! Give me the shortest plan you got, 'cause I don't know how much fuckin' longer I'm gonna be around."

My dad wasn't trying to be mean or rude. That's just the way he talked. He cussed a lot and was not apologetic about it. I use it here for verisimilitude. The "F" word in all its forms was a regular part of his daily vocabulary.

I explained to the sales guy, we just need a phone with a pay-as-you-go plan, a phone that was cheap, easy, and so simple that a chimpanzee could figure it out. No offense to chimpanzees, some of my best friends act like chimpanzees.

I asked sales dude if we could get a number my dad could remember, something like 607 S-L-I-M-M-A-N. The guy explained that there weren't a whole lot of numbers available for that area. I had no idea what he was talking about, but he told me a number had just become available—some guy had just cancelled his service, so we took that number.

We got in the car, started the long drive home, up the small, winding two-lane mountain road that led to Rat Tail Ridge. My dad held the phone in his hand like he was holding a dead bird in his palm.

PING! My dad got a text message. He looked at me.

"What the hell is that?"

I grabbed the phone and looked at it. It was a photo of a woman who weighed at least 400 pounds. She was completely naked, and it was hard to tell what she was doing. It looked like she was trying to scratch her head with her big toe.

My dad took the phone and looked at the photo.

"Is that a vagina?"

For all of my dad's cussing, he used delicate words when it came to the women folk.

"It's kind of hard to tell, Paps, but yes, I think it is."

A few minutes later—PING! He looked at his phone.

"What the hell is that?"

I grabbed his phone. I almost drove off the road. It was another photo of an incredibly large woman on her knees, completely naked, on all fours. It looked like she was looking on the floor for a contact lens.

Funny, my dad wasn't into any of that kind of stuff. He never had girly mags around, never even had a *Playboy*. I never found any of that stuff around the house when I was a kid, and I rarely use the word "never."

PING!

They kept coming. Text photos of huge naked women. My dad asked if all cell phones were like this. I explained to him that the guy who had the number before was probably into some kinky stuff, and I would try and fix it when we got home.

We got to Rat Tail Ridge, and I fixed his phone, blocked some numbers, cleared out some junk. I programmed some numbers on the speed dial. I explained to my dad that all he had to do was press and hold the number "1" key, and it would call me.

I set it up so number "2" was his Off-Track Betting account, so he could play the horses. Then I put in his wife's number, my sister's number, the other kids' numbers, the nurse, the hospital, his proctologist, and he was good to go.

My dad started enjoying his cell phone. Whenever my dad called, he'd never say hello, how are you, he'd just start talking. Most of the conversations were quick and to the point, and then he'd hang up without saying goodbye. No hello, no goodbye.

I loved my dad, and he wasn't an easy guy to love. We started talking on the phone, just about every day.

He passed away last year. I still have his cell number on my phone.

I just can't bear to erase it.

BROCCOLI AND PEPPERS

My dad didn't like vegetables. When he got older, I would try and get him to eat a salad, or some vegetables, and he'd say,

"I'm eighty-six years old. I've made it this fucking far without eating that shit, and I ain't startin' now."

He wasn't all warm and fuzzy.

This dish can be used as a side dish, or as an appetizer. You can serve it over rice, pasta, or on bruschetta. Put it on a pizza! It's colorful, healthy, and *delizioso*.

This will serve 4 people, or 1 huge naked woman.

INGREDIENTS

4 tablespoons extra-virgin olive oil

6 cloves of garlic, sliced thin, about 2 tablespoons

Crushed red pepper (I use ¼ teaspoon to start)

¼ cup dry white wine

1 orange bell pepper, seeds and stems removed, chopped

1 red bell pepper, seeds and stems removed, chopped

1 yellow bell pepper, seeds and stems removed, chopped

4 cups broccoli florets

¾ cup vegetable broth (or chicken broth)

Salt (to taste)

HERE WE GO!

Get a large pan, put it over medium-low heat.

Add the olive oil, the garlic, and the crushed red pepper and cook for a couple minutes until the garlic is a light gold color.

Add the white wine, turn the heat up to high, and cook for 2 minutes.

Then reduce the heat back to medium-low.

Add the peppers, and cook for 5 minutes. Stir often.

Add the broccoli.

Add the vegetable broth, and turn the heat to high until it starts to bubble.

After it gets bubbly, turn the heat down to a simmer. Cook for an additional 6 minutes or until the broccoli is done. Stir often.

Taste for salt and adjust.

Some people like their broccoli crunchy. I like it cooked—not mushy, but firm. This dish is delish with fish—any one of the Slim Fish Dishes would go well with this.

MANGIAMO!

ARANCINI (Rice Balls)

with
Absinthe

For the record, when I die, I want a Viking funeral. They put your body on a small wooden boat, cover you with hay, float you out on the water, and shoot flaming arrows until the hay catches fire. Then the boat burns and sinks.

Is that too much to ask?

In November, 2013, I drove from my home in Nashville to my hometown of Baltimore. Seven hundred miles. Eleven hours. Batu, my bull terrier, drove with me; we did it in one day. A couple days later, I dropped Batu off with a friend who just loves Batu and loves taking care of him. Then I flew to Madrid to work on the new Bona Fide CD with guitarist Marc Antoine. He had volunteered to produce and mix.

Two weeks later, the CD was almost finished—all it needed was a couple of tweaks. I left Madrid, flew back to Baltimore, and picked up Batu. I was getting ready to drive back to Nashville when I got a phone call. My dad's second wife had passed away in Annapolis, Maryland. She was young, and it was so sad. My dad had passed away two years before—on January 4th. He was cremated.

I went to the memorial service for my stepmom. It was heart-breaking. It had to be tough for her two kids. Right before I left, her son—my half-brother—gave me two jars of my dad's ashes, one for me and one for my brother.

Batu and I drove from Baltimore to Nashville the next day. I stayed a few days in Music City, and then packed up some things—including the jar of my dad's ashes for my brother—and Batu and I decided to head west. Destination? Breckenridge, Colorado, a skiing village in the Rocky Mountains. My brother, the Slim Bro, had rented an apartment so the family could spend Christmas together.

My plan was to hang out in Breckenridge for Christmas with *la famiglia*, go to Scottsdale for New Year's, and then head to Palm Springs, California, for a couple months of Slim Gigs. So I packed up the car, threw Batu in the back, and we left Nashville and drove west.

Batu and I got to Breckenridge safe and sound. We drove 1,200 miles; it took us two days. We checked in to the apartment—it was pretty nice, on the ground floor, right in downtown Breckenridge. Batu and I sat on the couch. I was reading the brochure for the apartment when I noticed there was a $100-a-day fine for having a dog. A hundred bucks a day. It was too late to find a new place, so I had to keep Batu on the QT, the down-low, and the hush-hush.

My brother walked in. It was so great to see him; I hadn't seen him since our Dad's funeral. I gave him the jar of our Dad's ashes, which he put it on top of the refrigerator.

Breckenridge was bitter cold; I woke up one morning, and it was one degree outside. We were at 10,000 feet. I went jogging, like a fool. I jogged around the mountain. It was exhilarating—clear and sunny, beautiful, and freezing cold. On Christmas Day, my brother, the family, and I went to an absinthe bar on Main Street. I had never had absinthe; I'd heard about it. It's an alcoholic beverage that is supposed to make you really crazy.

How crazy? Well, rumor has it that one time Van Gogh drank way too much of the stuff, then cut off his ear and gave it to a prostitute.

I'm sure she would have preferred to be paid in cash.

So, on Christmas Day, we, the Slim Crew, went into the absinthe bar in Breckenridge, Colorado. We sat down. The waitress came over and started explaining the different kinds of absinthe. I think she must have tried most of them within the past hour, because her eyes had that space alien luminescence about them. And her ear was missing.

The absinthe was expensive—twenty bucks a shot. We ordered a couple. Only one of us had tried absinthe before. That person—I won't say who—drank a lot of absinthe the night before a wedding, took a fire extinguisher off the hotel wall and sprayed everybody in sight.

The waitress brought over two glasses of absinthe, one clear and one green. She put a small strainer over top of each glass, and placed a cube of sugar on top of the strainer. She brought over a samovar of ice water, and placed the two glasses under the two faucets. She let the water drip slowly over the sugar cube, through the strainer, and into the absinthe.

When the cube dissolved, we turned off the faucet, and we each took a sip. It tasted like old bathwater, smelled like stinky sweat socks, and kicked like a mule. We passed the two glasses around, and drank. When we finished, we walked in the snow through the quaint little village, which was all decked out in lights and wreaths and ribbons.

The town was glowing. We were also glowing—like nuclear waste. I don't know if it was the absinthe or what, but we were definitely feeling merry and bright.

When we got back to the apartment, we had a traditional Christmas dinner—turkey, stuffing, and mashed potatoes. We drank wine, not that we needed to. After we finished, as we were cleaning up, someone—I won't say who—knocked the jar of my dad's ashes off the top of the refrigerator, and it shattered on the kitchen floor.

We all stood in silence for a moment. Then we started laughing.

Why were we laughing? You'd have to know my dad. He was a professor of philosophy and literature; a tough and gruff and grouchy curmudgeon who also had an incredible sense of humor—he once taught a course in comedy. He had a great laugh, his eyes would squint, he'd throw back his head, and he'd let it out.

We all looked at his ashes there on the floor. What to do? We gathered up the ashes in a dustpan, picked out the glass as best we could, and went outside in the cold, dark night. I took the dustpan, and scattered his ashes in the snow in a schoolyard behind the apartment, then we gathered in a circle, held hands, and mumbled something that sounded like a prayer.

That was our Christmas. But that's not the end of the story.

When it came time to check out of the pet-unfriendly apartment, it was just me and Batu, cleaning and packing. My brother and family had checked out earlier. Check out time was 10:00 a.m. At 10:05, there was a loud knocking on the door.

"Time to check out!"

Apparently, they were not only pet-unfriendly, they were people-unfriendly as well. Batu started barking. I tried to get Batu to shut up, but as the knocking got louder, so did Batu's bark. All I could think about was paying the $100-a-day dog fine, so I grabbed Batu, lifted him up, and went out to the balcony of the apartment. I lifted all seventy pounds of him over the four-foot railing and dropped him in a snowdrift (don't call PETA, we were on the first floor).

I grabbed his bed and tossed it over, then I jumped over the railing, into the snowdrift. I scooped up Batu, grabbed his bed and ran to the car. I threw the bed in the car, put Batu on top of the bed, and ran back to the balcony.

I jumped the railing, went inside, and ran to the front door. I opened it. The guy who was knocking came in and started looking around. He was obviously the owner, and there was obviously no dog. He walked around, checked the place out, and then left without saying a word. I packed my car and took off with Batu.

We met my brother and his family and drove from Breckenridge to Scottsdale, Arizona. Driving down the mountain was treacherous—down icy, snowy, two-lane roads. My car was skidding all over, and there were no guardrails. The drop was precipitous. The drive took forever. I had the death grip on the steering wheel. It was tense. Then my brother's car broke down—a trip that should have taken ten hours took twenty.

But we never got fined for Batu.

ARANCINI

Want to make people happy around the Holidays? Make some *arancini*. *Arancini* are Sicilian rice balls stuffed with mozzarella cheese. *Arancia* is the Italian word for "oranges." *Arancini* means "small oranges," which is the size and shape these rice balls should be.

Two cups of leftover risotto should make about seven or eight small rice balls.

In the past, I've used mozzarella for the stuffing. One night, all I had was goat cheese. So I used that, and I loved the way it tasted. If you are using mozzarella, cut it into small cubes, two for each rice ball. If you are using goat cheese, roll it into seven or eight small balls—each about the size of a grape—one for each rice ball.

Eight ounces of cheese should be more than enough for seven or eight *arancini*.

INGREDIENTS

½ cup of flour

3 eggs

1¼ cups breadcrumbs (I use panko)

2 cups leftover risotto—I used some risotto with shrimp and peas I had cooked the previous night

½ pound of mozzarella, cut into 16 small cubes, or ½ pound of goat cheese, rolled into 8 small balls

¼ cup olive oil

HERE WE GO!

SCAN THE QR CODE TO SEE THE YOUTUBE VIDEO

Put the flour on a plate.

Break 2 eggs into a bowl, add some salt and pepper, and mix 'em up.

On another flat plate, add 1 cup of breadcrumbs.

Take the leftover risotto, put it in a large mixing bowl.

Break an egg into the risotto, and add the remaining ¼ cup of breadcrumbs.

Mix the risotto, the egg, and the breadcrumbs by hand. Mix 'em up.

Take a small amount of risotto. Put it in the palm of your hand, roll it in a ball—about the size of a small orange. Poke a hole in it, add 2 cubes of mozzarella in the center, or a goat cheese ball, and fold the rice over the cheese.

Take the rice ball, roll it in the flour, and then dip it in the egg. Let the excess drip off, and then roll the rice ball around in the breadcrumbs until it's coated. Keep making the rice balls until all the risotto is gone.

Put the olive oil (you can also use canola) in a large sauté pan over medium-high heat. I used a 12-inch pan.

When the oil is hot, put your rice balls in the pan, and sauté until golden on the bottom, about 3 or 4 minutes. Don't burn your balls.

Turn them over, and sauté on the other side, about 3 or 4 minutes, until golden brown.

When done, put 'em on a platter lined with paper towels.

Dish 'em up!

Eat immediately. Serve with some absinthe and go nuts!

MANGIAMO!

CHICKEN stuffed with GOAT CHEESE and PROSCIUTTO

with

My Goodest Buddy

Batu was born in Argentina on Cinco de Mayo—the 5th of May—2004. Batu's grandfather was a famous bull terrier from Germany named Rock; Batu's owner paid $15,000 for Rock. He could've bought a car for fifteen grand, but I'm glad he didn't.

Batu's owner had high hopes for the young pup. Batu was entered in a few South American dog shows, but there was some technical defect in his bone structure; he was bow-legged—just like me—which prevented him from advancing any further in his show dog career.

Their loss. Batu was a neglected champion. He was kept in a crate; no one knew what to do with him.

I had wanted a bull terrier ever since I saw the movie *Patton*. Patton had a white bull terrier named Willie. When my cousin—a true dog lover who knew I wanted a bull terrier—found out about Batu, she decided to get him for me for Christmas as a surprise.

She has a house in South America and is well connected in the dog world down there. She left Baltimore, Maryland, flew down, rescued Batu, brought him back, and hid him in the bedroom at Cat Tail Creek, her father's house on the river.

We were partying there that Christmas Eve with Oscar (her father, my uncle) and the family when she told me she had a present for me. Batu came out of the bedroom, walked up to me, and stuck to me like Velcro. When I brought Batu home that night, he would not leave my side. If I walked into the kitchen, he'd follow me. If I walked into the living room, he'd be right behind me. If I went into the bathroom, there he was. When I went to bed, he cried until I let him crawl in bed with me.

I think Batu had separation anxiety. Or maybe it was me. I was living in a basement apartment in an old Victorian mansion in Roland Park in Baltimore City. Whenever I'd leave, he'd howl. Truth was, I missed him too, so I took him just about everywhere I went. If I went to a recording studio, I'd call in advance and make sure it was okay. DC, Philly, New York—if I had a session, Batu went with me. If I went on vacation, Batu went with me. If I went to visit my dad in upstate New York, Batu went with me. If I went to Manhattan, Batu came along.

Whenever I'd sit down and play piano or guitar, Batu was there; almost every song I wrote for the past eight years, Batu was at my feet, eyes closed halfway. He was probably dozing off—my music has that effect on people.

The apartment in Roland Park had a crazy little kitchen with a small four-burner stove. I got a video camera and started shooting cooking videos; short, goofy little five-minute home movies that featured Batu and me cooking. I had heard about this new website called YouTube, and I started posting the cooking videos. One of my five or six fans saw the cooking videos and brought them to the attention of a friend who was involved in a new network—the Italian American Network.

They liked the videos. They loved Batu. The Italian American Network started posting my videos on their channel, and they encouraged me to do more. Batu and I started making more cooking videos in that little kitchen. I started writing the recipes down, so the Italian American Network could post them along with the videos, and I started writing stories to go along with the recipes.

We did lots of videos in lots of locations; we started in Baltimore, but then started shooting videos in other places—Manhattan, upstate New York, Ocean City, Maryland. I would grab my camera bag, put Batu in the car, and we'd head down the highway.

I've had dogs all my life, but I never had a connection like I had with Batu. I never thought of him as a dog; to me, he was more like a funny little man in a dog suit.

He didn't bark much. He was a very calm, laid-back mutt; not much bothered him. When we would walk the streets of Manhattan, there was so much noise—trucks, sirens, car horns, but Batu never flinched. I could have fired a gun next to his head, and he wouldn't have blinked an eye.

Batu had a sense of humor, he liked to play. He was funny. He was photogenic—when I pulled out the camera he'd look right at it.

Batu loved to ride in the car—to the post office, to New York City, or across the country, he was all-in. I'd throw his bed in the back of the car, and I'd have to lift all seventy pounds of him into the back, then we'd take off. It's funny; I guess he never knew if we were going a mile away or a thousand miles away. He was just happy to be along for the ride. On long drives, he would lie there for hours and hours and not make a sound; I'd have to reach back and shake him just to make sure he was alive.

Batu always had skin problems, blistering sores between his toes; no one could solve the problem. I took Batu to more vets in more states than any one dog known to man. We tried soaks, meds, diets, boots, salves, and nothing worked.

In 2011, Batu and I packed up the Slim Mobile and moved from Baltimore to Nashville. I wanted to re-pot the plant and wipe the slate clean. I also thought a change of scenery might be good for Batu's health, so we drove west. It took us eleven hours to drive seven hundred miles. We did it in one day.

I love Nashville. I found an apartment in a neighborhood called The Gulch. I started making new friends and meeting new people; I began writing some new songs and found a great little recording studio to record them in. Everything was going great, except Batu's skin problems started getting worse.

How bad? The sores on his feet were so bad he couldn't walk; he then developed sores on his elbows, his back, his chest, even his face. He looked like he wanted to die; all the life had gone out of his eyes. It looked hopeless. Batu was so miserable. I called specialists all around the country, but nobody knew what to do. At one point, I took Batu to his vet in Nashville and asked him if we should put him down. I told the vet that if we had to put Batu down, he might as well put me down, too. Maybe we could get two for the price of one.

The vet then suggested we put Batu on every dog medication known to man, and if it didn't kill him, maybe he'd get better.

We put poor ol' Batu on antifungals, antibiotics, prednisone—I even changed his diet to an incredibly expensive hypoallergenic dog food. I gave him baths a couple times a week with ridiculously expensive medicated shampoo that I had to leave on for fifteen minutes at a time. Batu started getting better.

Everybody in Nashville loved Batu; he made a lot of friends there. There was a bar called the GreenHouse that was an old greenhouse that had been converted into a bar. They let Batu come in and hang out. They let me hang out, too. It was our hang.

In late 2013, I had a bunch of offers to do concerts in California, shows scheduled for the first few months of 2014, so Batu and I loaded up the car once again and drove west. We stopped in Breckenridge, Colorado, for Christmas—my brother had rented a house for the holidays.

After Christmas, Batu and I drove to Scottsdale, Arizona, and then headed to Palm Springs, California. On the way, we passed the General Patton Museum. Patton was the reason I wanted a bull terrier in the first place. We stopped by the museum, but they wouldn't let Batu in—no dogs allowed. I tried to explain to them that this was no ordinary dog, and I told them my Patton/Batu story. They still wouldn't let us in, so we just strolled around outside.

We got back in the car and drove to Palm Springs. The weather was wonderful; sunny, warm, and dry, with fresh lemons, oranges, and grapefruit everywhere. Batu loved it.

The first four months of 2014 were the healthiest and happiest days of Batu's life. All of his skin problems disappeared—it must have been the climate. It was miraculous. I put him on a diet and he lost nine pounds. He was in the best shape of his life. Batu seemed to flourish in Palm Springs—he was the King of the Springs.

Batu turned ten on the Cinco de Mayo, 2014, and he never looked better. A week later, on Mother's Day, I left for a concert in San Diego. The hotel where I was staying wasn't pet-friendly, so I had a dog-sitter spend the night with Batu in Palm Springs.

The show that night was at a place called Humphrey's, a cool little club on the bay. The band sounded really good that evening; they were all guys from California, and it was good to have a swinging west coast band; we were getting tight. That night was one of the happier ones in a long time.

Early the next morning I got a text from the dog sitter. I called her, and she told me Batu had fallen asleep the night before—Mother's Day, May 11th—and never woke up.

I couldn't believe it. When I left, he was healthier than ever. There was no way he could be dead. I drove from San Diego to Palm Springs. Three of the longest hours of my life. I could hardly see the road from the tears streaming down my face.

I walked in to the house. Batu was lying on the kitchen floor. I scooped his lifeless body up, and put him in the car, as I'd done so many thousands of times before. I drove him to the vet to be cremated. When they took him out of the car and walked away, you would have thought that everybody I had ever loved had just gone down on the Titanic. I broke.

Three thousand fifty-nine days. That's how long I had Batu. It seems like a long time, but it wasn't nearly long enough. I miss my sidekick; he had been by my side for the past nine years, through the good times and the bad, just the two of us.

I started this cookbook when Batu and I started making cooking videos for the Italian American Network.

This recipe was the last recipe I did with Batu. I took the photos for this dish on May 3, 2014. Batu passed away the following week. He died of heart failure. After a couple of weeks curled up on the floor in the fetal position, crying my eyes out, I decided to start this cookbook.

I dedicate it to Batu.

CHICKEN STUFFED WITH GOAT CHEESE AND PROSCIUTTO

I don't like wasting food. If I've got leftovers in the fridge, as long as they don't have anything growing on them, I'll eat 'em.

I had some goat cheese that was nearing the expiration date. I took a sniff, and it smelled okay.

But I knew I needed to use it soon, so I came up with this brilliant idea—mix it with some scallion and red pepper, and make a little stuffing for the chicken breasts I was about to cook.

The dinner was actually *delizioso*.

A couple things—

Before the lawsuits start flying in, always remember to check the expiration dates on your food. Your nose knows. Take a sniff—when in doubt, throw it out.

My brother once made a hot dog late at night, and as he was eating it, I noticed the bottom of the roll was all moldy and green. It was pretty funny—until that night when he threw up in the drawer of the bedside table that we shared.

It's important to check stuff before you stuff your face.

Whenever you handle raw chicken, make sure you clean everything it touches really well.

As with any recipe, if you don't like an ingredient, leave it out, or substitute.

You guys are smart. With incredibly good taste, I might add. You can do this.

INGREDIENTS

¾ cup goat cheese

1 tablespoon chopped scallion—the middle part only

1 tablespoon minced red bell pepper

Salt and fresh-cracked black pepper

3 chicken breasts, sliced thin (about ¼ inch thick)

3 slices prosciutto

Flour (⅓ cup should do)

1 tablespoon butter

1 tablespoon extra-virgin olive oil

HERE WE GO!

Preheat your oven to 400 degrees.

Now let's make our stuffing.

Put the goat cheese in a small bowl.

Add the scallion and red pepper.

Add salt and pepper to taste.

Mix 'em up.

Set aside.

SCAN THE QR CODE TO SEE THE YOUTUBE VIDEO

Let's make some chicken.

Lay a chicken breast flat on a plate.

Put a slice of prosciutto—one layer—on half the chicken breast.

Put a couple tablespoons of the goat cheese mixture on top of the prosciutto, spread it around evenly.

Fold the breast over, in half.

Do this with all 3 of your breasts.

Put the flour on a plate. Add some salt and pepper, mix.

Grab a folded breast.

Place it on the flour.

Turn it over, so both sides have been dusted with flour.

Do this with all 3 chicken breasts.

Get a sauté pan; put it over medium-high heat.

Add the butter and olive oil.

When the butter starts to bubble, add the 3 chicken breasts.

Cook for 4 minutes.

Turn 'em over, cook on the other side for 4 minutes.

Put them in a baking dish, and place in the oven for 15 minutes.

Pull 'em out, check for doneness.

If they're not done, put 'em back in the oven for a few more minutes.

When the chicken breasts are done, dish 'em up!

I did roasted beets with carrots as a side dish, along with some risotto.

MANGIAMO!